Eric Newby was born in London in 1919 and was educated at St Paul's
School. In 1938 he joined the four-masted Finnish barque *Moshulu*
as an apprentice and sailed in the last Grain Race from Australia to
Europe by way of Cape Horn. During the Second World War he
served in The Black Watch and Special Boat Section, and was a
prisoner-of-war from 1942–45. After the war his world expanded still
further – into the fashion business and book publishing. Whatever
else he was doing, he always travelled on a grand scale, either under
his own steam or as Travel Editor of the *Observer*.

Mr Newby's other books include *Something Wholesale, Slowly Down
the Ganges, Love and War in the Apennines, A Short Walk in the
Hindu Kush, A Book of Travellers' Tales, A Traveller's Life, On the
Shores of the Mediterranean* and *Round Ireland in Low Gear* – all of
which are available in Picador.

Richard:

Happy 39th (1st of)

1990

Jane, Sharon & Sons.

Also by Eric Newby in Picador

A Book of Travellers' Tales
Love and War in the Apennines
On the Shores of the Mediterranean
Round Ireland in Low Gear
A Short Walk in the Hindu Kush
Slowly Down the Ganges
Something Wholesale
A Traveller's Life

ERIC NEWBY

The Big Red Train Ride

PICADOR

published by Pan Books

First published in Great Britain 1978 by Weidenfeld & Nicolson Ltd

This Picador edition published 1989 by
Pan Books Ltd, Cavaye Place, London SW10 9PG

9 8 7 6 5 4 3 2 1

ISBN 0 330 30805 X

Printed and bound in Great Britain by
Richard Clay Ltd, Bungay, Suffolk

To the Peoples of Siberia,
who have to live there

Contents

Acknowledgements

I would like to express my warmest thanks to all those who helped and encouraged me while writing this book, and especially to Joan Bailey of the London Library, without whom I should have been permanently lost in its transepts; Venetia Pollock, who reduced a mountainous text to more portable and readable proportions; Christine Kirk and Barbara Bearne of Newton Abbot for their beautiful and rapid typing of the original manuscript; Barbara Gough of Weidenfeld and Nicolson for her reassuring editorial presence; Anne Dobell for checking Russian names; John Price, editor of Cook's International Timetable (that astonishing and invaluable work), who read the proofs for railway errors; and John Silverlight, author of *The Victor's Dilemma*. Finally, I would like to thank Wanda, the indefatigable traveller, who kept me going while I wrote the book in a Devon winter of near Siberian severity.

Lynx-eyed rail enthusiasts may detect discrepancies in the distances given between some stations. Such discrepancies also exist between official Russian and other timetables. They should address themselves to these authorities rather than to me.

The photographs were taken by Wanda and myself.

OCEAN

80°

CHUKCHI
SEA

E. SIBERIAN SEA

GULF OF
ANADYR

60°

CAPE CHELYUSKIN

LAPTEV SEA

Nizhnekolymsk

Kolyma

A R C T I C   C I R C L E

Magadan

KAMCHATKA

Lena

Okhotsk

SEA OF OKHOTSK

50°

Tura

Yakutsk

E. SIBERIA

SOVIET FAR EAST

SAKHALIN IS.

Olekma

Berkakit

Stanovoy Ra.

Vitim

Komsomolsk-on-Amur

TATAR STR.

Ust-Kut

Amazar

Bam

Tynda

Zeya

atsk

LAKE
BAIKAL

Primorsky Ra.

Shilka

Amur

Birobidzhan

Sovetskaya Gavan

Yablonovyy Ra.

Blagoveshchensk

Obluchye

Khabarovsk

Irkutsk

Chita

Nerchinsk

Vyazemskiy

Ulan-Ude

Argun

Sikhote Alin Ra.

hanar

Dab

Ra.

Ingoda

Ussuri

Kyakhta

Onon

Harbin

Ussuriysk

Selenga

Nakhodka

40°

Ulan Bator

C H I N A

Vladivostok

GOLIA

SEA OF JAPAN

110°

120°

130°

140°

When the trains stop, that will be the end.
Lenin, during the Civil War

The Big Red Train Ride

Prelude

Long Ago in Leningrad, or New Year's Night on the Red Arrow

The whole of snowy Asia, by way of Moscow ends in this city that looks out on a frozen sea.

Valse des Fleurs, Sacheverell Sitwell

LENINGRAD is a city of canals, a northern Venice of such beauty that there is no absurdity in the comparison, and as the taxi raced down the Nevski Prospekt, here nearly 120 feet wide. over what looked like pure ice to the station where I was to catch the night express to Moscow, it seemed, with the huge flakes of snow drifting down into it out of the darkness of the northern night, yet another enchanted, frozen waterway, brilliantly lit.

It was New Year's Eve 1964. At 11.30 pm, having entrusted a two-kilo tin of the finest procurable caviar to the engine driver who stuck it on the front of his steam locomotive in order to keep it cool, I boarded the *Krasnaya Strela* (the *Red Arrow*), and after disposing of my baggage took a seat in the restaurant car.

The *Krasnaya Strela* is one of the Soviet Union's most famous trains. It covers the 410 almost dead straight and completely bump-less miles to Moscow in eight hours and thirty minutes, arriving at the Leningrad Station on Komsomolskaya Square at 8.25 the following morning, on the dot. The line has a sentimental place in the hearts of Russian railwaymen as it was the first major line to be built entirely within the frontiers of Russia; it took 50,000 serfs working from sunrise to sunset – and who were flogged for the privilege of doing so – eight years to complete. Thousands of them died.

Almost everything about the *Krasnaya Strela* was good. It was warm, even too warm, and the dark blue brass-buttoned greatcoats and fur hats worn by the conductresses who sometimes smiled, sometimes scowled, sometimes were inscrutable – Russian officials of either sex are as unpredictable as fruit machines – were of the finest quality. And it was not only the conductresses who were fitted out in a sumptuous manner: the appointments of the two-berth 'soft-class' compartments, which is how the Russians describe their first-class *wagons-lits*, were redolent of another age – the headboards fitted with linen covers embellished with drawn-thread work, the dark green curtains, the pleated silk shades on the massive cast-iron table lights, the glittering water decanters, the long druggets in the corridors (instantly soiled by the snow-covered hooves of the passengers as soon as they boarded the train), the dazzling white curtains and bed linen, the multiplicity of mirrors – all were satisfactory to the most exacting bourgeois taste and therefore not only to me but to the sort of Russians who were my fellow travellers in 'soft class', many of whom had the air of commuters. It was not surprising that at one period of the war this rolling stock had been used by Hitler and other top members of the Nazi Party, or so someone told me later that night.

In fact, the only remotely criticizable thing about the *Krasnaya Strela*, apart from the thought that I might be occupying a berth once used by Himmler, which was rather off-putting, was the menu in the restaurant car, of which I had been offered an English translation covered with gravy stains, in which all the more agreeable items and most of the less agreeable ones were unavailable. 'Beluga Belly Flesh', 'Goose', 'Roasted Duck wit Garnisch' and 'Plum Cake "Stolichny"' were all out of stock. All that was currently on offer was some luke-warm noodle soup, great gobbets of some unidentifiable meat which looked as if it had been hacked to pieces by a maniac with an axe, and what were literally smashed potatoes.

It was therefore little wonder that I and my fellow diners, all of whom were Russians and therefore endowed with the native facility of making the best of what would have been disastrous for anyone else, had recourse to the bottles with which the restaurant car was well supplied, and on which they had already made a start before I arrived.

The only other passenger at my table was a large man as tall as an early Romanov with glossy black hair, wearing an expensive, hand-built black suit, a black knit tie and a white shirt with a Madison Avenue-type button-down collar with a fashionable swerve to it. He was in his early forties and looked a formidable customer. Anywhere west of the Iron Curtain I would have put him down as the man in charge of the J. and B. Rare or the Smirnoff Account. Here, I identified him as a member of the *apparat*, and a trusty one who had spent a lot of time abroad.

He was uncommunicative – just a very curt nod – but hospitable. He had just filled a large-size glass with Stolichnaya from a 500-gramme bottle and now he did the same for me, which emptied it. We clinked the big glasses and turned them bottoms up in the Russian fashion. I ordered another bottle. Into the Valley of Death.

It was now a quarter to twelve.

'Where are you going?' he said suddenly. He spoke English with a fine voice as deep as he was.

'To Moscow.'

'Of course,' he said impatiently, making me feel like a small boy of about seven, 'but after Moscow?'

'To London.'

And that was the end of that conversation. At 11.50 the *Krasnaya Strela* left for Moscow.

In the course of the next ten minutes of what was becoming a New Year's Eve carouse we emptied the second bottle. I must say it is a boring way of drinking, this ritual. Then, having ordered a 500-gramme bottle of Ukrainian pepper vodka a minute or two before midnight by the restaurant clock, he leant forward across the table and said, portentously, 'Do you know Nakhodka?'

It was like the beginning of that boring joke that begins, 'Do you know Omsk?', which I had heard so many times in my years as a commercial traveller, but instead of waiting for a couple of hundred *versts* to pass as do the protagonist and the blundering reciters of this chestnut half as old as time, he carried straight on.

'You should go to Nakhodka,' he said, 'by the Trans-Siberian Train. From it you will see Siberia and the great progress our peoples have made in developing the country. It is the longest railway in the world and it was built by Russians.'

By now, somewhere in the outer suburbs of Leningrad, it was 1 January 1965, and any further conversation of a coherent sort in the restaurant car was rendered impossible by great gusts of singing, the drinking of further enormous toasts and an outbreak of bear-hugging among the entire company. It was half past one before I finally got to bed, having sung 'Auld Lang Syne' three times by popular request to great applause and having drunk to peace in our time so often that it should last at least two thousand years, leaving the rest of them still hard at it. Nevertheless, overcome as I was, the man in the black suit had planted the seed of an idea in my fuddled brain.

At 8.26 am I was decanted on to the platform of the Leningrad Station in a city still shrouded in gelid night and one that I have never really grown to like however hard I have tried. There I re-possessed myself of my two-kilo can of *beluga malossol* which was thickly coated with hard snow – it had been a risky business sticking it on the front of the engine as caviar begins to disintegrate around 20°F, but less risky than having it simmering itself into a Russian version of *bouillabaisse* inside the *Krasnaya Strela* where the temperature was up in the 70°s and 80°s.

Then I queued for a taxi to take me to the National Hotel, where I planned to leave my treasured possession in a cool caviar chamber for the next week or so before taking the Ost–West Express to Liverpool Street by way of Brest, Warsaw, Berlin, Rotterdam and the Hook. It was a long queue with few taxis at the end of it, and while I was shuffling forward in it I suddenly recalled through a haze of distilled potato juice the words of my brief acquaintance whom I was to see no more.

'You should go to Nakhodka [wherever that was] by the Trans-Siberian Train. It is the longest railway in the world and it was built by Russians.'

In my hand luggage I had a copy of *Cook's Continental Timetable* and in a few moments I was deep in the USSR section of that heady work, studying the timetable headed MOSKVA–IRKUTSK–KHABAROVSK–NAKHODKA. TRANS-SIBERIAN RAILWAY.

The whole thing appeared even more simple than my perennial optimism about travel would have allowed me to believe. The train, which was called the *Rossiya* (the *Russia*), was due to leave for Vladivostok in approximately one-and-a-half hours time from the Yaroslavl Station, which was so close that I could see it from where I was standing. There was no need for a taxi and I already had a porter.

By reading the small print I discovered that, being a foreigner and therefore not allowed to enter Vladivostok, which was a naval base, I would have to change trains at Khabarovsk on the Amur River, 5331 miles from Moscow and would arrive at Nakhodka on the Sea of Japan on the morning of the ninth day from Moscow. From Nakhodka I could take either a Russian steamer to Yokohama in about 52 hours or one to Hong Kong in 174.

I was terribly tempted. If I did decide to go I would have made the entire journey from the Nevsky Prospekt across Asia, a street of which Sacheverell Sitwell wrote (in *Valse des Fleurs*):

Down at the far end, which tails off as the crow flies, towards Moscow, the buildings, the people, and even the colour of the sky are already Asiatic, in the extent to which the word means wars and plagues and barbarian invasions. The first suburbs of another and an endless world, all plains and distance.

This is what, in spite of feeling rather ill, my heart yearned for at this moment – those vast nomadic steppes which in their southern parts extend for more than 4000 miles without interruption from the Danube to the Great Wall of China. For I am one who believes that a golden opportunity once rejected is seldom put on offer again.

With me I had everything I needed: a Russian visa which was valid for another ten days and which, as a transit passenger on the railway, I would have little difficulty in extending if the need arose. Even if I failed to get an exit permit at Nakhodka for Yokohama or Hong Kong, neither of which was the exit point named on it, I could always fly back from Khabarovsk to Moscow and get my exit visas there for Poland and East Germany. For once I even had plenty of money on my person. There was time, too, to buy food for the journey, which seemed a good idea as 'Roasted Duck wit

Garnisch' would presumably, more often than not, be 'off'. Anyway, with a couple of kilos of caviar to hand I would not lack for friends *en route*, and if I did I could always stick it on the front of an engine.

It would be a quiet time, something in parentheses in a life that was sometimes almost too full of movement, and yet I would be moving, cocooned in the white sheets and with the heavy water decanter to hand (I would steer clear of burly men in black suits and button-down collars who gave me 200-gramme slugs of Ukrainian Pepper Vodka and bear-hugs at midnight into the bargain), and I would re-read Tolstoy's *Resurrection*, something of which currently I was badly in need.

But this moment of euphoria soon passed. I was also a newspaperman with a piece to transmit to London, and there were others to be written in Moscow in the next few days. How I wished I had a brace or two of carrier pigeons which I could release at intervals beyond the Urals. 'National Hotel,' I said, sadly, when my turn came to board a taxi. More than twelve years were to pass before I finally caught the *Rossiya* from the Yaroslavl Station and made the journey of the Trans-Siberian Railway.

I

Under Starter's Orders

FOR eleven years I roared around the world, but during that time the opportunity to travel on the Trans-Siberian Railway never arose, although I often thought of writing a book about it. Railways, like rivers, are difficult subjects for writers because they go on and on. They are less difficult for writers of fiction who can populate their trains with corpses, villains, beautiful people and *wagons-lits* attendants with seven o'clock shadows. If they get bored they can blow them up or derail them. A non-fiction writer is lucky if anyone pulls the communication cord.

When the opportunity finally arose I discovered that there were three possibilities open to me. One was simply to apply for a transit visa for the USSR, buy a ticket from Intourist in London and make the journey from Moscow to Nakhodka without getting off the train at all, except to inspire fresh air on the station platforms along the route. An alternative would be to make the journey, stopping over for a day or two at Novosibirsk, Irkutsk and Khabarovsk, these being the only cities along the route open to foreign visitors in 1977. The third way, and the most complicated and expensive, was to make the journey under the aegis of the Russians themselves and let The Agency provide one of their representatives to accompany me. The Agency is regarded by Western intelligence services as an arm of the KGB. The theoretical advantage of this was that it might be possible to stop off at places that were not on the normal Intourist agenda and see things denied to ordinary foreign tourists, and this was the course that I eventually decided upon.

Which was why, in the depths of Arctic January 1977, I found myself keeping a tryst with a senior representative of The Agency in a sauna bath in the West, not much more than a biscuit's toss from the Iron Curtain.

Mr Oblomov (for that is what I shall call him to spare his blushes), whom I was now regarding through a haze of steam in this subterranean hothouse, was a splendidly endowed fellow in every way, both physically and mentally. Dressed in a Western bespoke suit he had been impressive; now, wearing nothing but a piece of towelling and flagellating himself with a bunch of birch twigs, he looked like a pentathlon gold medallist, and when we plunged into the spacious pool after the torture was over he swam like one.

Later, when I had swum two lengths of the bath under water to show him that, although I was not in the same class as he, I also kept fit, we sat swathed in towels, drinking beer and mapping out a programme for him to present to his superiors.

Two days and three bottles of whisky later – there were others in on this act – I left for London. It had been a thoroughly successful meeting so far as I was concerned. Mr Oblomov had a list of Siberian Wonders as long as your arm, which if I was able to see only a few of them would have turned me into a Siberian Marco Polo. It included visits to active volcanoes, to the coldest place in Siberia where the temperature descends to $-90°F$, to the descendants of the Golds, aboriginals, who until comparatively recently had worn suits of fish skin, to railway construction sites in the remotest wilderness, to gold and diamond mines, ginseng root-collectors and bring-them-back-alive Siberian tiger-hunters. 'I shall also,' said Mr Oblomov, 'recommend that at least part of your journey should take place while there is still snow on the ground. A visit to Siberia without seeing it under snow is like ...'

'A rose without a thorn?' I suggested.

'I was going to say', he said, mischievously, 'like a writer without a head.'

The day after I got back to London I received a message to say that I would not be able to make the journey through Siberia with snow on the ground. No reason was given. I suppose they think it makes the place look untidy.

'Your other proposals', the message said, 'are being considered.'
They were still being considered when I caught the train.

Unlike the English, who have largely destroyed their railway system
and the morale of its employees, the Soviet Union is actually involved in building more and more railway lines, some of them
enormously long. In Siberia, where road-building can cost anything
up to a million rubles a mile and the cost of maintaining them is
equally astronomical, railways are the only means of communication
that can carry heavy freight all the year round. In fact, the Trans-
Siberian is still the only continuous land route from Western Europe
to the Pacific coast of the USSR. At the time of writing there is
no continuous motorable road across Siberia from the Urals to the
Soviet Far East, although work has begun on one.

In the course of this immense journey the train crosses nearly
a hundred degrees of longitude in Europe and Asia and traverses
seven time zones. By the time it reaches the Pacific it is seven hours
ahead of Moscow time; but it has observed Moscow time throughout, as have the clocks on all the stations along the route. The journey for a Soviet citizen takes seven twenty-four-hour days, or to
be more precise 170 hours and 5 minutes, if it is on time, to cover
the 5810 miles from Moscow to Vladivostok, on the Sea of Japan,
where it arrives soon after noon on the eighth day.

For foreigners, who are not allowed into Vladivostok in case they
might espy some more modern version of the battleship *Potemkin*
but have to go to Nakhodka, the only Soviet port facing the Pacific
that is open to them, and from which they can take a ferry to Japan,
the distance is 5900 miles and the journey consumes almost eight
twenty-four-hour days – 192 hours and 35 minutes, which includes
a stopover from day 7 to day 8 at Khabarovsk on the Amur River,
and a change of trains for the last, exciting lap along the frontier
with China, reaching Nakhodka on the morning of the ninth day.
There is no railway journey of comparable length anywhere in the
world. Even New York–Los Angeles on the *Sunset Limited* via New
Orleans is a mere 3420 miles. The Trans-Siberian is *the* big train
ride. All the rest are peanuts.

There were four of us travelling to Siberia together: Otto, a

German photographer on a mission of his own, who was Jewish and with whom we were travelling as it was cheaper to share an interpreter; Mischa, a member of the Agency, who had spent some time in India and who was almost certainly godless; me, as British as a Bath bun and a lapsed member of the Church of England (although still crazy about old churches, preferably with singing going on inside); and lastly Wanda, my wife, a Slovene and a Roman Catholic, who dislikes Mass in the vernacular and whose observations during our long journey together in the two-berth 'soft-class' compartment on the *Rossiya* were interesting to record. Put all these unlikely ingredients in the same compartment, stir in a bottle and a half of vodka, leave to simmer for a couple of hours, light the blue touch paper and stand clear!

Besides being singularly ill-assorted, we were also exceptionally heavily laden, apart from Mischa who was apparently set on going a quarter of the way round the world and back with two shirts and a mohair pullover. It was not altogether our fault. We had been warned to 'dress as you would for an English spring', which is a damn sight more difficult than being told that you are going to the Sahara in summer, or the Arctic in winter; besides which, we were loaded with the tools of our trade.

I had a barely portable library of Siberiana and all sorts of other works which included a timetable for the entire route in Cyrillic. I also had two 1:5,000,000 maps which took in European Russia, Siberia and most of the rest of the USSR.

These maps were contained in a four-foot-long cardboard tube which drove everyone mad who had the custody of it for more than two minutes, including myself. I also had, among others, an underwater camera (because it was also dustproof), six Eagle H pencils, a rubber, a pencil sharpener, three pens and a Challenge duplicate book. All of which worked extremely well throughout. Otto had a large, highly professional metal box, which although made of aluminium was as heavy as lead, full of cameras, and a tripod which also drove everyone mad who had anything to do with it.

On the way to the Yaroslavl Station, the boarding point in Moscow for the Trans-Siberian train, we made a detour to the National Hotel in Manezhnaya, now 'Jubilee of the Revolution', Square where Lenin, who had as keen an eye for the bourgeois comforts of the bed and the board as any of his successors, put up for a spell in March 1918. As we drove to it we passed through Dzerzhinsky Square, so named after the Pole, Felix Dzerzhinsky, whose statue has brooded over it since 1958. Dzerzhinsky was head of the Secret Police from its formation in December 1917, when it was called the CHEKA (Extraordinary Commission for Combating Counter-Revolution and Sabotage), until his death in 1926 from natural causes, something rare in his profession, by which time it had become the OGPU (the State Political Administration). Now, in 1977, its direct lineal descendant the KGB was, almost unbelievably, preparing to celebrate the first sixty Glorious Years of the existence of the Secret Police by giving parties.

At the top end of this square, which is the size of a modest airfield, an immense wedge-shaped reddish building rises on a desirable island site. The pre-revolutionary headquarters of an insurance company, it has been added to and rebuilt many times, the last time in 1946. The back of these premises faces on to a dark and draughty street which for years was shunned by Muscovites like the Black Death, and by almost everyone else in the USSR who happened to be in its vicinity – and still is by those who cannot rid themselves of the habit.

'What's that building?' I asked Mischa. It was intended as a joke. I knew what it was, or what it had been, as well as he did, and so did everyone else in Moscow, where it was as well known as Wormwood Scrubs and the Bloody Tower to Londoners, or the Tombs to the inhabitants of New York – so infamous that some years previously my son, while still a schoolboy of the smaller sort, had tempted providence by photographing it with a rather noisy camera. 'It's some kind of office block,' Mischa said airily. I was damned if I was going to take this from anyone, let alone a 'fellow journalist', even if he was a card-carrying member of the you-know-what. '*You* know what it is, don't you?' I said to the taxi driver, a cheerful fellow who spoke some English. 'Yes,' he said, 'I know what it is.' 'Well, what is it?' 'It's the Lubyanka,' he said.* And he roared with laughter, exposing a perfect row of stainless steel teeth in the upper storey.

The Yaroslavl Station at which we presently arrived is the setting off place not only for Yaroslavl on the Volga, which was its original terminal point when the railway was first built in the 1860s, but also for the Soviet Far East: Archangel, Murmansk, the shores of the White and Kara Seas – for those who like the seaside and pad-dling – as well as for Kotlas, Seregovo, Ukhta and Vorkuta – for those who only go to such places because they are sent to them with one-way tickets.

The station, at which we arrived one-and-a-half hours before the train left, is an astonishing building, even in Moscow, where this epithet, especially when applied to architecture, can become seri-ously over-used. From the outside it looks like the work of a horde of gnomes of the class of 1900, although actually built in 1907 by F. O. Schechtel.

The inside is very different. Entering the waiting room, I had expected to find the customers perched on toadstools. Instead I found myself on an Eisenstein set for a twentieth-century sequel to *Ivan the Terrible* – medieval-looking chandeliers powered by elec-tricity, a complete absence of natural light, squat black marble columns with granite capitals, and filled to the brim with all the extras waiting for the stars to appear and the cameras to roll, hundreds of what could have been Tartars, Komis, Udmurts, Mordvins, Nanays, Chuvashs, Buryats, Koreans, Latvians, Ger-mans, Kazakhs, Bashkirs, Maris, Evenks, Tofas, Ukrainians and possibly some genuine Russians – just some of the people who in-habit the regions through which the Trans-Siberian Railway passes on its way to the Soviet Far East.

I say 'could have been' because even an ethnologist might have found himself stumped, unless he had an identikit with him. None of them, apart from a few Uzbeks in little round hats, whom even I could identify, having once visited their country, wore anything remotely resembling a national costume, so well had the rationalists done their work. The men were dressed in Western-type suits that

* One of the three prisons in or near Moscow which housed political prisoners, and since December 1917 the headquarters of the Secret Police.

looked as if they had been cut with a chopper – the Soviet tailoring industry shares the same master-cutter with the Turks – although some of the younger ones were wearing plastic jackets. Most of the adult males had on the sort of cloth caps worn by British working men before the war. The women wore headscarves and velour top-coats which made them look as if they had been dumped in the waiting room in sacks.

The Uzbeks were at the wrong station, anyway, although they probably didn't know it and if they did, being Uzbeks (and therefore by nature nomads), probably didn't care. They should have been next door, at the Kazan Station (architect A. W. Shchusev, who was also responsible for Lenin's Tomb), waiting for Train No. 24 – 'soft' and 'hard' class, with dining car – to whirl them to their capital Tashkent, 2094 miles away, beyond the Aral Sea. They had plenty of time to find out that it wasn't the Kazan Station – their train didn't leave until 11.20 pm, and it was now 8.30 am.

As in every other railway waiting room in every other communist country I had ever visited, this one was the exclusive preserve of the *lumpen proletariat*, the hoi-polloi. There was not a single traveller to be seen in it of what one might call the administrative or managerial class. I knew, from previous experience, that if any such chose to travel by train they would arrive at the station by taxi or office car, as we had, not as the occupants of the waiting room appeared to have done, on foot and a couple of days early; and they would arrive just before the advertised time of departure. Then their neat luggage would be wheeled up the platform in front of them by porters to whom they would give tips, just as their counterparts in East and West Berlin, Paris, Prague, Warsaw, Rome, Bucharest or Peking would do; everything here is just as it was under the last of the tsars, and just as it still is at Waterloo, King's Cross, Victoria, Euston, Paddington and Liverpool Street under Elizabeth II in my own country – that is, if anyone can find a porter to tip at any of these six last-named termini.

It was a bit different in the waiting room. Here, the submerged classes, most of whom displayed a stoic attitude which under the circumstances was most surprising, were laid out for inspection, in some cases quite literally. The majority of them were sitting or sprawling on the varnished wooden settees with which, just as in every other waiting room in a main station anywhere, this one was inadequately provided: sleeping, sawing away at huge, dark loaves as if they were cellos, talking, quarrelling, belching, smoking cigarettes, laughing, crying, taking milk from the breast, extracting gobbets of meat from horribly greasy parcels, engaging in dreadful spasms of coughing, or just sitting, surrounded by black bags made from American cloth, cheap suitcases and cardboard boxes, all bulging at the seams and held together with bits of string. Those who could not find a seat – and I never saw one unoccupied for an instant unless it was piled high with bags or coats which indicated that it was already somebody's property – either stood, supporting themselves with unfurled, unopened umbrellas, or squatted among their possessions with which they had walled themselves in like settlers preparing to resist an attack by Red Indians. Some simply lay on the floor. Of these, the most determined to find peace and quiet had flaked out in a little enclave that led off the ticket hall one floor up, built in 1964; vast, airy, full of natural light, the complete opposite of this lugubrious place, but almost empty because there was nothing to sit on except the floor.

Meanwhile, down on the ground floor others queued to buy lumps of boiled chicken and equally pallid sausages, Scotch eggs and delicious-looking macaroons, washing these delicacies down with Russian coke, squash or coffee – no beer, vodka or even tea available at the station, apparently, except possibly in the restaurant on the upper floor, outside which a queue had formed. A good thing, too, judging by the Bacchanalian scenes enacted outside in the vicinity of Komsomolskaya (Young Communists') Square, even at this unseemly hour, by what I hoped were non-fellow-travellers.

Over all hung the smell of Russians *en masse*; no worse than the smell of an *en masse* of English or Italians, or inhabitants of the Côte d'Ivoire, or any other nationality; but just different. A smell that one traveller compared, I think inaccurately, to that of a laundry basket on the weekly collection morning; inaccurate not because it is impolite – it is impossible to describe smells of people *en masse* politely – but because the smell to my mind is more pungent, and I think comes in part from eating the strong, black bread. I wondered what we smell like to them.

In these surroundings it was not surprising that Otto, a somewhat conspicuous figure in Russia, although he could never understand why (his jeans – the going black market rate for which was in the region of £100 – his Nikons and Leicaflexes were under continual offer from the locals) contrived to get himself arrested twice in the space of an hour: the first time by the Railway Police for photographing an elderly lady on one of the platforms in the rain (which, apart from one miraculous day, had been falling more or less incessantly ever since our arrival in the country); the second time, which was far more serious, by the Military Police, for taking pictures of some conscripts from the borders of Outer Mongolia, who were on their way to be turned into soldiers elsewhere in the Soviet Union.

The clothing of the conscripts was exiguous. Mischa explained that they were wearing their oldest clothes because, on their arrival at their training depot, their clothes would be burned, as was the Red Army custom. One had a paper hat on made from a sheet of *Pravda*. It seemed a shame to burn that. They looked cold, tired, hungry, fed up, and far from home. I felt sorry for them and I felt alarm for Otto, but I also sympathized with the lieutenant in charge of the draft who had called on the Military Police to take Otto away to their home-from-home in the station. He was as grumpy as an Irish Guards officer would have been at Paddington Station, lumbered with a similar collection of recruits straight from the back blocks of Connemara and Mayo and on his way with them to the Training Depot at Pirbright, if he found them being photographed by a Russian.

It was fortunate that I saw Otto being marched off as Mischa was elsewhere; otherwise we would have started looking under trains for him or calling up hospitals. As it was, Mischa had to produce the small, oblong red pass entombed in plastic, the one I never managed to get a really close-up look at in the weeks to come, which sometimes worked in difficult situations. This time it did work; but only after much serious telephoning.

2

The Way to Zagorsk

By now it was 9.45 am. The *Rossiya*, otherwise Train No. 2, was due to leave at 10.10. Train No. 1 is the *Rossiya* from Vladivostok to Moscow. Both ways the service is daily.

It was time to board. With the recently-released Otto, savouring his freedom, and preceded by a porter wheeling our eighteen pieces of assorted luggage, including several cardboard boxes of drink and more or less imperishable food – we had all heard gruesome reports about the quality of the food on the train, and the cost of it, from survivors of the journey – we plugged up the platform against intermittent rain squalls and a blustery north-easter, past a bunch of tough-looking soldiers wearing fore-and-aft caps and loose-fitting uniforms, to all of whom I was tempted to say, and would have done if I had been in charge of them, 'Dirty Boots!' (The only clean army boots I saw in Russia were on the two men guarding Lenin's Tomb.) All the cars on the *Rossiya* were steel-built in East Germany. On every other passenger train except the *Rossiya* No. Ones, which in the course of the journey we saw from time to time flashing past in the opposite direction on the way from Vladivostok, the cars were pea-green with two horizontal yellow bands around them. On the *Rossiya* they were red. In addition each car was embellished with a metal plaque embossed with the coat-of-arms of the USSR: a golden hammer and sickle against a brown and yellow globe, golden wheat-sheaves wrapped in red scrolls with the names of the constituent republics on them picked out in gold, and a red star over all. And, to me, most exciting of all, beneath the plaque, there was a sign with the magic words MOSCOW–VLADIVOSTOK inscribed on it in Cyrillic characters.

Awaiting the customers at the door of each car was a pair of conductresses, dressed in black jackets, peaked caps and mini skirts. Some were comely, some were so-so, some were really rugged. Those with knobbly knees could have done with some inches on their hems. What sort of pair were we going to field?

Our car was about halfway up the train, but there was no cause for alarm. One of ours was a platinum blonde, going on for twenty-four with rather weak legs and the peroxide just beginning to grow out, and a mouth with some bits of steel filling showing, but otherwise OK. The other was in the prime of life, with chestnut hair, good legs and a really charming smile, with some real gold in it. Short of getting the twin daughters of Helen Osekina, the top Russian fashion model in the sixties – that is, if she *had* twin daughters old enough to be conductresses – or Pola Negri out of a deep freeze, it would have been churlish to complain. For a moment I wondered if it was chance. Then I dismissed the thought as unworthy. Soviet Railways must have more important things to worry about than whether a bunch of foreigners get conductresses who are easy on the eye.

The windows on the corridor side next to the platform were all locked, presumably to prevent foreigners escaping into the USSR, a temptation that we were all able to resist during our journey to the Pacific. There was, therefore, no possibility of shoving the luggage through the windows, which is what Italian and French sleeping car porters often do when loading bags into sleeping cars. This meant that the luggage had to be ferried down the corridor, piece by piece, past other passengers who, like passengers in corridor cars everywhere, prefer to have their toes trodden on twenty-four times or more by an assortment of individuals rather than withdraw into their compartments, even for an instant.

Meanwhile, up at the head of the train, with the underwater camera, I was just about to photograph the big Czechoslovakian electric engine, Type CHS2, which was to haul the *Rossiya* over the first 210 miles of the course, giving it, and the two motormen (one scowling, the other grinning like a before-and-after ad for Dr Collis Brown's Chlorodyne), 1/125th sec at f5.6. By now the weather was redolent of Clapham Junction in December rather than

Moscow in May with spring, at least in theory, breaking out on every side. Then, just as I was pulling back on the shutter release lever (a peculiarity of this camera is that you pull rather than push), a large, soft hand the colour of lard closed over lens and viewfinder and for the first of what was to be dozens of times I heard the dread words '*Nyet razreshayetsa!*' ('Not permitted!').

On the other end of this massive organ of prehension was one of the less comely conductresses. She looked like a full-length cast of Khruschev fitted with tits.

Fortunately, I had my phrase book open at page 13, 'Some Basic Expressions'. 'Mee*noo*tahchkoo, *yah* pahsmah*tryoo* smah*goo*lee yah yee*yo* nigh*tee* v *knee*zhkyee,' I said, which was what it told me to say, or as near as I could get to it. ('Just a minute, I'll see if I can find it in this book.') Finally, after skimming through the Russian equivalents of 'What is your telephone number?', 'Thank you it has been a wonderful evening', 'Where's the nearest filling station?', 'Excuse me. May I park here?' and 'Suppose I come back in half an hour?' I found something that might be more to her taste on page 22, under 'Passport Control – IF THINGS BECOME DIFFICULT'. 'I'm sorry. I don't understand. Is there anyone here who speaks English?'

'Here, you read it,' I said giving her the book and taking the picture of the CHS2 from the hip which is a piece of cake with this sort of camera. I wasn't pointing it in the right direction. All I got was a Moscow sky.

In the course of this little adventure, besides having it confirmed that there is such a thing as reincarnation ('KHRUSCHEV LIVES!' – I could just see the headlines in *The Sun*), I learned that altogether there were fifteen passenger cars on the train, a restaurant car with a kitchen belching steam and a girl peeling spuds in a bucket at an open door, a mail van, and a compartment containing a radio transmitting set with an operator already bent over it, in case we hit an iceberg – '*Sparks!*'

I had also discovered that, of what I estimated to be the 500 or so passengers on the train (the number of adults, including staff, was actually nearer to 650), none were the sort of people we had seen in the waiting room; but thoroughly urbanized, solid citizens,

THE WAY TO ZAGORSK

well-off workers, mostly young, mostly married with one or two children and sometimes with grandparents in tow. The men wore white drip-dry shirts if they had not already changed into track suits of a poisonous shade of royal blue for the journey, which were marginally better than the ghastly striped pyjamas, that gaped in the wrong places, I remembered from the train journeys on my previous visit. The women were positively formal in shiny print day dresses covered with cabbage roses or sunflowers and some of them had huge bouffant hairdoes. Their children were as spick-and-span as if they had been given the man-made fibre treatment at Marks and Sparks, or Ohrbach's. I wondered then, and still do, when and by what means Eisenstein's extras were destined to leave the Yaroslavl Station and whither they were bound.

There was one late arrival, and he was very late; he was a junior *apparatchik* in a suit of pure new wool and with luggage all of a piece, which was being propelled up the platform ahead of him by a porter travelling flat out. He had cut it a bit too fine and although only about the same age as Mischa, about thirty-five, he was puffing like a steam engine on a 1:30 gradient.

By 10.10 am the people seeing the *Rossiya* off had been reduced to two, a girl wearing white shoes who had a Soviet sailor in a crafty hold, and an ex-fighter pilot turned journalist from the Agency who had been seeing us off with a farewell picnic of vodka and cold meat. At this precise time the CHS2 uttered the sort of noise a snake makes while being crushed underfoot, which communicated itself to our car by way of some rubber pipes; the conductresses on the platform (now reduced to one per car – the others having gone to get their heads down until they came on shift) held out their yellow batons which looked like corn-cobs, stepped aboard and closed and locked the doors; and we were off on the line to Yaroslavl, the carriages swaying backwards and forwards with the sort of gentle movement that a car on a big dipper makes just before it finally comes to rest, or that a horse makes when swimming a river. We had been told that we would not be allowed off the railway till we reached Novosibirsk 2089 miles up the line.

Almost at once the view from the train windows became much more rustic than one would normally expect on a main railway line near the centre of a city of more than seven and a half million people. Lime trees and silver birches plugged the more horrible vistas. To the right was the Sokolniki Park, named after the imperial falconers whose hunting territory it was, which certainly didn't look like falcon country any more. Now for a moment we were in marshy land in which lengths of cement pipe leading nowhere were semi-submerged in a sort of pond. Then we crossed the little river Yauza and passed through a marshalling yard somewhere near the Yaroslavl Highway full of flat cars loaded with thousands more pipes, *en route* for the oil and gas fields beyond the Urals.

Standing around in this marshalling yard was a squad of dumpy women, a small detachment of the million or more women who make up about a third of the 3,500,000 Soviet Railway workers, wearing headscarves, padded black cotton jackets, yellow plastic waistcoats to make it more difficult for drivers to run them over, short black skirts, thick black stockings and sensible boots. They were supposed to be lubricating points with what I assumed to be, having greased wire ropes with it when I was a sailor, a filthy mixture of grease and tallow. (This is just one of the troubles about travelling by train. You can never find out about important matters like this. Next thing you find yourself writing to the Head of the Russian Railways asking him what he thinks they grease them with, and he doesn't know either.)

Instead of getting on with this horrible task, and in spite of the rain, to which they appeared oblivious, they were having a bit of fun with a group of male railway workers. Two of the men had their arms around two of the women's waists, or as far round them as anyone's arms could go around a couple of short-waisted hip 44s with something like five layers of clothing between themselves and the outside world. The rest of the party, apart from a couple of do-gooders who were working with all the animation of the participants in a slow-motion film of a coronation, shrieked with laughter, slapped their thighs and waved derisively at their bourgeois-type female comrades with the bouffant hairdoes on the train.

Now the *Rossiya* ran through Mytischi, where an enormous factory produces subway cars. In 1926 it made the first electrically powered railway cars in Russia for a line at Baku.

This was the last stop, although the *Rossiya* didn't make use of it, before the *dacha* land of the Muscovites, the wooden weekend and holiday houses, ownership of which is the dream of every citizen. Some of the dachas were so small that they must have fitted their occupants closely round the hips. Each one had a television aerial and a small patch of garden, and looked out on to a muddy but arcadian lane lined with lime trees.

Ever since the *Rossiya* had got beyond waving distance of the platform at Moscow, not that there had been anyone left on it to wave to when it did leave (even the girl in the white shoes who had been saying goodbye to the Navy had by then sloped off), the Russian passengers, who appeared to make up about 90 per cent of the total cargo, began to run hither and thither like a nest full of ants which someone had stirred with a stick, and the corridors were filled with milling humanity.

Small boys and girls zoomed up and down continuously, licking hideously sticky toffee apples and caressing the door knobs of the compartments thereby turning them into miniature replicas of toffee apples; sailors in uniforms that looked as if they had been designed by Bakst and soldiers who looked as if their greatcoats had been designed by a blanket manufacturer clonked past with armfuls of beer bottles on their way to orgies; some of the large, determined-looking matrons in floral prints swayed down on us like clipper ships under stun'sails, carrying everything before them; and old men in striped pyjamas that made them look like survivors of a concentration camp tottered on their way, stopping to have a look at the big yellow samovar with which our car was equipped. It was all extremely Russian and interesting; but when, in spite of the crowds, the blonde conductress arrived with one of those recumbent, wheel-less vacuum cleaners and began to give the corridor carpet a going over, it was too much, and we took refuge in our compartment. 'If it's going to be like this for the next 5800 miles all the way to the Pacific, I shall go mad,' Wanda said. 'Well, what about me?' I said. 'Perhaps we should get off at the next stop. Breathe it to Mischa.' 'You breathe it to Mischa,' she said, 'it was your idea, this crazy journey.' 'I didn't know it was going to be like this,' I said. 'And anyway, what are you doing on this train if you thought it was a crazy idea?' 'I came to see that you didn't get drunk,' she said, pronouncing it 'dronk', 'and say things you might be sorry for.' 'Thank you very much,' I said, as I closed the door, becoming nice and sticky in the process.

We now took a closer look at our deluxe, 'soft-class' compartment, which was one of nine such two-berth compartments in the only soft-class, two-berth car on the train. It was certainly a bit different from the Russian sleeping car on the *Krasnaya Strela* in which I had snatched a few hours' sleep on New Year's morning in 1965, and less ample than the first-class sleeper occupied by Maurice Baring, poet, man of letters, diplomat, war correspondent and linguist, while on his way to report the Russo-Japanese war in Manchuria in 1904, which had a 'bathroom and a small bookcase of Russian books'. Some trans-Siberian trains had at that time a church car on them. On this May morning in 1977 the compartment was almost as dank as the weather outside, but only because the heating had not yet had time to seep through the pipes to it from the furnace at the end of the corridor, which was fuelled with coal.

The compartment was clean and, apart from a brown tabletop and a strip of carpet similar to that in the corridor, remarkable for its lack of colour. The walls and ceiling were the palest of pale greys; the cotton covers on the upholstered back rests and the curtain on a rod, which obscured the view from the lower half of the window and kept falling down, were off-white, not because they were dirty but because this was their natural colour. All the metal fittings were of some pallid alloy. Altogether it was rather like looking at a photograph of a sleeping compartment that had been heavily over-exposed.

There was a ceiling light which could be dimmed to a sinister, frigid blue and a couple of well-meant but rather inadequate reading lights above what would be the beds when they were made up. These were side by side, opposite one another on the ground floor – no nasty little ladders leading to upper berths which make going to bed in the upper regions of a four-berth compartment on a train as dangerous as footling about on the Eiger without a rope.

But there was nothing wrong with the design of the appurtenances. The folding table was a miracle of ingenuity. There was a water carafe, stable and heavy enough to survive a force 9 gale in the Bay of Biscay. There was sufficient space in the containers under the seats to take a folded corpse, as well as a large suitcase, and the seats had enough overhang to accommodate a couple of small suitcases behind one's feet. There was also a space in the bulkhead above the door ample enough to take a small trunk. At present it was occupied by our two sets of bedding: a mattress fitted with a sheet covering, a top sheet, two pillows and a blanket and two hand-towels, which had to last all the way to Novosibirsk, although we did not know this, two nights and two days to the east.

Between us Wanda and I disposed of two large suitcases, two small ones, not much bigger than document cases, a formidable black overnight bag which looked as if it might contain a brace of human heads, Wanda's handbag, as commodious but somewhat less sumptuous than a buyer's from I. Magnin, the cardboard telescope containing maps, a camera bag, and a pile of raincoats, windcheaters and sawn-off Wellington boots, all of which had defied our efforts to contain them in any sort of portable container, plus the food-and-drink box. The various luggage depositories swallowed all these impedimenta quite effortlessly and with room to spare. I began to wish we had brought more.

We now received a visit from the ticket inspector, a man of about fifty. With his mahogany, Mayan-type face and thick, straight, greying black hair he looked as if he had just pole-vaulted the Bering Strait. He was unable to clip our tickets as Mischa had them in the other compartment further up the car where he and Otto were, one hoped, making the best of it.

Instead we had a chat, in agonizing, sub-O-level German which was the best he or I could manage. Personally, I would never have started it.

'Ich,' he said, banging his chest to emphasize who was speaking – it emitted a sound like a broken drum – 'Ich arbeit acht Uhren jeden Tag. Hundert ziebzig Uhren jeden Monat.' And he stood back so that he could better take in the effect that this pronouncement was having on such an obviously shiftless fellow.

It was difficult to know whether to congratulate him on having a cushy job, or commiserate with him on having a rotten, overworked one. What *were* the German equivalents of 'Cor!' 'Ripping!' or 'Hard Cheese!'?

'Wieviel Uhren arbeiten Sie?' Now he was banging *my* chest, which gave off no sound at all, as if I might be in doubt as to who I was.

'Ich weiss nicht.' How boring foreigners tend to be. No one would dream of asking me such a question on the 9.30 to Penzance – certainly not a ticket inspector.

'Weiss nicht? Warum weiss nicht? Was sind Sie? Americanets?'

'Nein, Anglichanin.' The Russian for 'English' sounds like something smelly you rub on your chest when you're not feeling so good. 'Anglichanye arbeiten nicht zu viel,' he said triumphantly.

'Well, you can hardly accuse the Russians of overdoing it,' said Wanda who had been listening to this conversation with increasing impatience.

His mood changed. Now he looked solemn, if not gloomy. For a moment I thought that he would ask me some impossible-to-answer-without-giving-offence question, such as 'Do you like Russia?', while I was still searching my peanut brain for some shattering reply to 'Anglichanye arbeiten nicht zu viel.' But he didn't.

'So, Anglichanin,' he said. 'Dann warum haben Sie ein so schrecklich Wetter aus ihrem Land gebracht?' pointing at the sodden landscape whirling past outside the window. Then he went on his way in search of other tickets to clip, laughing at his little joke.

'And next time you come to England don't bring any of your snow with you,' I shouted after him in English; but it was too late, he was already in the next coach.

By this time things had quietened down and the corridor was practically deserted. It seemed a good time to have a look at the lavatories, something we had been putting off. We approached them with the trepidation that all travellers experience when visiting such places for the first time.

There were two lavatories, one at each end of the car, and we inspected them with care, knowing that we were going to be stuck with them for the foreseeable future whether we liked them or not. There was however no cause for alarm – at least at this stage of the journey, when few passengers appeared to have discovered their existence.

The washbasins and the loos were clean and the basins both had plugs, thus rendering superfluous the black squash ball (a dog ball for the smaller sort of dog will perform the same function) which we had brought all the way from England to serve as a plug and which we had guarded with our lives. It had been a godsend in Moscow at the Ukraina Hotel where, if our first-class accommodation was anything to go by, there are more than 1000 plugless rooms.

On the deficit side there was no trap under the washbasin, so that if you dropped your toothbrush, earrings or contact lenses down the hole they would end up on Russian soil. These basins were also equipped with those devilish taps, which they also have on ships to prevent the user sinking them from the inside, that work only with the exertion of superhuman pressure, and when they do, finally and grudgingly, deliver either scalding hot or freezing cold water, but never at the same time.

The lavatories were huge, large enough almost to accommodate a Siberian mammoth, and fitted with seats. These mammoth traps came from the same factory as the taps, shooting up, when there was no weight on them, with a vicious and resounding clang, revealing two non-skid plaques on the pan itself, intended for those who, like me, prefer to stand rather than sit on strange, outlandish objects. On the other hand there was a big bar of pink soap, an adequate supply of tough paper and a 220-volt, two-plug socket for electric razors (of which there were more out in the corridor for those who like to shave in public). I have spent many a night in far worse places.

It was 11 am. The *Rossiya* was running among pine trees. The *dachas* were behind us. Now the country began to open out and there were green fields between the trees. It was a bit like any stockbroker belt but without the houses and without the stockbrokers. The only human being in sight was a man carrying a heavy pack on his back making his way across a clearing and getting nice and wet.

Now the girl whom I had seen peeling potatoes appeared, wearing a potato-stained white coat and a limp little white hat, from beneath which strands of damp hair hung down over her face, partially obscuring it and making her look indescribably pathetic, like a waif who has been crying over a sinkful of washing up – in her case about a dozen bucketfuls of potatoes. She offered us cream in bottles, borsch, rice, and meat the colour of the weather outside swimming in a sort of greasy bouillon, all of which she carried in nesting aluminium containers – the potatoes were, presumably, reserved for those brave souls who had reached the restaurant car, that undiscovered country from whose bourne no traveller returns – none of which we felt like trying, especially the meat which was distinctly off-putting. Mustering a brave little smile in answer to ours, she dragged off down the corridor.

Now, as in a play in which no time can be wasted as it invariably is in life, the blonde conductress who was named Irina appeared bringing glasses of lovely hot tea in shiny metal holders embossed with figures of cosmonauts, sputniks zooming through space, battleships ploughing the seas and Soviet-type skyscrapers like the ones on Stolichnaya vodka bottles, all commemorating fifty years of communism, and therefore almost ten years old, having drawn the boiling water from a bright yellow samovar which she kept fuelled with blocks of peat. This samovar, which looked like a trench mortar, stood in a recess at the end of the corridor outside the den of whichever girl was on duty, and alongside it was an exploded plan of the thing in case it blew a gasket or needed other help.

Irina also brought some little cakes which cost 19 kopecks each and some small chocolate bars, labelled 'Red Front' in Russian, at a colossal 1 ruble 80 each – colossal to the English, anyway, with the ruble, which is divided into 100 kopecks, currently standing at 1.26 to the pound. Wanda had a cake; Otto had a choc'bar – perhaps the Germans were getting a better exchange rate – and so did Mischa, to whom rates of exchange meant nothing. The tea was free unless you took sugar, in which case it cost 4 kopecks a glass.

Irina was petite, slim and slightly anaemic-looking, as many Russian women seemed to be. In an attempt to redress her rather transparent pallor she had gone to work on herself with an orange lipstick and some eyeshadow of an unfortunate shade of green. Now, having removed her clumsy uniform jacket which was rather like that of a London bus conductress, she was dressed in the tight black uniform skirt, a white shirt with a railway badge pinned to it and black, sling-back sandals. She looked as if she had been asked to go to a fancy dress party as Monroe and had done her best to comply.

Outside in the corridor there was a rack loaded with helpful literature in English, French, German, Japanese and Spanish, with a polite notice inviting all and sundry in 'soft class' deluxe (the service did not extend to other parts of the train) to study this material at no further cost to themselves. A lot of it emanated from The Agency in Moscow. These boys miss few if any chances to make their mark in the world about them.

As always undecided when it comes to choosing literature, especially when it is of an ostensibly improving nature, and because there were no other contenders for it anyway, I took the whole lot back into the compartment with the intention of sifting out some bedtime reading for the next 1125 miles or so to Novosibirsk.

The choice narrowed itself to: *Marx–Engels–Lenin: On Socialist Revolution* and *L'URSS vue par un Étranger: Notes de Séjour*. All four of us were now crammed into our two-berth suite with Mischa sitting opposite me. As I skimmed through the stuff I realized that I only had to utter one 'Ha!' or 'Ha-Ha!' to bring him in on the act and I would then be up to my neck in dialectics. I therefore preserved an air of gravity.

The first to go was the *Marx-Engels–Lenin: On Socialist Revolution*. Page 22 recorded an interview granted by Marx to a correspondent of *The World*, in London, on 3 July 1871.

Interviewer: It would seem that in this country the hoped for revolution, whatever it may be, will be attained without the violent means of revolution. The English system of agitating by platform and press until minorities become converted into majorities is a hopeful sign.

Dr Marx: I am not as sanguine on that point as you. The English middle class has always shown itself willing enough to accept the verdict of the majority so long as it enjoyed the monopoly of the voting power. But mark me, as soon as it finds itself outvoted on what it considers vital questions we shall see a new slave owners' war....

Notes de Séjour were the thoughts of Arthur Feslier, chief public relations officer of New Zealand Airways, which had surfaced recently while he was being interviewed on a Soviet radio programme, rendered for some inscrutable reason into French.

Question [it read] (often propounded, but not on radio): Do the Soviet People have some characteristics which do not please you?

Reply: No, they have their own characteristics, we have ours. And who am I to make absurd comparisons?

Question [The questioner obviously getting bored with this subject which could go on being batted about until kingdom come]: Have you met any Soviet women?

Reply: Only on official occasions. I have seen some in offices and at Radio-Moscow.

Question: Do you consider that the absence of unofficial meetings constituted a gap in your programme?

Reply: Yes I do. But I have not given the matter much thought. Certainly, I would have liked to meet some Soviet women: some intellectuals, some employees, some officials, some housewives, and have a talk with them in private. I will do it the next time.

Eventually I decided to put the leaflets back in the rack where I had found them, but when I reached the rack, padding along the drugget, it had already been replenished with a fresh, identical supply. It was like being at the source of a river.

At 11.14 am the *Rossiya* trundled past some melancholy brickfields and through a rustic-looking station at Zagorsk, 46 miles from Moscow.

For almost 550 years Zagorsk was called Sergiev after Saint Sergius, the son of a boyar from Radonezh in the Rostov region who lived and died there. In 1930 it had the honour of exchanging it for the name of Vladimir M. Zagorsky, secretary of the Communist Party, who was blown up by a bomb in Moscow in 1919.

And now a few hundred yards away to the left of the line the great brick towers and pale, machicolated walls of the Troitsko-Sergievskaya Lavra, the Trinity Monastery of St Sergius, came into view, dwarfing the trees and clapboard houses beneath them. Within this perimeter a mass of spires and domes, one a belfry about 300 feet high designed by Rastrelli (the architect of the Winter

Palace at St Petersburg), rose against the sky: bulbous domes, domes shaped like helmets, some gilded, some painted cerulean blue and studded with gold stars – all of them, spires and domes, topped with glittering gold crosses supported by spidery antennae, all shaming the unutterably gloomy weather.

Sergius founded the monastery in 1340. He died in 1392. In 1408 the Tartars sacked Moscow and the monastery, burning the wooden church that he had built and in which he was buried. It was Nikon, his successor as abbot, who recovered the body of Sergius from the smoking ruins, still miraculously intact. As a result the monastery became immensely popular as a place of pilgrimage, as it still is to this day. Between 1422 and 1427 Nikon built the Cathedral of the Trinity to house the remains of St Sergius. He himself was also sanctified, and his body lies in the Church of St Nikon, next door to the Cathedral of the Trinity.

Since its rebuilding the Monastery of St Sergius has survived every vicissitude in a way that, if not actually miraculous, is as near miraculous as makes no difference. It was never visited by plague (in 1570 200,000 persons died of plague in Moscow and its neighbourhood alone) or by cholera, which in 1892 killed more than 150,000 people in European Russia.

But perhaps the greatest miracle of all was that it was not plundered under the Bolsheviks. On 20 April 1920 a special decree was promulgated by the Council of People's Commissars establishing 'The Museum of Historical and Art Relics of the Troitsko-Sergievskaya Lavra'. The principal signatory was Stalin. It then became a museum and a refuge for savants; but by the time the English traveller, art critic and historian Robert Byron succeeded in visiting it in 1930, the savants had been dispersed, accused of plotting – 'some to manure Socialist fields, others to populate the Ural towns and lumber camps', as he put it.

Today it is the centre of Russian Orthodoxy, with a seminary and academy for young priests, and the religious capital of Russia. A day or two before setting off on the train we had visited the monastery by car from Moscow, although it is equally possible to go there by train. The coming of the train had been vigorously opposed by the Metropolitan of Moscow in 1860: 'Pilgrims would come to the monastery in railway cars, in which all sorts of tales can be heard, and often dirty stories, whereas now they come on foot and each step is a feat pleasing to God.'

It is difficult to think of any church building more austerely beautiful than the little Cathedral of the Troitska, with its glistening walls of smooth white stone, gilded roofs and helmet dome supported by a slender, soaring drum of masonry, pierced by tall, narrow windows; or one with a more memorable interior, its darkness and mystery enhanced by the long shafts of dust-filled light that stream down into it from above.

On the day we visited it, before boarding the train, it was crowded with pilgrims, the majority of them women, mostly poor (if one can properly use such an expression to describe citizens of the USSR), the younger ones the sort of women whom I had just seen greasing points on the railways. They were buying candles from a little stall in the narthex, which also sold Soviet-made ikons, and were setting them up before the iconostasis, the screen separating the sanctuary from the main body of the church, on which the ikons are displayed, in an atmosphere heady with incense and resonant with the constant chanting of the plea *'Gospodi pomilui!'* ('Lord have mercy upon us!') It was this iconostasis that displayed until after the Revolution the 'Trinity' by the monk Andrei Rublyov, which he painted in the early part of the fifteenth century – one of the finest, perhaps the finest icon ever painted, now in the Tretyakov Gallery in Moscow.

There were hundreds of pilgrims awaiting their turn to kiss the jewel-encrusted silver sarcophagus given to the monastery by Ivan the Terrible, which houses the mummified remains of Sergius and stands beneath an enormous heavy, solid silver baldacchino, presented by the Empress Anna Ivanovna. There they were, confessing their sins ('instead of greasing points near Babushkin I allowed a fellow railway worker to put his arms around my waist, as far as he was able'); paying their respects to St Nikon; drinking and taking away holy water from the miraculous well housed in a little multi-coloured chapel close by; and crossing themselves before the sarcophagus of the usurping tsar, Boris Godunov.

I was told that I might ask questions of the civil administrator of the monastery and of two young priests who sat on either side of him, so I inquired whether the membership of the Church in the USSR was declining or increasing and what was the estimated number of members at the present time. To both of these I received the reply, 'We don't know.' After this I gave up and concentrated on the monastery.

These two priests, one of whom was deputed to act as guide – a portly young man with a fine, glossy beard which looked as if it had been given frequent goings-over with brilliantine – I did not find attractive. They were too well fed, too well groomed and too self-satisfied. Nor did I find agreeable the offhand, impatient way in which the fat one offered his ring to be kissed by pilgrims during our tour of the monastery. Admittedly, there were many who asked the right; but it was a great day for them, and he should have complied with better grace.

3

The Way to the Volga

THE *Rossiya* now left the Moscow *oblast* for that of Vladimir, two of twenty-two such *oblasts* that make up the Central Economic Region. This enormous region has a population of over 28 million people or 11 per cent of the entire population of the USSR. It is a gigantic industrial area, some of whose industries had first been set up in the seventeenth century by Peter the Great. Now it produces more than half of all the textiles in Russia, which is saying a great deal, for Russia is the world's biggest producer of cotton textiles, not to mention silk, wool, linen and synthetic fabrics.

The USSR is divided up into fifteen Soviet Socialist Republics (SSRs) of which the largest and most populated is the Russian Soviet Socialist Republic. In addition some major ethnic and other groups have been given the status of Autonomous Soviet Socialist Republics (ASSRs). An *oblast* is at the same level of political jurisdiction as an ASSR but it is a unit without any ethnic significance which has been created solely for reasons of economic convenience.

The Central Region goes in for shoe and clothing manufacture, food processing, steel rolling, the production of every kind of machinery from diesel engines and aeroplanes to watches and cameras – in fact everything that a Central Economic Region in a capitalist country would produce and which everyone in a capitalist country takes for granted.

This is a distinctly chilly part of the world. Its northern limit is in 59°N, about the same latitude as Uranium City, Saskatchewan, far north of the effective limit of settlement in North America; temperatures can go down to −45.6°F, and below-freezing temperatures occur in every month except July and August.

Here, on the line of the Northern Railway, we were in a rural part of the Central Region. There was no doubt about that. It stretched away among woods of birch and conifer with reaches of clover and alfalfa meadow running between them. This was country which, long ago, had been covered with dense forest, but forest that had been cut again and again until it assumed its present aspect. Now, according to the Russian *Atlas of the USSR*, it was cattle and dairy country, although there was not an animal to be seen.

In it the villages were mostly long lines of *izbas*, single-storey log cabins with corrugated iron or tarred roofs. They stood behind picket fences, each with its own vegetable plot, in which the dark, sodden earth had only recently been dug, and to every six or seven cabins there was a well for drinking water, worked by a windlass; in some of these little villages, but not many, there was a wooden church.

At 11.52 am, 70 miles from Moscow, the *Rossiya* came to a halt for one minute at Alexandrov on the Seraia River, the first of the ninety-three scheduled stops it would be making on its way from Moscow to Vladivostok. As we trundled over the bridge into the station, the Cathedral of the Trinity could be seen hemmed in by factories and yards full of cans.

This was the place to which, at the end of 1564, Ivan the Terrible retired with only a few followers, to make it his temporary capital. One would have thought that the boyars, the territorial nobility, would have been delighted to have got shot of a ruler so ingenious in the infliction of cruelty; but, in fact, it was the boyars who actually travelled to Alexandrov in order to implore him to return. Which he did, setting up a regime in which even more blood flowed, culminating in 1570 in the butchery of 60,000 of the inhabitants of Novgorod, which had been rash enough to consider opening its gates to an army of invading Poles.

Novgorod, one of the oldest cities in Russia, was founded by Scandinavian Vikings, whose principal business had been trading furs with the Hanseatic and Scandinavian cities. By the twelfth century a German settlement was established at Novgorod, the 'Deutscher Hof'. It also had close commercial ties with Constantinople by way of the Dnieper; and it was strong enough to resist the Tartars and at the same time to remain on reasonably good terms with the Khan of the Golden Horde on the Volga.

Sir Jerome Horsey, an English adventurer and traveller who was for a time Ivan's envoy to Elizabeth I until he fell into disfavour because of alleged frauds, left a profile of the Tsar which he wisely put off publishing until after his death.

Thus much to conclude with this Emperor Ivan Vasiliwich. He was a goodlie man of person and presence, well favoured, high forehead, shrill voice, a right Sithian, full of readie wisdom, cruell, bloudye, merciless; his own experience managed by direction both his state and commonwealth affares; was sumptuously intomed in Michell Archangel church, where he, though garded daye and night, remaines a fearfull spectacle to the memory of such as pass by or heer his name spoken, who are contented to cross and bless themselves before his resurrection againe!

After Alexandrov the *Rossiya* entered the first time zone beyond Moscow, so we were one hour ahead of Moscow, three hours ahead of Greenwich. The line now crossed an open plateau on which there were big plantations of pines and broad-leafed trees. For some time the sun had been trying to break through the low cloud, and now it finally succeeded and for a few minutes bathed in an unearthly yellow light the sombre dripping woods, the fields in which the earth was all sorts of shades from black to claret, newly sown with potatoes, oats and barley, and the birch trees in the snow breaks along the line. Then the weather closed in again and everything was as before.

Just over two-and-a-half hours from Moscow the plateau began to fall away in a long, gradual descent towards the basin of the Volga, and now the *Rossiya* picked up speed, racing down past big freight trains, mostly loaded with lumber, which were slogging up the incline in the opposite direction. While it was going what seemed to me flat out, Otto made an excursion to the restaurant car, which was about half a dozen cars downhill in the direction of the engine. When he returned it was with a whole heap of depressing news. The food was as unappetizing as that being hawked up and down the train, and the kitchen was equally so. In the course of gaining this information he had nearly lost his nose and the front part of one of his cameras when the head cook – Otto could not bring himself to call him *chef* – had slammed a door in his face. There was no beer or vodka on board, and the only wines on offer were Russian champagne at 5.40 rubles a bottle and what appeared to be some sort of dessert wine of a sinister brown colour which cost 5.25 rubles.

By now the other conductress was on duty, the more mature one with the chestnut hair. She was called Lilya and she had a charming smile which lit up the whole sleeping car – nothing like the sort to which we had already grown accustomed, which were switched on and off like 40-watt bulbs, but a real one filled with gold which was itself a welcome change from the everlasting stainless steel. She could speak a little English, but she understood much more than she spoke.

Vodka was no longer served on the *Rossiya*, Lilya said, or on most other trains in Russia. The reason was obvious. In the short time we had been in the USSR I had never seen so many drunks anywhere in the world, with the possible exception of Finland, and at such odd times of day – early in the morning, when most people are still contemplating having breakfast. In Moscow it had been commonplace to see men embracing lampposts.

I could understand about the vodka; but why no beer? Anyone would have his work cut out to get even mildly drunk on any of the Russian beer I had tasted.

'Why no beer?' I asked Lilya.

'Because there is not enough beer in Russia.'

'But why isn't there enough?'

'Because not enough is made.'

We were in the Yaroslavl *oblast* now and around a quarter past one we all opened up our 'tuck boxes' and ate delicious slices of buttered, black rye bread and cuts off a 2-foot-long German-type sausage, and drank vodka and Carlsberg beer. All these items we had bought from one of the eight Beryozka shops in Moscow, which accept foreign currency for food, drink and other items of a sort that few Russians ever see unless they are invited in, or unless they are armed with what are known as certificate rubles, a special currency issued to those who have earned money abroad, which can sometimes be obtained on the black market. We ourselves would have done even better if we could have visited the so-called 'Bureau of Passes' at 2 Granovskovo Street, where the Soviet nobility shop or send their chauffeurs to collect what they have ordered by tele-phone – just like Harrods.

Just as we began this feast, as if as a warning against excessive indulgence, a completely paralytic Red Army soldier was propelled past our compartment towards the administrative part of the train at the engine end by my friend, the German-speaking ticket inspector.

While eating I kept a sharp look-out over the rather swampy country through which we were now passing for the miraculous Church of St John-upon-Ishnaya, which, in the sixteenth century, had floated along the river Ishnaya from Lake Nero, rather as if an Edwardian houseboat had broken its moorings at Henley-on-Thames and drifted down towards the weir at Hambledon Lock. Fortunately, instead of prolonging its drift indefinitely (the Ishnaya flows into the Volga, which ends up in the Caspian Sea), it had come ashore at a place called Bogozlov, all ready to be worshipped in. Unfortunately, at the very moment when the *Rossiya* flashed over the Ishnaya, I happened to be trying to recover a piece of dropped sausage from the floor and therefore failed to catch a glimpse either of Bogozlov or the Church of St John. I also missed Lake Nero, which lay somewhere on the corridor side of the train, to starboard; but by trampling on the feet of what had up to now been my friendly companions on this venture and completely disorganizing their eating arrangements I managed to reach the corridor in time to see, away to the east beyond the railway station, 140 miles from Moscow, another lot of domes, spires and crosses, this time of the city of Ros-tov-Yaroslavl, rising behind earthen ramparts.

I was looking fleetingly, for Rostov-Yaroslavl is not a stopping place for this train although it is one of the oldest towns in Russia. Here, in AD 862, according to the chronicle of a monk named Nestor, which is based on legend, the Slavs of Novgorod invited three Vik-ing chieftains, Ryurik, Sineus and Trivor, to come and protect their trade routes. 'Our land is great and fruitful, but there is no order in it; come and reign and rule over us,' were the words of the invita-tion. And they did. On the death of his brothers two years later

Ryurik became the sole ruler. 'From them our land is called Rus,' Nestor wrote.

Rostov-Yaroslavl was situated on the bank of Lake Nero, which was the scene of an astonishing mass baptism, one of many such that took place all over Russia in the year 989, when Vladimir I, the ruler of what was then a completely pagan country, ordered the conversion of the entire population to Christianity.

Until the previous year, when he himself had been converted, Vladimir had been a monster of cruelty and depravity. He had become sole ruler after killing his brother, the ruler of Kiev, who had previously killed *his* brother.

While on a visit to Constantinople, Vladimir, already much married, married Princess Anna, younger daughter of the Emperor Romanus II, and was converted to Christianity. On his return to Kiev he ordered an idol that he had set up on a bank of the Dnieper – it represented Perun, the Slavonic god of thunder – to be over- turned, beaten with staves and thrown into the river. The following day the inhabitants of Kiev and its environs were assembled on the right bank of the river. They were then ordered into the water where they were baptized by priests from Constantinople. The baptisms at Lake Nero were performed with even greater economy of effort. The entire population of the area was made to enter the water in small groups, each numbering between ten and fifteen persons; and there they waited while the priests from Constantinople – there were no Russian priests as up to this time there were no Christians – sailed or had themselves rowed around the lake, baptizing each group with a single name.

As a result of this vast operation, in the course of which the whole of Russia was Christianized without any recorded dissent on the part of the inhabitants, both Olga, his pious but terrible grand- mother, who had been converted in 955, and Vladimir were canonized, which is rather like canonizing the bosses of Cosa Nostra and Union Corse.

I could go on for hours about Rostov, without having seen it for more than fifteen seconds: about the great fair that was held there every year far into the nineteenth century and which attracted thousands of Russians, Greeks, Armenians and Tartars; about the trade in linen, vinegar, white lead, vermilion, soap, candles, leather, hemp, corn, chicory, dried sweetpeas, apothecary's herbs and enamelled pictures of saints (the manufacture of linen and the production of enamelled work, though probably not entirely devoted to sacred pictures, still persists to this day), together with the manufacture of coffee from chicory, and treacle. I could go on; but now we were nearing Yaroslavl, on the last heights above the Volga. To the right, on an escarpment, factories, chemical plants and/or refineries – being scientifically illiterate I had no way of knowing which was which – were belching smoke into a sky so dark that it was immediately assimilated without trace. Whatever they were, they looked too large and important to be producing treacle or the enamelled heads of saints. More likely they were churning out some of the things Yaroslavl is famous for: motor tyres and engines, scientific instruments and paint.

To the left of the line the land fell away, lightly wooded here and there, to the basin of the Volga, a plain full, according to the *Atlas of the USSR*, of flax fields, pigs and dairy cattle, none of which were currently on view. This plain extended northwards as far as the eye could see. It was reminiscent of one of those spacious landscapes by Koninck, but without the luminous light cunningly inserted by the artist, which would have transformed this particular scene for the better, too. There was no sign of the Volga. Had the Russians with their current passion for pipes run it underground?

At 2.11 pm Moscow time and 3.11 pm local time the *Rossiya* slid into Yaroslavl through the south-eastern industrial district, which was as lovely as south-eastern industrial districts are anywhere, and came to rest in front of the station building, a large, bilious-looking structure which would have effectively blocked the view of anything that was worth looking at in its immediate vicinity. There wasn't, as I discovered when I took a quick look out of the front door.

The *Rossiya* remained immobile in the rain for ten minutes, in the course of which Otto took a picture, I think of someone with an umbrella up – one of the few of the half million people of this, the largest city after Moscow in the Central Economic Region, who was visible to the naked eye – for which he was rebuked by an official. I for my part employed what was left of the time after my

little excursion to the station building hunting for wh
Chekhov had written upon alighting here from the train in
weather conditions while on his way to Siberia in April 189

In Yaroslavl the rain beat down so hard that I had to put on my leather
coat [he wrote]. My first impression of the Volga was spoiled by rain,
the tear-stained windows of the railway compartment, and the wet nose
of Gurlyland (a law student of Yaroslavl), who came to meet me at the
station.... There are many signs grossly misspelled, it is dirty, jackdaws
with huge heads stalk the street.

While we were still there I read Otto the bit about photography
in the 1914 Baedeker, which I thought he would appreciate:

The taking of photographs near fortresses is naturally forbidden; and
even in less important places the guardians of the law are apt to be over-
vigilant. In order to escape molestation the photographer should join the
Russian Photographic Society. Imperial châteaux and the like may not be
photographed without the permission of the major-domo.

'Remind me to ask the major-domo for permission next time I
photograph Brezhnev's *dacha*', he said.

Most of the interesting things in Yaroslavl, which in 1914 included some sixteen churches and monasteries and many fine old
houses, are congregated in the part of the city called the 'Strelka',
developed in the seventeenth century on the high ground above the
right bank of the Volga, at which time Yaroslavl was renowned for
its art and architecture and had a considerable cultural influence
on the rest of central Russia.

Baedeker made it all sound very attractive. One could stroll along
the Volga Promenade which was carried over three ravines on via-
ducts; take a steam-ferry across the river from one of the landing-
stages ('The appearance of the town, especially as seen from the
Volga, is very picturesque'); and in the evening frequent one of the
restaurants on the Kazansky Boulevard, which runs along the west
side of the town and 'which presents a scene of great animation,
especially in the evening' – '*Restaurant Buttler*, to the north of the
theatre', sounded a likely one. There one would have sat on a warm,
bright night in the summer of 1914, struggling with the *St Peters-
burger Zeitung* and wondering whether, what with all these goings-

on by funny little men in the Balkans, shouldn't one be thinking of getting back to St Petersburg and catching the *Nord Express* to London? Time to order an *izvoschtchik*.

Droshkies or *Izvoschtchik* [I read] are one-horse vehicles with the well-known Russian harness. The horse runs between the shafts under a wooden arch or hoop. They have barely room for two persons and often lack a cover ... Disputes should be referred to the nearest policeman. The driver often does not know how to read; he does not always know his way about the town and sometimes raises difficulties about giving change.

It is just as difficult for a traveller on the Trans-Siberian Railway to get a sight of the centre of Yaroslavl today, unless he breaks his journey – which would be pretty difficult – or manages to cadge a lift in a police car, as it was sixty-three years ago.

Soon a far-off voice, like someone fallen down a mine shaft calling for the elevator, announced that the *Rossiya* was off, after which it trundled obediently through an outlandish tract filled with little home-built garages made of painted tin sheet. There was not a car to be seen. All the mini-Zaporozhets and five-seater, 4-cylinder Zhigulis (the Soviet version of the Fiat 124, made at the Volga Motor Vehicle Plant at Togliatti, designed and built by Fiat with other Western aid), the apples of their owners' eyes, the reward of years of waiting, scheming, knowing the right people or being one of the right people (which it was unlikely that the owner of a home-made tin garage on the swampy side of Yaroslavl would be), were securely locked away, or else had taken their owners to the factory or the office. Unless he or she is a member of a privileged class, a Soviet citizen has to wait anything up to five years before taking delivery of an automobile, at a cost of between 4000 and 10,000 rubles – between two-and-a-half and six years' salary for an industrial worker.

On the other hand, some of these garages might be empty, all shiny and bright inside and awaiting the delivery of the new motorcar, like nurseries got ready by expectant parents. Or perhaps the owners couldn't afford a motorcar and hadn't ordered one, but had built a garage to keep up with the Brezhnevs.

In this labyrinth of garages and mud there was only one human being to be seen, an elderly male Yaroslavlian oiling his padlock. Was he one of my carless garage-owners, or was he really getting everything ship-shape for a spin when spring eventually arrived? There are so many questions that have to remain forever unanswered when one travels by train....

4

Over the River
and into the Trees

THE *Rossiya* was high up on an embankment now, and from it I looked down into a little coppice on the northern outskirts of Yaroslavl which someone had omitted to cut down. In it two small boys were warming themselves at a blazing fire and smoking what I hoped were their first cigarettes – they weren't more than eight or nine – from a packet that didn't carry a Government Health Warning.

And now we were running out towards the big bridge over the Volga, the Spies' Delight, with Mischa in an agony of indecision as to which foreigner to stay with in order to ensure that no photographs were taken of this highly secret construction which was originally set up here about the time of the Boer War and was probably rebuilt soon after the First World War: Otto, whose pictures might reasonably be expected to be more attractive and rendered in colour, or Newby, whose more conventional method of aiming might produce results more useful to some foreign power getting ready to destroy it – forgetting, too, that it is almost impossible to take pictures of bridges when one is actually on them.

Meanwhile, as we chugged up to it, I zipped through *Rules for Cine-Camera Fans and Photographers*, a little brochure published by Intourist and intended to help one to survive in the USSR.

It is forbidden [it said] to photograph, film or make drawings of all kinds of military weapons and equipment and objects of a military nature, sea ports, large hydro-electric engineering installations, railway junctions, tunnels, railway and highway bridges, industrial plants, research institutes, design bureaus, laboratories, power stations, radio beacons, radio stations. It is forbidden to take pictures from a plane, to photograph or draw pictures of industrial cities on a large scale, or to take pictures and make sketches within 25 kilometres of the border. 'Intourist' hopes that you will take home many interesting photos and films of your visit to the Soviet Union.

It is also forbidden to take photographs of any railway station, or photographs from trains, as it is to take photographs of any factory or government office, or of anyone in service uniform, without special permission.

By the time I had tried to figure out whether these regulations applied to station platforms, on which everyone seemed to object to photographs being taken, or to the trains themselves, provided that they weren't loaded with tanks or hydrogen bombs, and what size paper I would need to make a large-scale drawing of an industrial city, we were well out on the bridge, high above Europe's longest river, here several hundred miles from its source in a swamp in the hills north-west of Moscow. Now, some six weeks after the break-up of the ice, which in this part covers the river from the end of November to the middle of April, it looked like Brown Windsor soup.

To the right, as the *Rossiya* rumbled slowly through the webs of girders in the spans, the oldest part of Yaroslavl came into view on the high, right western bank of the Volga, what the people who live along it call the Nagorny Bereg, the Hill Bank; the low, left, eastern bank which we were now approaching being known as the Pugovoy Bereg, the Meadow Bank. These banks are like this all the way down the middle and lower Volga, as far south as the salt earth steppes of the Caspian Depression, which form the real boundary between Russia in Europe and Russia in Asia.

Now the sun came out, and the whole scene was transformed. The white steamers tied up at the landing stages, to which an *izvoshtchik* driver would have taken me from the station in 1914 for 50 kopecks plus the customary tip, were as spick-and-span as yachts moored in a river not more than half a mile wide, now, in the eye of the sun, flowing away, slowly and majestically into the mist, down towards the Caspian Sea.

If all the tributaries of this river – which drains an area larger than the whole of France, Germany, Italy and Britain put together – are delineated in black ink on white paper without any extraneous

detail, as they have been by Soviet cartographers, the effect is of
a wind-blasted thorn tree devoid of leaves and something like 1120
miles high. Its roots (its delta) are in the Caspian Sea. Its trunk
(the main stream before it receives any real tributaries) is some 370
miles long, with an almost right-angled bend in it at Volgograd,
and is almost branchless until the river Torgun joins it from the
east. And above this, reaching upwards and outwards for another
750 miles or so as the crow flies, is an increasingly dense and tortuous
labyrinth of branches (the tributaries of the Volga) from which
sprout countless thorns (the lesser streams that feed them). Knowing all this, I thought it would look bigger. It was, it's true, a wide
river, but not as grand as I'd expected. I would like to have seen
it lower down.

Now the *Rossiya* was running off the bridge, which was guarded,
as are all the bigger bridges and all the tunnels on the Railway –
this one by a very small sentry in a very large greatcoat, who looked
as if he could do with a spring clean, and who was giving himself
an airing outside his sentry box, a sight that would have cheered
the Pentagon. From here I could look down the embankment on
to the low-lying Meadow Bank of the river, on to orchards, fields
of what looked like heavy brown clay which was sown with something, probably potatoes or flax, and on to the rooftops of wooden
houses which were painted in shades of ochre, ginger and the same
dark brown as the earth: a scene that a few moments ago would
have been gloomy in the extreme, now transformed by the brilliant
early afternoon sun. Could it be that spring had really come at last?

Chekhov too took a less jaundiced view of Russia as soon as the
weather took a turn for the better. In April 1890 when he was travelling, there was no through road to the Urals and work on the Trans-
Siberian had not yet begun. Instead, after he had reached Yaroslavl,
he boarded a steamer to go to Kazan, where he boarded yet another
steamer which took him to Perm.

On waking I saw the sun [Chekhov wrote to his sister]. The Volga is
not bad: water meadows, sun-drenched monasteries, white churches, an
amazing expanse; wherever you look it's cosy, inviting you to sit down
and cast a line ... now and then a shepherd's horn is heard. White seagulls
hover over the Volga....

'What I want to know,' I said to Mischa (never one to let sleeping dogs lie), 'is why your government gets so steamed up about bridges. This book I've got describes every bridge on the Trans-Siberian Railway in detail, and there are photographs of all the really big ones. I know we're not in Siberia yet; but I bet there's another book with pictures of all the bridges on the way to the Urals. Anyway, what difference does it make? They all get photographed from satellites.'

'I have never seen such a book,' he said.

'Well, would you like to look at it? Here!'

'I do not want to look at it.'

'Well, just listen to this then: "At the 1328 verst* the line crosses the river ..."'

'Which river?'

'The Ob. Would you mind if I get on with it, as it's rather long?'

'The line crosses the river by a bridge 372.50 sahzens† long having seven spans. The I and VI openings are 46.325 sahzens, the II, IV, 53.65 sahzens, and III and V, 53.15 sahzens. The upper girders of the bridge are on the Herber's system.'

I'm going to cut it short: 'The stone abutments of the bridge are laid on granite rocks, the right pier, No. 1, near the bank is not supported on a caisson, the other piers, Nos. 2, 3, 4, 5 and 6 are laid on caissons sunk to a depth of 1.81 to 3.40 sahzens below the lowest water level. The minimum elevation of the trusses above the low water mark is 8.23 sahzens and 4.42 above its highest level ...

'Look, there's an awful lot more: you don't want me to go on do you? It's terribly boring.'

'You should not be in possession of such a book,' said Mischa, severely. 'Such a book is a confidential publication.'

'But this is the official Russian guide to the Trans-Siberian Railway, published in English in 1900. And it's a reprint. I bought it in Britain a couple of weeks ago. Look, it's even got a picture of the Boss.' And I tried to show him the frontispiece, a photograph of that supreme twit His Majesty Nicholas Alexandrovich, Autocrat of All the Russias, Most August President of the Committee of the

* 1 *verst* = 0.663 mile; 3500 feet
† 1 *sahzen* = 7 feet

Siberian Railway, without whose untiring efforts to bring about the Revolution I would probably not have been sitting here on the *Rossiya* arguing with Mischa.

'You should not have brought this book into the country. You should have declared it to the Customs authorities.'

(A facsimile of the *Guide to the Great Siberian Railway*, first published in St Petersburg in 1900, has been published by David and Charles of Newton Abbot, Devon, which is how I came to acquire it, it being otherwise a rare work.)

'No one asked us to declare anything. We've got *Vogue*, *Harper's and Queen*, the *Observer*, *Sunday Times*, *Sunday Telegraph*, *The Times*, *Guardian*, *Time Magazine*, Italian *Panorama* and *Country Life*. We thought you'd be interested. Anyway, it was you who took us through Customs.'

'You shouldn't have all those either.'

'That's a fine thing to say when I've already given you my *Observer*.'

The woods closed in again, and so did the weather. The *Rossiya* was heading almost due north now by Otto's car compass, after having been on a north-easterly course ever since leaving Moscow. To the left was the highway to Archangel, where the driver of CHS2 would end up unless he took some avoiding action pretty soon.

Archangel, terminus of the Northern Railway from Moscow, the great fishing and timber port, is near the mouth of the northern Dvina. The Archangel *oblast* is the biggest timber producer in the North-West Economic Region, which is itself the larger wood producer in the USSR. Not even eastern Siberia, which is more than two-and-a-half times as large, can equal it. The northern Dvina is the principal vehicle by which this timber, in the form of huge rafts, is brought down to Archangel from the unimaginable interior (although some survivors of the logging camps in it have left accounts of what it is like) during the summer months. From Archangel, having been cut up during the winter into more manageable lengths, it is exported all over the world. I found it an awe-inspiring thought, and one to which I had reverted frequently during our journey, that I only had to take the wrong sort of photograph, hit Mischa on the nose or say 'Fuck the USSR' in public – the last two outrages preferably at the same time – to find myself engaged in tree-felling on the northern Dvina or other rivers in the region for the rest of my life. But soon we rolled into Danilov, and I knew we were on the right line for the Urals.

Mischa (whom I had not the slightest desire to hit on the nose), worn out by his duties as policeman, interpreter, nursemaid, general factotum and purveyor of filleted information, all of which tasks he performed to the best of his ability, was asleep. I must say I wouldn't have had his job with us for all the tea in Russia. How he had come to accept it was a mystery. It must have been a carrot of the kind that has so often been dangled before me during my own life with the promise of bigger carrots, which, if one accepts it, leads to a life of misery as an employee of the Carrot Marketing Board.

Feeling like schoolchildren whose teacher has failed to turn up owing to laryngitis, fallen arches or the heebie-jeebies, the three of us skipped down into the fine drizzle that was currently descending on Danilov Station.

In front of the station house two ancient, pear-shaped ladies dressed in black coats, black felt boots and white headscarves, who in Britain would have been considered ripe to be carted off to a geriatric ward if they so much as put their noses outside their doors, were vigorously digging and hoeing the dark earth in the station flower beds, at the same time talking away to one another nineteen to the dozen.

Meanwhile, other equally ancient protagonists of free enterprise, who were certainly old enough to remember the real thing, were peddling tulips and white peonies in pots to the passengers, who purchased them eagerly. Lilya bought a couple and hung them in wire holders in the corridor of our coach. It would have been difficult to imagine such a happening on British Rail, or any other Rail for that matter; less difficult to imagine it in Russia, because all Slavonic peoples are mad about flowers to the point of sometimes breaching the law in order to acquire them. (At the age of seventy-seven my mother-in-law, in London on a visit to us from the Carso, near Trieste, managed to take extensive cuttings at the Royal Botanical Gardens, Kew, while 'lagging behind', ostensibly because of her sciatica. These cuttings did very well on her native heath, if one can use the expression to describe something that is about 99.999 per cent limestone; and their progress was noted with interest by a son of the Curator when, some years later, he dropped in by chance and was invited to stay the night while down there on a visit.)

Danilov Station had a small shop. It was about the size of the smallest sort of ticket office but crammed with jars of rice, biscuits, earth-covered objects which looked like ginseng roots but were obviously something more mundane, jars labelled 'KOK' in Cyrillic, which contained various sorts of vegetables steeped in vinegar, little bowls of smoked fish, matches, blocks of soap and the proprietress herself, large and jolly, whose face entirely filled the small window which was the only means by which anyone could do business with her. No sooner had the train come to a halt than she was besieged by eager customers to whom the mere idea of taking their turn in a queue was something they had left Moscow to forget. It was only by a display of equally powerful Slavonic determination that Wanda managed to buy some honey biscuits, and even so it took the best part of the sixteen minutes that the *Rossiya* remained in Danilov.

If I had been attempting to buy honey biscuits, or anything else in competition with about fifty Russians, and at the same time trying to look up the equivalents of 'Excuse me!' and 'Sorry!' in my phrase book but continually turning up expressions equally useless such as 'Good evening. I'd like a table for three', I would have been a non-starter. Instead I went to say goodbye to Czech engine, Model CHS2; but by the time I arrived at the head of the train it had already been replaced by another Czechoslovakian model, a CHS4, which looked much the same to me, whose interest in engines went out of the window at the end of the steam age and to whom any subsequent development in this field is about as exciting as a new car taken in part exchange for one of the same sort, traded in after two years in order to save buying a new battery.

Nevertheless, I waved in friendly fashion to the crew, who presumably didn't see me as they didn't wave back. Mind you, you don't get as much change out of diesel engine drivers in Britain today as you used to from the drivers of the big steamers when I was a boy, who were always ready to listen to my childish prattle and on one or two memorable occasions even allowed me to sling a shovelful or so of Welsh nuts into the firebox unaided, an act which, today, would immediately bring about the immediate paralysis of the whole of British Rail's Western Region, and all the other regions, on which the threat of non-union labour raises its hideous head.

Then just as I raised my faithful Nikkonos to take a shot of this, to me, boring engine, a charming local official told me in easy-to-understand language, using only one hand, to desist.

After tying a knot in my handkerchief to remind me to ask Intourist what was the position *vis-à-vis* photographing locomotives, old ladies and people sheltering under umbrellas, and if the response was a thumbs-down would they please arrange to have all three added to the 'Forbidden' list before I passed this way again, I said hullo to a rather somnolent horse that was standing outside the station, harnessed to an unsprung, two-wheeled cart, otherwise a *telega*, an instrument of torture in use since tsarist times. I also said good afternoon to its owner, who was comparatively full of fight. Nothing from the horse, but I did get a grunt from the owner, which was better than a slap in the eye with a wet fish, I suppose; although this kind of thing is hurting to a person like me who has been brought up to say 'Sorry' when someone treads on my toes in the lift.

This individual, who was actually old enough to know how to speak, being all of thirty-eight, was sitting on the box of the *telega* and wearing a piece of headgear popular in the fifties and sixties, at a time when the pigeon-chest, minimal lapel suits were also very much a vogue with the boys in the garment industry, door-to-door salesmen, bailiffs, morticians and other men-of-good-cheer: that is to say, a hat with a minimal brim and a vaguely Tyrolean crown.

The difference between those prototypes and this particular model was that it was constructed not of felt, nor of plastic, as was some of the headgear in the good old days of Mr Khruschev, nor of cardboard, with YIPPEE! I LOVE EVERYBODY! written large across the front, but of wood shavings, this station being on the borders of the lumber country.

'Did you photograph that man with a horse and cart outside the station, the one who was wearing a wooden hat?' I asked Otto, who never missed much, when we were once more safely aboard the *Rossiya*.

'I didn't even try,' he said, gloomily. 'It's all impossible. I've a good mind to give up and go home. All I want to do is ...'

'I know,' I said, having travelled with photographers before, '"take smashing pictures". Well, maybe we're on the wrong train. I'm beginning to think that we should be on the *Settebello*, or the *Train Bleu*, or even the 8.18 am from Wimbledon by way of Earls-field, Clapham Junction and Vauxhall to Waterloo, something with local colour on board which you don't have to join a society to photo-graph. Anyway, give us enough time to get our bags out too, if you do decide to leave.'

Now the *Rossiya* was running past a village built along one side of a dirt road, parallel to the line. The houses were very small, built of solid tree trunks with gardens to scale, much the same size as gardens backing on the line in an inner London suburb; but here, in the depths of vast, rural Russia, seeming a bit stingy. And there were goats on long, shiny chains, ponds full of ducks and squads of officious geese who hissed malevolently at the *Rossiya*.

We were now on the southern fringes of the Forest of Forests, which more or less covers the whole of Europe and Asia north of the 55th parallel, from the Atlantic coast of Norway to the shores of the Sea of Okhotsk, an arm of the Pacific: a wilderness of pine, fir, spruce, larch and in its southern parts, through which we were now travelling, of hardy deciduous trees such as birch, aspen and alder.

In those parts of the forest that lie in Norway, Sweden, Lapland and around Murmansk on the Kola Peninsula, the forest extends far north of the Arctic Circle to 70°N and beyond.

Not counting those huge expanses of the forest in Finland and Scandinavia, the USSR still has the world's largest forest, covering over 2 billion acres; or, to put it another way, it accounts for a quarter of the entire forest area of the world. If the whole tract in

European Russia is then subtracted, what remains east of the Urals in Siberia and the Soviet Far East is still one-third larger than the whole of the United States. Of all the trees in the forest east of the Urals, 38 per cent are Siberian larch. I began to think that I should have packed a chain saw.

About an hour out from Danilov, we entered the *oblast* of Kostroma. According to my books the country we were passing through was good for flax-growing, cattle and pigs, although up to now I had not seen a single specimen of either. Perhaps they hibernated in this part of the world and still had their heads down. One could scarcely blame them. Here, in the woods of Kostroma, where silver birches far outnumbered conifers, later in the year, if there was enough sun, innumerable fungi would be emerging under the trees and on the fringes of the clearings, popping up in the mysterious, unpredictable fashion of fungi everywhere, which obey such abstruse laws that they sometimes drive even the most experienced fungi hunters round the bend. Of these some would be edible, some inedible because they have a nasty taste, or cause diarrhoea or disturbing visions, and some would be downright poisonous.

Of the poisonous varieties that occur here, as they do in other parts of the world, none are more lethal than the terrible *Amanita phalloides*, which comes in various shades between white, the pallor of a sickly child, and lemon. Even a taste of *Amanita phalloides* is a sentence of death, as lingering and awful as that from rabies. Until very recently attempts to effect a cure invariably ended in failure. In Czechoslovakia, another huge producer of fungi, one treatment was to feed the victim raw, chopped rabbit brains; but doctors noted for their acumen soon realized that it was difficult in the pre-delirium stage of the illness to get the patient to co-operate by ingesting them.

Of the edible varieties none would be more delicious than *Boletus edulis*, known to the Russians as *borovik*, to the French as *cèpe*, to the Germans as *Steinpilz* and to the Italians as *porcino nero*. One of the many varieties of *Boletus*, not all of which are edible, it is a fungus with a thick, squat stalk, tapering from the base, like the trunk of an old, pollarded tree, and sometimes so thick that the stalk is wider than the cap.

When these delicacies finally appear, able-bodied Russians everywhere with the right kind of woodland within range, which includes the *dacha* country around Moscow, are out in force, armed with baskets (bags, especially plastic bags, are no good as fungi soon go off when deprived of air) and with sticks with which to root among fallen leaves which often conceal them from view.

Forgive this digression. I may not currently be in sufficiently good training to give Anatoly Karpov a good game of chess; but I will take on anyone in the *borovik*, *Steinpilz*, *porcino* or *cèpe* stakes.

At around 5 pm we came to a halt at a place called Buy on the upper waters of the Kostroma River, a navigable tributary of the Volga. Behind what would have been the guard's van on a British train, the caboose on an American one, but which on the *Rossiya* was simply the last coach of the train, with a fine view of the permanent way aft through the glass in what was literally the back door, the sky was now clearing rapidly to the cerulean blue of the blue domes of Zagorsk.

There was nothing to be seen of Buy except the station, which was one of the smaller variety, or of any of the 30,000 inhabitants, apart from about a dozen characters who in tsarist times might well have been Maris or Tcheremisses, or Tartars, but who now were more likely to be Russians. Today the Maris, who are Finnish, have their own Autonomous Soviet Socialist Republic between Gorkiy and Kazan, although only 44 per cent of the population are Maris. The rest are Russians.

Like most of the places on this stretch of line, the inhabitants of Buy devoted themselves to the timber business and to making various wooden objects, as well as to producing cheese, chemicals, fertilizer and fibre from flax. Here Lilya bought us a *vatrushka*, a tart lined with sour cream.

Attracted by the sight and/or smell of this freshly baked object, a small boy of about seven, although still in the thumb-sucking stage, appeared in the doorway of our compartment where the four of us, Mischa having awoken from his siesta, were preparing to demolish it. I recognized him as the son of an unforthcoming couple two compartments away who had given me the same treatment when I said good morning to them as had the train drivers at Danilov.

'What's your name?' Wanda asked him four times in her Slovene Russian, having discovered that the phrase book omits this useful phrase even under 'Dating', where you have to make do with 'You've dropped your handkerchief!' (I know, I'm trying to get rid of it!) or, 'What time is your last train?' If you said that to a girl on the *Rossiya* she would think you were trying to get fresh, or had escaped from a home, and as like as not she would call the conductress, unless she was the conductress.

No reaction. This child had the same, spine-chilling way of observing the world about him and filing the information away in his noddle for future and probably disastrous use as the small, pop-eyed one with a sorbo ball, the midget von Stroheim, in Carol Reed's *The Third Man*.

'What's your name?' Mischa, who also had a son, asked him, but even he had to say it three times before this miniature traveller accepted the fact that they both worked for different branches of the same firm (and I was surprised that he did this without the production of the oblong red pass); upon which the combination began working, things began to click inside the cranium and the door opened a few fractions of an inch. It seemed to me that Mischa should have been getting him down on a short list for The Agency intake of cub reporters in about 1990. 'His name is Vladimir,' he reported eventually.

Wanda cut him a slice of *vatrushka*, using one of those murderous French folding knives with '1er Choix-Opinel-La Main Couronnée' stamped on the handle, which in aircraft can travel only in hold luggage unless you want to be given the treatment, and which she happened to have about her – nice class of girl I married. By the time she'd finished dismembering it and we'd all had a slice, including Lilya, it was time for someone to write the lyrics for a song beginning 'Goodbye Vatrushka, you delicious sour sweet ...'

The only time when time flies on a train is when you're either asleep or eating, so by the time we had finished the *vatrushka* and Lilya had brought more tea and Vladimir had been given the interrogation by Mischa (which was painfully slow as no truth drugs or red-hot irons were available), which elucidated the information from him that his father was an engineer, his mother – the one with the sourer face of the two – was a schoolteacher, and that they were on their way home to Novosibirsk, I had failed to see a river called the Veski, as well as Lake Galichskoye and the town of Galich itself which Batu 'Watch-it-Come-Down' Khan had demolished in 1228. It seemed an appropriate moment to give up for a bit and have some sleep, and after making sure that CHS4 was still pounding away up front I did so.

By 6 pm I was awake again. The *Rossiya* was running almost due east. It was a golden evening, with a gentle wind blowing from the south. The trees in the forest were mostly tall, slender silver birches and their leaves were shimmering in the sun. Once we stopped, and so by a coincidence did the terrible music and singing that was relayed throughout the train from the radio room, and which, even though we kept it permanently switched off, nothing could prevent from seeping into our compartment from the one next door. Then, for some minutes it was so quiet that with the window open one could hear the wind sighing in the tree tops, like the sound of the sea running up on a distant shore. Once we passed a village with a wooden church with a white dome where two boys on one bicycle tried to race the train and rode into a ditch; once we saw a girl driving some geese home; otherwise we saw no one at all in the country we passed through.

At 6.56 pm we came into Nicola Pomola, which sounded more like a beautiful Russian spy than a railway station and was just as elusive. Although the name of the station appeared in the official timetable as a stopping place, it did not figure on the official route map. It was memorable also because on the common land on the outskirts we saw the first herd of cows since leaving Moscow.

Here, we stopped for one minute while two heavily laden ladies who could have done with the services of a porter clambered aboard. This station, as did so many others all along the route, had a larger-than-life, silver-painted statue of the founder on it in what one was later to recognize as one of a number of standard poses. This one, so far as I can remember, was '*Hi! Taxi!*'

Out beyond Nicola Pomola, as the sun went down the wind died away and the pale trunks of the birch trees closest to the line accentuated the darkness of the forest behind them. But it was not all forest. There were big, green clearings in it, meadows in which the grass was short, as if it had already been cropped by sheep, only there were no sheep.

In the settlements along the line – they could scarcely be called villages – the lights were on behind the drawn blinds in the *izbas*. There was not a breath of wind and the smoke from the cooking fires rose straight into the air.

Then, with the sun gone at last, the afterglow illuminated the pools and ponds in the marshy ground near the line over which long swathes of mist were forming. How beautiful Russia was at this moment. Soon the forest closed in again, dark and eerie, and now the sky above it was huge and pale, the colour of pearls. And so it would remain until dawn, the perpetual gloaming of a spring night in the latitude of Juneau, Alaska; Dunnet Head, the most northerly point of mainland Britain; Stavanger in Norway; and, allowing a degree or so, Cape Farewell, the southernmost extremity of Greenland.

Supper was a re-run of lunch, more or less. There was no room for all four of us to dine together, as Otto and I had each contrived to make a shambles of our respective compartments, in which our companions had very little to look forward to – he with camera bodies and lenses and motor drives all over the place, but worst of all with his tripod which had a Nikon with a 50/300 mm zoom lens stuck on the end of it, and which now stood permanently in the space between the two bunks – about as convenient for Mischa as having a Red Indian erect a wigwam in it – and I, with my now-unfurled maps which kept on falling on the floor and rolling themselves up; my twenty-one assorted books, including The Notebook; my cameras and, Wanda's contribution, the rather sticky honey biscuits with which the folding table was now covered.

In the course of this repast, Otto and Mischa, with no gentle female company to distract them from the bottle, managed to get slightly tiddly. I, on the other hand, with Wanda in charge of the drinking arrangements and determined not to let me get drunk in Russia and make a fool of myself, had failed to become even mildly elevated; but after a while the two of them joined us in our compartment and soon I found myself beginning, albeit slowly, to catch up.

I was, I must say, rather surprised at Mischa, not for any moral reasons but simply because he had been at considerable pains to tell us, while we were still in Moscow, in what I now identified as his 'the-Lubyanka-is-some-kind-of-office-block' voice, that Russians drank vodka only with meals.

At first everything was very genteel, everyone talking about how we could all work together to make the trip better (or was it the world?) etc. Then the Second World War came up like a storm on the horizon and we would have been well advised to have begun digging slit trenches among the mattresses; and then one thing led to another and, oh dear! Mischa was saying how rotten Britain had been to leave Czechoslovakia to be overrun by Hitler in 1939.

'Almost as bad as Stalin making a non-aggression pact with a bunch of Fascists' I heard myself saying, like an actor thinking about how long the show will run, and will he be able to pay the gas bill if it doesn't, while spouting, except that in this case I was thinking how much nicer Russia was outside the window.

'He was playing for time,' Mischa said. He had very thick, dark eyebrows which were now meeting in the middle and he looked more angry than he probably was, at least I hoped so. 'Stalin was a great realist.'

'Do you think it was right, what he did?'

'The end justifies the means.'

'Lissun, Mischa,' Wanda said, already bored with this verbal ping-pong among persons already patently half-cut. 'What is your definition of fascism?'

'Fascism,' said Mischa, 'is a regime which, for the purpose of attaining complete power, eliminates everything which gets in its way.'

'Tank you,' said Wanda, in her best fractured English, 'that's what I tought you said about communism – about the end justifying the means.'

And she leaned back in the corner of her bunk with the air of a lawyer in one of those thirties B-movies, when he sits down and says, 'Mr Attorney, *your witness!*'

Up to this time, and for a little while longer, Otto has kept out of this dreary business, which is the sort of thing sixth-formers used to go on about over cocoa; but quite soon, after some fairly straight talk about the Freedom of the Individual, which raises the temperature some more, the conversation switches to the Jews, and Mischa is not too nice about them either, forgetting present company.

Now Otto, who normally wouldn't hurt a fly unless it walked on one of his Leicaflexes, and who only wants to take smashing pictures, as he has already told me a number of times (and will continue to do so throughout this trip), being Jewish, or partly Jewish, goes into action with arms metaphorically flailing, rather like Kali, the ten-armed Hindu deity who is represented with a hideous and terrible countenance, dripping with blood, encircled with snakes and hung around with skulls and human heads.

Deciding that I had done enough to spoil Anglo-Russian and German-Russian relationships for a decade, not forgetting Wanda's own attempt to wreck any *entente* between Yugoslavia and the USSR that might still exist, I bowed out, mumbling something about having to go to the lavatory.

Instead, I went on past it to the end of the car where the exit was and where, by some lucky chance, one of the girls had forgotten to lock the window.

While I was leaning out of it, inspiring the pure air of Russia and on the rebound expelling the fumes of demon vodka on the environment, the *Rossiya* came to a halt to let a big train of brand-new Uniflex containers from the United States go past to the west, after which it continued to remain where it was for what seemed ages but was probably not more than ten minutes.

From it came the sounds of sporadic singing, distant laughter, the hiss of the samovar and the rumbling of acrimonious voices from our compartment, like a thunderstorm that is almost over but refuses to go away completely. Outside the forest was completely silent. There was no wind sighing in the tree tops, and not a scream, howl, growl, hoot, grunt, groan, whistle or any other sound from the creatures reputed to inhabit it: wolves, great grey owls, northern bats, Eurasian ground and flying squirrels, brown bears, stoats, mink, marten, foxes and capercailie, to name a few. Nevertheless, I was very impressed by this forest. In theory, if I chose my alignment to avoid settlements and labour camps and the big pulp and paper complexes around Kotlas, it should be possible to travel northwards from where we were on the railway, through this forest belt, here about 450 miles wide, then across another 200 miles or so of mossy, fearfully marshy tundra, to reach the head of the Kanin Peninsula on the shores of the Barents Sea, more than 600 miles north of the railway, without encountering a single human being. With which thought, having heard the party break up in our compartment, I returned to find Wanda, who could have worked the halls in vaudeville as a quick-strip artiste, already in bed and murmuring something that sounded like 'stupid bogger', while working hard at going to sleep. Whether she was taking about me or Mischa wasn't clear. I didn't ask.

It was obvious, I thought to myself as I undressed, that things were not going to be easy. Perhaps they would be impossible. How sensible I had been to bring Wanda; for a moment I almost made the mistake of calling her Wendy – it was difficult not to think of the male members of the party as The Lost Boys. Our most acrimonious matrimonial difficulties in the course of a not uneventful life could only barely compete with what had already taken place in our compartment on the *Rossiya*.

I was woken by what sounded like a flight of Kamikazis being given the multiple pom-pom treatment off Okinawa, which immediately elevated the top half of me into a vertical position.

The *Rossiya* had come to a halt and a freight train was racing past it in the opposite direction. It was made up of coal waggons, refrigerator cars, boxcars, flat cars loaded with tree trunks, steel girders, generators, transformers, tractors, unidentifiable objects covered with tarpaulins, and more of the brightly coloured containers that had come overland from Nakhodka in the Soviet Far East, our ultimate destination; and as each individual piece of rolling stock flashed past our partially opened window it went *whumph*.

How extensive was this train going to be, I wondered, as it went on *whumph-whumphing*, and I had counted to forty-six, having missed the first ones. Was it going to be longer than the American one that I had looked up in the *Guinness Book of Records*, which had been assembled on the Norfolk and Western Railroad in 1967 on the Iaeger, West Virginia, to Portsmouth, Ohio, stretch, which was about 4 miles, six diesel engines and 500 coal wagons from end to end and weighed nearly 42,000 tons? It seemed unlikely that the Russians, in whom the spirit of emulation burns with the intensity of one of their own 600,000 candle-power xenon arc lamps (another record), would not have been spurred to put together something even longer. I hoped they hadn't. If they had many trains like that on the go we wouldn't see much of Siberia from our north-facing compartment.

But almost immediately the last car flashed past. It was probably a fifty-waggon train, weighing altogether about 4500 tons and for all its *whumphing* probably not travelling at more than about 30 miles an hour. On the tablecloth, among the honey biscuits and other debris, was a souvenir, a proof that it wasn't a ghost train – a small, shiny nugget of coal, the size of a diamond in a generous engagement ring.

It was 11.20 pm. I had only been asleep for twenty minutes, which included an eight-minute stop at Atsvezh, to which no map which I possessed referred.

I abandoned the idea of going back to bed. Sleep was not what I had come for. I switched on my bed-head light and opened a map, inadvertently rustling it.

'Quiet!' said Wanda. I felt like asking her if she had heard the freight train.

The next station of any consequence would be Kotelnich, the junction for the line to Gorkiy, formerly Nizhny Novgorod, now a city of over a million people, the seventh largest in the USSR. At 11.36 the train stole, ghost-like, into Kotelnich. The station house was a charming building, the sort of place where, before the Revolution, a grand duke might have got down to go shooting. In front of it there was a garden surrounded by white-painted, ornamental iron railings, in which fruit trees with whitewashed trunks grew. It was difficult to believe that somewhere on the other side of this rustic facade, which seemed likely to produce a chorus of peasant

girls in pigtails and embroidered blouses, there were factories producing machinery.

Here, Irina, the blonde, let down the steps, without which it is
almost impossible for anyone but an acrobat to get in or out of a
Russian train (unless there is a built-up platform, which is the
exception rather than the rule in Russia and Siberia), and herself
got down on the line; but no one left the train and no one joined
it. Apart from one or two other conductresses there was not another
human being in sight.

At the end of the statutory three minutes stopping time the train
left as quietly as it had arrived, without so much as a hoot or a
whistle; so quietly that I wondered if the driver and his mate had
got down to stretch their legs, having forgotten to put the brakes
on and we were now off on a down-gradient, heading for a spectacular disaster – possibly on the bridge over the Vyatka River, up which,
by way of the Kama and the Volga, the Novgorodians had pioneered
a route in the twelfth century to Kirov, which was the next treat
in store.

However it was not to be. As our car drew abreast of the station
entrance I saw the station-master standing rigidly at attention in
full uniform and pointing a baton at the train, rather in the manner
of an imperious monarch banishing a subject to Siberia, which in
a sense was what he was doing. This is the official way in which
station-masters-and-mistresses (in which Russian railways abound)
indicate that the doors are closed, the train has its full entitlement
of wheels, the driver and his mate are in the cab, and all is well.

5

How the Railway
Came to Be Built

'THE question of the construction of the Great Siberian Railway,
which for a third of a century had occupied the attention of the
Government and society, was now settled, representing the most
important event of the century, not only in our country, but in the
whole world.' Thus says the *Guide to the Great Siberian Railway*
in 1900.

As I sat in my seat gazing out over Russia, I could not help
wondering how and why they had started to build this immensely
long railway line, the thought of which must have daunted all but
the bravest. As I hunted through the guides and books that I had
brought with me, I found that it was a complicated business, for
the line had begun first at each end and had then proceeded in fits
and starts piecemeal in the middle, these middle sections running
from main river to main river. For many years people crossed
Siberia using railway, steamboat, horse-drawn *tarantass* or sledge
and railway again, zigzagging along as best they could.

The first passenger line in Russia was built in 1837 and ran
between St Petersburg, where the Tsar ruled, and his country
seat, Tsarskoye Selo, a distance of 14 miles. Later on it was extended
an extra mile to Pavlovsk, where there was another magnificent royal
palace. There, a terminus with buffet and ballroom was built. The
train ride to it became a very popular outing for the citizens
of St Petersburg, and provoked a famous remark by the very anti-
train Minister of Finance, E. Kamkrin, to the effect that in other
countries railways led to industrial centres, in Russia to a tavern.

In 1851, after nine years of technical difficulty and considerable
suffering on the part of the serfs who built it (as many as 50,000

were in the field at one time), the line linking St Petersburg with Moscow was completed with the help of American artisans working for two well-known American locomotive builders, Ross Winans and Partners of Baltimore and Eastwick and Harrison of Philadelphia. All the locomotives and rolling stock for this factory were constructed at the Alexandrovsky gun foundry. It was a great commercial success.

The first man to suggest building a railway through Siberia was the dynamic Lieutenant-General Nicholas Muravyev. As he had been governor-general of eastern Siberia since 1847, he wished to start from the Pacific end. In 1857 he cut a road from Alexandrovsk, a newly founded Russian post opposite Sakhalin Island, to Sofiysk, on the lower reaches of the Amur River, a distance of some 40 miles through the wilderness. Having done this he then proposed to the Government that a private company should be formed which would build a line over the route his men had opened up, thus bypassing the mouth of the Amur which was dangerous to shipping. In making this suggestion he blandly ignored the fact, as did his superiors, that this and other vast territory over which he exercised control, and which he was busy exploiting, was in fact part of China, and had been ever since the Qing Emperor, K'ang Hsi, had made such a show of force in 1689 that the Russians had been compelled to conclude the Treaty of Nerchinsk which deprived them of the use of the Amur as an easy route to the Pacific. However, in spite of the fact that there had not been a squeak out of the Chinese over Muravyev's spectacular violations, the idea of a Russian railway on Chinese territory was too much for the Government, and they turned it down.

In 1857 an English engineer named Dull, of whom nothing is known as an individual, not even his initials (and no one is even sure that his name was not Dall), asked the then Minister of Ways of Communications, C. V. Chevkin, for permission to build a tramway with cars drawn by Siberian wild horses, of which he believed there was an inexhaustible supply, all the way from Nizhny Novgorod to the Pacific by way of Kazan, Perm and across Siberia by some unspecified route – 'the most commodious way' was the one he suggested.

Chevkin, a man noted for his irascibility and a masterly obstructionist to boot, showed him the door, as he did to Suprenenko, an ex-governor of Tomsk, who wanted to build 1825 miles of horse-tramway from Tyumen to Irkutsk completely boxed in, so that the horses could trot through a sort of wooden tunnel.

Sleigh, Horn and Morison, three rather raffish Englishmen, also came up against Chevkin. They wanted to build a steam railway from Nizhny Novgorod to Alexandrovsk on the Tatar Strait. One of the three was already a bankrupt.

A very different sort of contender, and one whom Chevkin had to take much more seriously in order to circumvent, was an American, Perry McDonough Collins, who later won a thirty-three-year imperial concession to build what was to be the abortive overland telegraph from Nikolayevsk on the lower Amur to the Bering Strait, which the Russians had agreed to link with Irkutsk, thereby completing the telegraph link between North America and Western Europe.

In the spring and summer of 1857, having previously had himself appointed 'Commercial Agent of the United States at the Amoor River', Collins sailed from Chita, the capital of Transbaikalia, 2200 miles down the Ingoda, Shilka and Amur Rivers to Nikolayevsk in order to satisfy himself that they were navigable by cargo-carrying vessels.

Collins proposed to form the Amoor River Railroad Company, with a capital of $20,000,000, to build a railway from Irkutsk to Chita by way of Kyakhta, an important trading place on the Russian–Mongolian frontier, which was on the caravan route to Peking. From Chita steamers would carry cargoes downstream to the Pacific, and return up-river with merchandise.

Inevitably, the Government referred the whole matter to a Siberian Committee, which, equally inevitably, had as one of its members C. V. Chevkin. The plan was vetoed.

In the course of the next thirty years the authorities were bombarded with schemes for Siberian railways, some of them emanating from lunatics, others from foreign consortiums, provincial governors, merchants and local big-wigs anxious that when a railway finally was built it would pass their doors and not leave them marooned in the wilderness (which was precisely what was to happen to the old city of Tobolsk). Some of these schemes, and not only those proposed by lunatics, were pretty dotty; all of them were turned down, or in the last resort shelved by committees, if they got as far as being considered by committees.

There were various reasons for turning them down, even if the schemes were well thought out, as they sometimes were: the war with Turkey in 1877–8 was one, a terrible famine another; and the most ineluctable reason of all was that, for much of the time, in spite of the splendour and conspicuous consumption that was associated with the Empire and its ruler, there was a serious shortage of cash. In 1875, when the Minister of Ways and Communications, Constantine Posyet, submitted a report to Tsar Alexander II and his Committee of Ministers, advocating the building of a railway from the Volga to the Amur, or failing that as far as Irkutsk, the cost of the entire project was estimated at $125 million.

Meanwhile, a whole network of lines was gradually being extended towards the Urals and beyond, to serve the developing industries there. In 1862 the Moscow–Nizhny Novgorod line was completed; in 1870 the Moscow–Yaroslavl; in 1878, the Perm–Yekaterinburg, the first line to cross the Urals.

The first line built on Siberian soil, the Yekaterinburg–Tyumen, was completed in 1885. It was one of three projected routes traced out by surveyors. Another, completed in 1890 from Samara (now Kuybyshev) to Zlatoust by way of Ufa, was built with the approval of Alexander III, a tight-fisted giant, one of whose hobbies was twisting pokers into knots, who had succeeded his father, Alexander II, when the latter was blown up by anarchists in 1881.

Other events over a long period also conspired to make the building of the Trans-Siberian Railway inevitable. In 1869 the Americans completed the Union Pacific and Central Line, the first railway to span a continent. Naturally, such a construction, if not the rapidity with which it had been accomplished, became something that, possibly only subconsciously, Russia would want to emulate.

In 1872 Vladivostok, which Muravyev had founded twelve years previously, became Russia's principal port and naval base on the

Pacific, and this drew attention to its complete isolation from European Russia. Anyone proposing to make the journey overland had to be prepared to encounter enormous difficulties. The only alternative was to travel by ship, either from the Black Sea or the Baltic. If the Suez Canal, which was opened in 1869, was ever forbidden to Russian troop carriers and warships, as it most probably would be in time of war, the sailing distance from Kronstadt, Russia's naval base in the Baltic, to Vladivostok would be 12,655 miles. In spite of this danger, in the best traditions of Russian procrastination, nothing was done.

However, by 1886 the Tsar was himself becoming impatient at what seemed an excessive delay in even planning a route for the railway into Siberia, and after reading a report by Count Alexis Ignatyev, governor-general of Irkutsk, to the effect that the Chinese, after years of complete indifference, were beginning to take an interest in the Amur region, he added an irritable rubric to it in his own hand:

I have read many reports of the Governors-General of Siberia and must own with grief and shame that until now the Government has done scarcely anything towards satisfying the needs of this rich, but neglected country! It is time, high time!

Inspired by this spirited reaction, both Ignatyev and Baron Korf, governor-general of the Amur Territory, submitted petitions for the construction of two lines: one from Tomsk to Irkutsk, which was to be the mid-Siberian section of the railway; the other, the eastern section, to extend from the eastern shore of Lake Baikal to Sretensk, the highest point on the Shilka River to which steamers could navigate from the Amur.

The complete route from the west to Vladivostok would then be: from the Volga to Tyumen by river and rail; from Tyumen to Tomsk, in summer by boat on the Tura, Irtysh, Ob and the Tom Rivers, and in winter over the Trakt, the great Siberian post road, by sledge; from Tomsk to Irkutsk by the new railway and from the far side of Lake Baikal, by its new eastern extension to Sretensk. From Sretensk the route would be down the Shilka, Amur and Ussuri Rivers to the railhead of a line, the South Ussuri, which would be built from Vladivostok. A long route, but not so long as the two years that it then took for colonists to reach Vladivostok overland from the west.

Inevitably, because this was the only way it could be done, a ministerial committee was convened; and so effectively did I. A. Vyshnegradsky, the finance minister, stonewall against any sort of expenditure, even for a preliminary survey in Transbaikalia, that the Tsar, who had annotated the report with the words, 'Quite right. I hope the Ministry will practically prove the possibility of the quick and cheap construction of the line', was forced to dissolve it and convene another in 1887.

In the meantime (in June 1886) the Canadian Pacific Railway reached Port Moody, an inlet of the Pacific near Vancouver, 2893 miles from its starting point on the other side of the American continent. Two years later it was on the Vancouver waterfront.

At the second meeting, in spite of the presence of the Finance Minister, the Committee agreed to go ahead with surveys for the lines on both sides of Lake Baikal and these were begun towards the end of 1887. A greater sense of urgency imposed itself on the Committee in October that year when Baron Korf produced a report containing some alarming intelligence. It stated that the Chinese had built a telegraph in Manchuria; that they were said to be building river steamers for use on the Amur, vessels that might conceivably be used for an attack on Vladivostok; and that English engineers were planning a railway in Manchuria that would run northwards towards Vladivostok. It had also become known that, as a final turn of the screw, the British Government was subsidizing a steamship service between Canada and China.

In fact, the Russians had little to fear from any dramatic extension of the Chinese railway system. The only line that was currently functioning within the vast frontiers of the Chinese Empire was a mineral tramway with waggons hauled by the *Rocket of China*, so called by its builder, an English engineer named Kinder, because it began work on the 100th anniversary of the birth of George Stephenson. It only ran from some coal mines to the Po-Hai Gulf. Another eight years were to pass before foreigners began building full-size railways in China. Ironically, the first to do so were the Russians, who gained the concession to build the Chinese Eastern Railway through Manchuria which linked up with the Trans-Siberian.

It is impossible to go into all the happenings that preceded the final decision to build the Trans-Siberian Railway; but in June 1890, Vyshnegradsky again carried the day against the new acting minister of ways of communication, Adolph von Hubbenet (the unfortunate Posyet had resigned, having been held responsible for a train wreck in the autumn of 1888, in which members of the imperial family had been put in danger of their lives). The only decision that was made was to continue the Samara–Zlatoust line another 37 miles into the southern Urals, to a place called Miass, west of Chelyabinsk.

This was too much for the Tsar. Like Hilaire Belloc's chancellor in *Cautionary Tales for Children*, though scarcely the kindliest of men, he took his pen, on 12 July 1890, and wrote in the margin of Baron Korf's report on the Yellow Peril, which von Hubbenet had presented to him, the historic words: 'Necessary to proceed at once to the construction of the line.'

On 21 February 1891, a year of terrible famine in Russia which forced large numbers of peasant families to emigrate to Siberia, von Hubbenet's proposals to start work on the railway from Miass and Vladivostok simultaneously were accepted by the Committee, after a last stand by Vyshnegradsky, who prophesied ruin for Russia. The cost was estimated at about 90,625,000 gold rubles, or about 18,300 rubles a mile.

Events that up to now had moved with all the urgency of lady railway workers greasing points on the outskirts of Moscow now took upon themselves a new velocity. On 17 March 1891 the Tsar addressed an Imperial Rescript to his son, Nicholas, His Imperial Highness the Grand Duke Tsarevich. The Grand Duke Nicholas was at that time on an extensive tour of the East. Because of this he did not receive the rescript until he actually landed at Vladivostok on 24 May, having arrived there by warship from Japan where he had narrowly escaped being spitted on a sword wielded by a crazy policeman.

The rescript read as follows:

YOUR IMPERIAL HIGHNESS!

Having given the order to build a continuous line of railway across Siberia, which is to unite the rich Siberian provinces with the railway system of the Interior, I entrust you to declare My Will, upon your entering the Russian dominions after your inspection of the foreign countries of the East. At the same time, I desire you lay the first stone at Vladivostok for the construction of the Ussuri line, forming part of the Siberian Railway, which is to be carried out at the cost of the State and under direction of the Government. Your participation in the achievement of this work will be a testimony to My ardent desire to facilitate the communications between Siberia and the other countries of the Empire, and to manifest My extreme anxiety to secure the peaceful prosperity of this Country.

Beseeching the Lord's blessing upon the long journey through Russia which lies ahead of you.

I remain your sincerely loving

ALEXANDER

Vladivostok at that time was nothing to write home about. In fact it was a dump. The port was ice-bound for 110 days each year and its principal exports were sea-cabbage, ginseng roots, mushrooms found on oak stumps and lichens growing on corn. However, His Imperial Highness the Grand Duke Tsarevich did as he was bid and with his own hands filled a wheelbarrow with earth and emptied it on the embankment of the future Ussuri line, and then laid the first stone for the construction of the Great Siberian Railroad. Later he took part in the inauguration of the passenger station, laying one more stone. To commemorate this act an image of St Nicholas the Miracle-Worker was placed on the spot where he laid it. Whoever was going to build the railway would certainly need his help. As Harmon Tupper, author of *To the Great Ocean* wrote: 'Of all men engaged in monumental undertakings, few ever stood in greater need of supernatural aid than the builders of the Trans-Siberian Railway.'

6

The Urals

At 1.28 am on the second day of our journey the *Rossiya*, having emerged from the fringes of the world's greatest forest, came to an uncharacteristically shattering halt (normally its arrivals and departures are as smooth as those of a hearse from Harrods) in the station of Kirov, 598 miles, and 15 hours and 13 minutes, from Moscow.

It was, in fact, ten minutes behind schedule, as it often was, more or less, throughout the journey; but no traveller in his right mind would quibble about a few minutes, or even hours, provided that he was already on the train and not waiting for it at some god-forsaken station, on such a long trip – especially as the ferry to Yokohama from Nakhodka at the far end of the line always waits for the train (travellers in the other direction certainly have greater problems). For this reason, throughout the journey I have always referred to the scheduled times of arrival and departure.

There was nothing to be seen of the city, apart from a rather large but unremarkable station building which was brilliantly lit, as if in expectation of the arrival or departure of some important personage; but by now I was too chilly to get out of bed and check on whether one did actually arrive or depart. Instead I snuggled down under the blanket and checked up on Kirov.

Even a superficial study of my library told me as much as I wanted to know about Kirov at this ghastly hour: of its foundation in 1181 by adventurers and merchants from Novgorod who had trafficked here in the small horses of the region; honey, wax, beaver and squirrel skins with the indigenous inhabitants; of its continuing inaccessibility, except by way of the Kama and the Vyatka; and the difficulty that Ivan III, the humbler of Novgorod, experienced in reducing it before he finally annexed it in 1489. Today it depends to a very great extent on timber for its prosperity – it manufactures prefabricated houses, furniture, toys, educational aids and matches – but the forests to the north which supply it are almost exhausted and probably cannot last more than a decade. It is fortunate that it also engages in railway engineering, manufactures machine tools, motor tyres, and leather goods and deals in furs, which must be getting a bit thin on the ground, too.

Until 1780 the city was called Khylnov and from that time until 1934, Vyatka. In December that year Sergei Mironovich Kirov, friend of Stalin, his heir apparent and boss of the Communist Party in Leningrad, was assassinated in his office in the Smolny, the Party Headquarters there. It has been suggested that Stalin was responsible, and many Russians and experts on Russia in other countries believe that this is true. It has also been suggested that Stalin became unhinged, either before the murder of Kirov or immediately afterwards, which would be a charitable explanation of his subsequent behaviour but no more palatable for that. Whatever the truth, the death of Kirov precipitated the Great Terror, the Yezhovshchina, so-called after the awful Nikolai Ivanovich Yezhov, who succeeded the marginally less beastly G. G. Yagoda as head of the NKVD in 1936 on the latter's dismissal.

The Great Terror lasted from 1936 to 1938. Conservative estimates are that between January 1937 and December 1938, seven million people were arrested and added to the number (which did not include 'criminals') already in jails or labour camps, who numbered some five million. Of these twelve million, one million were executed in the course of these two years and another two million died. These figures are supported by the population statistics, which show a striking deficiency of males before the outbreak of war in 1941. The total death roll during twenty-three years of the Stalin regime from 1930 is very conservatively estimated at twenty million, and could be half as much again.

The Great Terror also set in motion the Treason Trials which, beginning in 1936, destroyed many of the highest in the land, including Yagoda himself. Yezhov did not get the chop until Christmas Eve 1953, when he, too, was finally executed.

No sooner was the breath out of Kirov's body than Vyatka was renamed after him. Today there are thirty-nine references to places named after him in the gazetteer of the *Atlas of the USSR*. In addition, his memory is kept evergreen throughout Russia in the form of Kirov clubs, streets, parks, stadiums, museums, theatres (the former Mariinsky Theatre in Leningrad is now the Kirov) and factories.

About 250 miles to the north now lay the country of Ivan Denisovich, around Kotlas where the dreaded *khanovey*, the wind of winds, howls across the tundra for more than a hundred days a year and where for more than eight months the temperature is below freezing. I thought of that one day in his life as the train left Kirov and began to run east under a sky in which a few stars were reluctantly competing with the pale twilight, and thanked God I was on the *Rossiya*.

The stars were showing more of themselves than the Kirov *oblast* was currently doing, with freight train after freight train rumbling westwards, almost nose-to-tail, making it impossible to see anything from the compartment.

Admittedly, I could have got up and stood in the corridor and admired the southern vistas; but I lacked the willpower at such an hour. Earlier on, with the window shut, it had been insufferably stuffy in the compartment, and now that it had been open half the night, if you could call such a feeble effort night, it was distinctly chilly.

During these rare gaps in what was otherwise a continuous wall of rolling stock – the intervals between trains was something like three minutes – I was able to see the forest, in which aspen and birch outnumbered pines, now all swathed with mist, and more of the great, green clearings in which the cropped grass was almost short enough to play cricket or baseball on, although the little haystacks built in the shape of sugar loaves around a long pole which were all over the place would have made either game difficult. Most of these poles, which protruded above the top of the stack, had crows perched on them, and these lent an additional air of melancholy to the scene, as the dark birds on poles do to the already sufficiently melancholy landscapes of Hieronymous Bosch.

Occasionally, but not often, we passed a wooden house standing on the edge of one of these clearings which looked suspiciously like an Edwardian cricket pavilion. They appeared unoccupied. No lights burned in them and no smoke issued from the chimneys: not surprising at around 2.15 am, even though it was light enough outside to read a newspaper, being 3.15 am in these parts.

By now I was terribly thirsty and, by the sort of coincidence that tends to afflict people who have lived together for years and years, Wanda had begun to mumble about tea; dragging on a dressing gown and trying to pretend that I looked like Noel Coward, I set off down the corridor to get some glasses from the little den where Irina was still on duty.

When I got there I found the door shut; lacking the courage to bang on it I went on into the next car to ask the conductress there if she could lend me a couple; but without much hope. Her door was open, which seemed a mistake as she was locked in what looked like a death grip with a slim boy with a Ronald Coleman moustache, whom I recognized as one who shared a compartment with a bearded Australian in our car. I coughed. No response.

'Excuse me,' I said, feeling a pig. There was no need. It was not death he was dispensing. He was giving her the kiss of life. You could have rung a gong or blown a whistle. It would have made no difference. I took two glasses and a couple of sputnik containers from the shelf over her head and slipped away to fill up at our own samovar.

Outside the landscape looked as if it had been executed in lead pencil on grey paper. Then, at 5 am outside, a miracle happened. The clouds opened, not to disgorge rain but to display a sun shining out of a blue sky so full of cirrus that it looked as if it needed filleting. Immediately, everything was transformed. The crows left their perches, stopped making gloomy Boschian noises and started zooming about in the sky. Beyond an invisible river were tree-covered hills, the outermost outworks of the Urals, which were several shades of green, each one of them delicious. Then the clouds clanged shut again and everything was as it had been.

28 May was a quiet day, like a Good Friday and with the sort of weather that accompanies a too-early Easter in Britain; everyone was subdued, with memories of the demon vodka and what it had done. When Russians attack a bottle of this material, which they assume that they are going to drink at a single sitting, with the help of one drinking companion, they do so without diluting it, which for us in the West is the equivalent of drinking half a bottle of whisky each without the addition of water or soda.

At 4.30 am we passed through Glazov, the most important town on this stretch of the line, and at one time, under the tsars, a place of exile. Its inhabitants were said to be engaged in engineering, sawing, lumber and producing food. Even at this hour about half a dozen of them were already on the platform dressed in rubber waders and carrying rods and umbrellas, waiting for the fishermen's special to show up. It was certainly Saturday, unless it was Sunday. Already, funny things were beginning to happen to my sense of time on the *Rossiya*.

At 5.30 we arrived at Balezino which was memorable only because here the *Rossiya* spent thirteen minutes trading in its part-worn CHS4 electric for another CHS2. It did this without any help from me. I was still smarting from the way the drivers had treated me at Danilov, now 521 miles back up the line. Besides, Mischa had promised us all a ride on the footplate later in the trip, provided we were good little boys and girls; but that was yesterday, before we blotted our copy books.

At 5.57, between Pibanshur and Cheptsa a train passed carrying thirty anti-tank guns to the West on flat cars, threatening to foul up still further the imbalance of military might in those parts. Abandoning my first, mad plan which was to put through a collect call to NATO headquarters from the *Rossiya's* radio car, as impracticable, I wrote in my Challenge Duplicate Book: '05.57. 30 ATGs gng wst', which I hoped wld pull the wl over the eyes of the most experienced delver among my papers.

'I vouldn't make jokes with Russians. They are not jokey' was what Wanda said when I told her what I had done, so I rubbed it out.

A few minutes later, at long last, the *Rossiya* crossed the Cheptsa.

It lay far below, compressed between steep banks, cold-looking and swollen with rain, running swiftly, and we crossed it by one of two 'grdr bdges', which I didn't make a note of, but tried to remember.

The *Rossiya* was travelling fast now through a dense forest of pine, fir and larch, some of them immense trees, and frequently it burrowed through deep cuttings in the hills that were little more than gentle swellings. Soon it began to climb, and now the views became wider as it ran out of the country of the Udmurts – middle-sized, fair or red-headed people – through which we had been passing, into the Perm *oblast* and approached the foothills of the Urals.

The views were more expansive now over what resembled Alpine meadows which were full of kingcups and violets. Here, there were many settlements with timber yards and houses with steep-pitched roofs on which the rain danced madly; but the interminable freight trains usually contrived to mask them from view, or else the wind-breaks performed the same service. Now we were on a wide, undulating plateau running down towards little valleys and ravines which seemed the top of the world, although according to the map it was less than 1000 feet above the sea. Somewhere here at a place called Kuzma, which I couldn't find between Kez and Vereschagino on the map – a large dilapidated-looking location enlivened by some green grain silos – we entered the second time zone from Moscow, which put everyone in it (apart from the occupants of the *Rossiya* and the stations along the line, who continued to observe Moscow time all the way to Vladivostock) two hours ahead of the capital.

I must say the landscape was a gruesome sight with the rain pounding down on it. Each one of us tried to come to terms with what was on view in our own way. Otto attempted some photographic 'effects', but soon abandoned the struggle; Wanda ignored it completely, Mischa played chess with the young man with the Ronald Coleman moustache, and I wrote things like, 'saw a cow' in my duplicate book and wondered what I was doing here.

Now the line behaved like a worm that had lost its gyroscope, wriggling madly through a district of low hills, intersected by streams and valleys, and with what looked like populous mining villages disposed around it. For the first time since leaving Moscow it was possible to see both ends of the *Rossiya* at the same time.

At 9.30 am, after travelling past some huge, dank marshalling yards full of flat cars loaded with enough timber to keep the pyromaniacs of the world in matches for the rest of their lives, the *Rossiya* clonked across the Kama, here about 1000 yards wide, a river as depressing as the Mersey on a wet day in spite of the wealth of shipping on it, and came to rest in the station at Perm, equally off-putting in this weather, 898 miles from Moscow.

From 1940 until 1957 Perm was called Molotov, after Vyacheslav M. Molotov, first deputy prime minister of the USSR at that date, who inspired the world's first undrinkable cocktail: one of nineteen places and one passenger liner named after him, at a time when ministers of the USSR were still, with an excess of optimism, thought to be for ever. In 1957, together with other old-guard Stalinists and reactionaries, such as Kaganovich, Malenkov and Saburov, he was given the air by Khruschev (he was lucky that was all he was given) and it became Perm again – not so quickly as Molotovabad and Kaganovichobad in the Tadzhik SSR in central Asia, which had their names changed the day before the news of the dismissals was made public. The good ship *Molotov* was renamed the *Baltika*.

Now Perm measured more than 35 miles from end to end, and was the chief port of the Kama River area. But such weighty matters did not really interest me at this moment, and neither did the almost unbelievable fact that somewhere out there beyond the solid curtains of rain, unless they had Saturday off, a large number of the 900,000 inhabitants of Perm were working away producing agricultural machinery, aircraft and tractor parts and excavators, and were tanning leather, pumping oil out of the bowels of the earth nearby, and making paper and, of course, matches. Something as unbelievable to me as the thought, every time I pass through Reading, Berkshire, on the *Cornish Riviera*, that biscuits are made there and that it was in Reading that Oscar Wilde was in gaol, matters to which I then give no further consideration.

We were not interested because, although it may have been 9.30 am on the *Rossiya* and on the station, so far as we were concerned it was 11.30 am on the western slopes of the Urals, and I, for one, had already been up for six-and-a-half hours. It was time for at least a slice or two of black bread and butter and a glass of beer (we were full of tea).

And so, accompanied by Wanda and Mischa, who, only temporarily I hoped, seemed to regard me as more worthy of surveillance than Otto, I set off to investigate the interior of the station building which at this time of the morning was bulging at the seams with damp humanity.

It took the best part of the thirty-three minutes that the *Rossiya* was due to remain in Perm to find out that there was no beer at the station, or anywhere outside it within walking distance. I also found out that any attempts to make contact with members of the public who were either marooned in it by the weather or were waiting to travel by train were received with the same enthusiasm as they would have been on a railway station anywhere else in the Western world.

When we did return to the train we found that Otto had again been in trouble with the authorities, this time for taking what promised to be some rather good pictures from a footbridge of a whole army of prospective passengers who were trying to join it without furling their umbrellas.

In revenge for this setback on two fronts we made Mischa – he was reluctant – buy a copy of *Pravda*, as we wanted to know what had been the fate of Mr N. V. Podgorny, chairman of the Praesidium of the Supreme Soviet since December 1965. On the eve of our departure from Moscow he had been sacked and replaced by Mr Brezhnev, who up to then had been president of the Central Committee of the Communist Party of the Soviet Union, since October 1964. In spite of this elevation Mr Brezhnev was, apparently, going to retain his original office in addition to becoming chairman.

While waiting for Mischa to digest the dense printed columns of the newspaper, I hunted up information on Perm.

Perm had been the place, before 1875, where east-bound travellers had had to leave the unfinished railway and take to their carriages and sleighs in order to cross the Urals. Exiles travelled on foot, carts and waggons being used to transport children and the infirm. Many of these exiles would have reached Perm by boat, for it was only about seven days' travelling time from Nizhny Novgorod, first down the Volga and then up the Kama river. On this section of their journey they were transported in steamers or in barges towed behind steamers. It is surprising to learn that the Kama had steamers on it five years after Napoleon had fled from Moscow. Before the days of steam, however, slogging up the Volga against the current would have been very slow work. Barges would have been towed upstream by bands of men yo-heave-hoing as they hauled from the bank, or else the boats would be warped up to a kedge anchor, using an enormous capstan turned by horses, or by gangs of anything up to eighty men.

At Perm foreigners had to obtain a *podorojna*, an order for horses. Usually, they were on their way to Peking by way of Mongolia, the only destination east of the Urals worth the expenditure of so much time and money. Travelling without intermission, London–St Petersburg–Peking took about fifty days in the 1860s and 1870s. The fastest travellers were the imperial couriers between Peking and St Petersburg. Before the telegraph was built linking the two capitals, they frequently covered the 3618 miles between Irkutsk and St Petersburg in sixteen days with 212 changes of horses, eating and sleeping in their sleighs, and averaging ten miles an hour for nearly 400 consecutive hours.

There were three principal sorts of conveyance: the *telega*, a springless, one-horse cart of the sort used by the wooden-hatted man at Danilov, which had a leather hood and curtain for bad weather; the *kibitka*, which was similarly equipped but could also be converted into a horse-drawn sleigh; and the *tarantass*, a sort of hooded and, except for the driver, seatless basket about seven feet long supported on a couple of long flexible poles mounted on the four axle trees which acted as springs.

The *tarantass* was drawn by a *troika*, a team of three shaggy Siberian horses. In it the occupants travelled lying prone on their belongings which acted as shock-absorbers. If one can use such an epithet about what were each in their own way unique instruments of torture, the *tarantass* was the most popular. All these sorts of vehicles were driven by a *yamschchik* (driver) who was invariably at least partially drunk.

Both *kibitkas* and *tarantasses* could be bought or hired in Perm, a *tarantass* costing between £12 and £15. The disadvantage of a *telega*, which was often used to transport the excess baggage of *tarantass* users was, apart from its truly hideous discomfort, that it had to be changed at each posting station at a cost of 8d a stage. This meant that the traveller's belongings had to be disembarked every two hours or so and re-loaded into another vehicle.

These posting stations were located at intervals of between 10 and 20 miles along what foreigners called the Great Siberian Post Road and Russians and the inhabitants of Siberia, the *Trakt*. They were two-room log cabins, too small for the number of travellers and drivers they were called upon to accommodate even temporarily, extremely dirty and lacking in amenity. However, they were havens of rest compared with the *étapes*, the stockaded stations and *polu étapes* that were half-way houses between the principal ones, built at intervals of between 25 and 40 miles along the *Trakt* in which the exiles were accommodated during their journey to the East, which they accomplished at a speed of about 330 miles a month with twenty-four hours' rest every third day.

The *Trakt* extended from Perm to Irkutsk and beyond it to Nerchinsk, where the Tsar's great silver mines were, in Transbaikalia, a distance of more than 3000 miles. Long stretches of it, deep in snow or mud or dust according to the season, apart from having been widened in the eighteenth century to 21 feet, were exactly as they always had been. In fact, to this day there is no continuous transcontinental road from the Urals to the Pacific that is motorable in the accepted sense, and until the mid-1890s, when large sections of the Trans-Siberian Railway were completed, it was quicker to travel from Vladivostok to St Petersburg by crossing the Pacific, the North American continent and the Atlantic than by travelling westwards across Siberia.

The never-ending rain on the way to Perm had thoroughly depressed all four of us. But an American, George Kennan, travelling to Siberia in June 1885 had been more fortunate with the weather, and had really enjoyed himself. He had found the scenery 'beautifully wild and picturesque' and as he steamed up the Kama towards Perm he had noticed that:

the crowds of peasants on the landing-stages were dressed in costumes whose originality of design and crude brightness of color showed that they had been little affected by the sobering and conventionalizing influence of Western civilization ... we certainly had not before seen in any part of Russia young men arrayed in blue, crimson, purple, pink and violet shirts, nor young women dressed in lemon-yellow gowns, scarlet aprons, short pink over-jackets, and lilac head-kerchiefs ... Neither in the weather, nor in the scenery, nor in the vegetation was there anything to suggest an approach to the frontier of Siberia. The climate seemed almost Californian in its clearness and warmth; flowers blossomed everywhere in the greatest profusion and luxuriance; every evening we heard nightingales singing in the forests beside the river; and after sunset, when the wind was fair, many of the passengers caused *samovars* to be brought up and tables to be spread on the hurricane deck, and sat drinking tea and smoking cigarettes in the odorous night air until the glow of the strange northern twilight faded away over the hills.

Kennan was born in Norwalk, Ohio, in 1845. His mother was related to Samuel Morse, the inventor of the Morse Code, and his father taught him telegraphy which makes his decision to become a telegraphist not really surprising. In the summer of 1865 he went to Kamchatka to take part in the Russo-American Telegraph Expedition which was to lay a cable from the Bering Strait to Niko-layevsk-on-Amur. By the time the Russo-American Telegraph Company went bust the following year for $3 million, following the successful laying of a transatlantic cable which rendered the whole scheme obsolete, the entire 4600-mile route had been explored. Kennan returned to St Petersburg overland by sledge in the winter of 1867, a journey of more than 5000 miles. Three years later he published an excellent book, *Tent Life in Siberia and Adventures among the Koraks and other Tribes in Kamchatka and Northern Asia*. In 1877 he was appointed night manager of the Washington Bureau of Associated Press.

In 1885 the American *Century Magazine* commissioned Kennan to investigate conditions among political revolutionists and other prisoners and exiles in Siberia. The number of revolutionists being sent to the mines in Transbaikalia had increased very sharply after the assassination of Tsar Alexander II in 1881 and it had become very difficult for foreign journalists seeking information about the

movement to contact members of it still at large. As Kennan wrote:
'Most of the leading actors in the revolutionary drama of 1878–9
were already in Siberia.' The obvious thing to do, if permission
could be obtained, was to visit them there.

In 1884 Kennan made a preliminary trip to Russia and in May
1885 he received permission from the Minister of the Interior to
visit Siberia, together with an artist, George A. Frost, a Bostonian.
Kennan was able to arrange this because, as he wrote: 'I then
believed that Russian Government and the exile system had been
greatly misrepresented by such writers as Stepniak and Prince Kropotkin ... and that the descriptions of Siberian mines and prisons
in the just-published book of the Rev. Henry Lansdell [*Through
Siberia*, 1883] were probably truthful and accurate.'

Interpreting this permission in the most generous way – 'In my
frequent skirmishes with the police, and with suspicious local
officials in remote Siberian villages, nothing but the letter which
I carried from the Russian Minister of the Interior saved me from
summary arrest and imprisonment ...' the two men were able in
the space of some ten months to make an extremely arduous journey
of more than 8000 miles, which took them to some of the most
remote and awful penal colonies in the Russian Empire.

The result was a remarkable series of articles by Kennan, illustrated by a collection of drawings by Frost which served the same
function as photographs. Both created a great impression when
they were published in *Century Magazine*, and in 1891 they were
reprinted in book form, with the title, *Siberia and the Exile System*.

A drawing of Kennan, made in about 1890, when he would have
been forty-five years old, and which forms the frontispiece of his
book on the Siberian prisons, shows a slight, elegant, rather delicate
looking individual with a droopy moustache. He is dressed in a comfortable dark suit, soft collar and what look like patent leather slippers with moiré bows. He is sitting writing, locked up in one of
those patent chairs-cum-desks in vogue at that time, an article of
furniture which could be taken to pieces and lashed on a drome-
dary's back in a matter of minutes. The room in which he is seated
– it could be part of a bachelor's chambers (or is it the inside of
a tent?) – has a good Asiatic rug on the floor and a collection of

Yaroslavl Station, Moscow

Railway workers

Hideous disorder in the Newbys' compartment

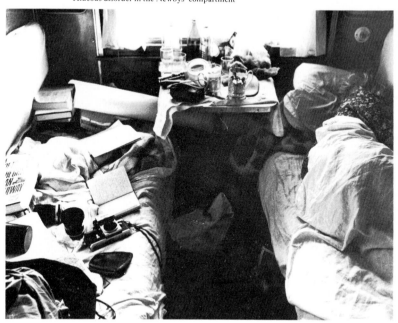

Very wet Russia west of the Urals

Boundary stone in the Urals between Europe and Asia

Platskartny car on the *Rossiya* with 58 'lying places'

Stationmistress seeing the *Rossiya* through Borodulino Station in the Urals

Conductress enjoying a joke

Girls from the Siberian
School of Choreography,
Novosibirsk

The Ob at Novosibirsk
Station concourse, Novosibirsk

Fond farewell at Krasnoyarsk

Steam engine east of Krasnoyarsk

Conductress in Eastern Siberia
Town in the Siberian Steppe

weapons on the wall. In spite of these warlike appurtenances it is difficult to associate this figure with the man who, on two separate expeditions, separated by twenty years, successfully overcame all the hardships, dangers and difficulties inseparable from travel in the most remote parts of Siberia in the second half of the nineteenth century.

But however difficult and dangerous Kennan and Frost found Siberia, they were at least allowed to go where they liked and to visit the places they wanted to. They were even allowed into Perm, although they had a lousy time there. Perm today is not on the very short list of cities in the USSR open to foreigners, so I was forbidden to go there.

Breakfast, eaten around 12.30 pm Urals time, with the four of us sitting down together for the first time since the previous evening, was a wary meal of bread and meat and tea, and apart from the tea, the only good buy on the *Rossiya* so far, a bit clammy.

'Tell us, Mischa,' Wanda said. 'What does *Pravda* say happened to Mr Podgorny?'

'Nothing.'

'Then what's all that stuff on the front page?'

'Nothing on Podgorny. There is nothing new; but I have news for you. You may go to the front of the train.'

'To travel on the engine with the drivers? Yippee!'

'No, that will have to be later, if the permissions can be arranged. Now you may talk with the people in the *platskartny* cars with the fifty-eight lying places, the "hard class" cars, if they don't object; and Otto can photograph them, if they don't object, also.'

'I don't like conducted tours,' Wanda said. 'I'll go later.'

An outing, even if it was with teacher – goody-goody, so far as I was concerned! Even if it hadn't occurred to me that I would have to ask anyone before drifting up and down the train.

Minus Wanda, with me bringing up the rear, hoping to drop off and speak to someone *en route*, and with Mischa in the van, we battled our way up the train towards Siberia through three sets of four-berth cars in which all the occupants seemed to have settled in the corridors, each car with two sets of doors with glass insets at either end, which either shut in one's face by their own weight or else were slammed shut in them by self-appointed door-keepers with draught-phobia; each car joined to the next one by a huge, slippery metal hump in the windy no-man's land over the couplings between them, which is so cold in winter that if you get stuck out there between two locked doors you're dead in twenty minutes; past four roaring samovars and four heating stoves ditto but less so; past four assorted conductresses, each of whom seemed to regard me with diminishing enthusiasm the further I got from my home-from-home, ruled over by Irina and Lilya, queens of the 'soft-class' car.

On, ever onwards, through the dining room in which a despairing throng was huddled, studying the greasy menus, wondering when the fun would begin, past Miss Cry-in-the-Bucket, now transformed into a waitress with a mini-apron and a sort of Mabel Lucie Attwell-type mob cap, on past 'chef', who actually snarled at Otto as he went by (they had already met); on through four more four-berth coaches in which the mixture was as before and past the radio compartment where the operator was deftly controlling the volume of what sounded suspiciously like a *kazakh* choir for the benefit of the passengers, while with the other hand making to headquarters that the ship was still afloat.

And so, on the second day of our journey we arrived at the first of the five multi-berth cars with 'lying places', as the Russians put it, for fifty-eight people, the last of which was separated from the engine by the mail van. These cars were open-plan and the passengers slept in two-tier berths, either athwart the car or parallel with the corridor. There was no discernible difference in the quality of the interior appointments of one of these 'hard-class' cars, built in 1975 for mass occupation in the classless atmosphere of Annendorf, East Germany, and the two- and four-berth cars. The classiest thing about them was the passengers themselves. As I had already noted before leaving Moscow, there were none of the submerged classes aboard. Presumably they were sweating it out in one of the slow trains that stopped at every station. All these citizens were cleaner and brighter than many of the passengers on a British Rail Inter-City from London to Birmingham, and just about as interested in us as their British counterparts would have been if a band of Russians in charge of an interpreter had irrupted into their car, that is unless they had snow on their boots. They simply carried on knitting, waiting in the perpetual queue for one of the two lavatories or showing one another the screamingly funny cartoons in *Krokodil*; or else they carried on the normal sort of high-brow conversation that takes place on long distance trains everywhere – about when next to eat, whether to start getting their belongings together in order to be ready to get off the train at Novosibirsk, now about 1100 miles to the east, or how to stop that otherwise nice sailor in bunk no. 7 snoring, as he is presumably going all the way to Vladivostok, where the nearest real sea is on this particular line.

But here we came to a shattering halt, held up by Khruschev Reborn, the conductress who had successfully frustrated my evil design to take a picture of her engine at Moscow. The next moment she was driving us backwards, in utter disorder, out of her dominions, shouting (she was damn near roaring) '*Nyet! Nyet! Nyet!*' at Mischa who was obviously unused to this kind of treatment and was becoming more and more red in the face. Eventually, he took out the famous red pass and held it within six inches of her nose.

'*Nyet!*' she shrieked, slamming the door in his face, locking it and then gibbering at him through the glass in a way that made me wish I'd brought my monkey nuts. At this moment I would not have swapped my weedy British passport for Mischa's bright red pass for anything.

The retreat began, with me leading the way. Should Russia tremble with women like this strung out along her life-lines?

'I tol' you,' Wanda said, when I got back to our compartment. 'I tol' you. Never go on conducted tours.'

I could have struck her. 'All right, Mrs Know-All, what am I supposed to do when the whole bloody thing's a conducted tour?' I shouted, sitting down as far as I could from her in this two-berth coffin, where I began to compose what turned out to be a distinctly off-colour Limerick which began:

> There was a young lady of Perm,
> Who had an affair with a worm.

Now the *Rossiya* ran south-east into the Urals, first over a wooded upland that was part of a detached range of hills, all the time following the line of the Trakt, here just a normal road, then down into the valley of the Sylva, a very winding tributary of the Kama which rises near the watershed of the main range, at first far away from it, then closing with it until, at Kungur, 63 miles from Perm, railway and river come together.

Kungur is built on a ridge above the Sylva. It was founded by Cossacks in about 1640 as a stronghold. 'Celebrated for its tanneries' – which it still is – 'and its thieves' was how Thomas Witlam Atkinson, architect, traveller and watercolour artist, described it. He was passing through it, also in filthy weather, in March 1849 with his newly wedded wife, an English governess from St Petersburg, while on their way to Siberia, Mongolia, the Kirghiz Steppes and parts of central Asia, a journey of some 39,500 miles which was to take them seven years. At this point they were still travelling with a driver and postilion, in a '*vashock*', which he described as 'a box-like machine, placed on a sledge; in fact a half-grown omnibus'.

At Kungur their other travelling companion, a deerhound, was stolen from them. Eventually, Atkinson traced it, by its whining, to some out-buildings.

I now walked towards the door . . . three black-looking scoundrels stepped forward to prevent my opening it; but my two barrels, suddenly pointed towards them, and the click of the lock, spoke a language they perfectly understood. Unresisted I pushed open the door, and out bounded the deer hound with a leather thong around its neck.

'Domes and very old one- and two-storey houses,' I wrote religiously in my duplicate book. The sort of thing that years ago, while flying low over central India with the temperature up in the 100°s Fahrenheit, I had detected Lord Reith (one time boss of the BBC, unseasonably dressed in black coat, striped trousers, starched collar and cuffs) writing in *his* memory book from Smythsons of Bond Street while on his way to a board meeting of British Aluminium at Jamshedpur – 'villages and views', he had written in a bold hand. Then I had thought him a figure of fun. And I still do. Although sitting a couple of feet from me in the opposite seat of a small private aeroplane, he had not even said 'good morning'!

There was only one other thing I noted as we flashed through Kungur. 'Interesting souvenirs can be bought at the station. They are made of local minerals and include stone sculptures of people and animals,' wrote the authors of *The Complete Guide to the Soviet Union*, ignoring the fact that the *Rossiya* doesn't stop there and you can hurt yourself quite seriously descending from a moving train (but no doubt only trying to make the USSR sound gay).

Onwards, ever onwards! Through green fields, some of them semi-inundated, on the left bank of the Sylva, spread out below the steep cliffs on its far side. In those lush meadows herds of cattle were huddled together with their tails turned to the driving, blinding, streaming, teeming, 'fucking rain', as Wanda described it more picturesquely, no doubt worrying about their milk yields and hoping that they wouldn't succumb to water-on-the-brain. Luckily, a lot of it was falling in the river, or the *Rossiya* would have had its periscope up.

Then over the Sylva, which here runs away to the south before curling back across the line of the railway high up near its source, close to the watershed; climbing now into the Urals – nowhere hereabouts were they more than 1600 feet above sea level, although they do rise to over 6000 feet further north.

Shalya had black wooden houses on its outskirts and black fences. Well, they looked black but it may have been on account of the rain. Once the *Rossiya* had sat down in the station for its five-minute obligatory rest, you could see precious little of the town centre with a goods train parked alongside on the other line. On the platform women were selling potatoes from buckets. Whether they were raw or boiled was impossible to say without getting down and having a look; but a Russian male passenger did brave the elements to buy himself a giant screwed-up newspaperful.

Then once more into the wilderness; or was it the wilderness? In the Urals any glade or nook may conceal a mine or blast furnace. It certainly looked like a wilderness to me. What we were rolling over was an apparently endless succession of fog-wreathed, grass-grown plateaux, all of them broken into by a labyrinth of ravines;

the plateaux crowned with stands of what to me through the mist looked like oaks, limes and possibly even elms but, whatever they were, were certainly deciduous trees; the ravines filled with dense growth of pine and larch.

Looking at the middle Urals from the window of his train in 1885, on what was the first line to be built across the range due east from Perm, about 250 miles to the north of where we were, George Kennan was reminded of West Virginia, where the Baltimore and Ohio Railroad crosses the Alleghenies. Looking at the middle Urals from the *Rossiya* in 1977, I was reminded of nothing.

It was difficult to believe that we were approaching the watershed of a 1400-mile-long mountain chain which almost succeeds in connecting the Arctic Ocean to the Caspian Sea and one that separates northern Europe from Asia. Difficult to believe, too, looking at its grassy, certainly not Alpine, meadows, that the Urals have concealed within them (or are reputed to have concealed within them) some 20,000 assorted minerals, and that for some 280 miles on either side of the line where we were at the moment, shifts of men were working away, digging some of them up, as they had done ever since 1558 when Ivan the Terrible had given the merchant family of Stroganov permission to exploit the salt and iron deposits on the banks of the Kama; the only difference being that now they were working on a wider range of materials: – not only iron and salt, but nickel, asbestos, potash, aluminium, gold, copper, coal (in rapidly diminishing quantities, but it is not so important now that they have natural gas), chromite, manganese and bauxite. Just a few of the exploitable minerals with which these mountains are loaded; not to speak of jasper, agate, emerald, topaz, tourmaline, malachite and diamonds, if their employers are lucky, although most of the diamonds come from the mines at Mirny in Yakutia, in eastern Siberia.

The Urals were the territory of hunting and fishing peoples: Zyrians, Permians and Yugrians, otherwise the Ostyaks, who were thought to be descendants of the Scythians and who also, to make it even more complicated, had affinities with Finns, Esthes and Lapps.

The Yugrians formed an effective barrier to Novgorodian expansion eastwards over the range into Siberia. The Novgorodians regarded the heathen Yugrians as impure, eaters of corpses, carrion and other filth; but filthy or not, the Yugrians had carried on a brisk trade in sables with Constantinople as early as the ninth century. Military expeditions sent out by Novgorod against them in the eleventh century in order to find a way through what was known as the 'Iron Gate in the Great Rock' had a depressing tendency to return either decimated or not at all, although individual freebooters, the Novgorodian *ukshuyniki*, succeeded in passing through the Gate from the beginning of the fourteenth century onwards.

It was not until after Novgorod fell to the Muscovites in 1478 that Stephen, a priest who was later sanctified for his success, managed to draw their teeth by converting them to Christianity and burning their temples. The route he followed into their country, by way of the Vym and Pechora Rivers, was the one used by the Muscovite Prince Semyon Kurbsky in the winter of 1499, when he crossed the northern Urals with an army. He reached the lower Ob in Siberia where, although he took a thousand prisoners from among the primitive Ostyaks and Voguls there and large quantities of furs as loot, he found it too unsafe to remain.

Soon the *Rossiya* closed with another river, the Chusovaya. I would like to have sailed down this tributary of the Kama, as Atkinson did, seeing the cliffs, the great jagged peaks called the Four Robbers, the immense extrusions of jasper and limestone, 'in strata which had once been horizontal ... now turned up, and curved into most extraordinary forms, with other substances forced through them', the curious rocks below the village of Ilimskoi; but riverlovers should not travel by train.

Now, the *Rossiya* swept across a vast open plateau, almost devoid of trees, so far as I could see. To the right of the line, to the south, queues of drab lorries, some with human beings huddled in the back under sacks, waited for it to go by at the level crossings from which roads with a surface of thin mud stretched away through sodden villages.

But then, as it ran in close to Pervuralsk, a city where the big pipes for the oil and gas lines are made, some curtains of rain were drawn back; low down on the southern horizon the sky cleared to

a brilliant, icy whiteness, and some of the huge plants in the industrial complex that surrounds the city were revealed in black outline
against it, belching smoke and flames: nightmare constructions in
a nightmare landscape, such as those in the painting by Pieter
Breughel of Mad Margaret, who is seen wearing a helmet and
breastplate, stalking through the ruins of the world. Then the
weather closed in, thicker than ever.

We were nearing the frontiers of Europe and Asia, something we
both wanted to be able to tell our children's children that we had
seen and crossed; and for what seemed an age we stood in the corridor squinnying through the rain-spattered windows hoping not
to miss it, while the rest of the occupants of the 'soft-class' car got
their heads down. All we could see were endless windbreaks and
the telegraph poles which, like the *Rossiya*, now seemed to be running downhill.

Finally, at kilometre mark 1777 (1110 miles) from Moscow and
at a measly height of 1345 ft above the sea, we had a fleeting vision
of a white obelisk to the right of the line with EUROPE inscribed
on one side and ASIA on the other (in Cyrillic). There is also a more
vulgar up-to-date monument somewhere hereabouts, a column with
a globe on top and a space-ship orbiting it; but we didn't see it.
We were in Asia, at last – but not, as we found out later, in Siberia.
There was nothing to see except a lot of deciduous trees in leaf,
which had been planted as windbreaks and which effectively
blocked any views. We should have come earlier, before the leaves
came out.

Now that it was on the eastern slopes of the Urals, the *Rossiya*
really began to pick up speed, swooping downhill through the big
bends that were frequent now, so fast that with my head thrust out
of the compartment window (to Wanda's disgust, who said she was
freezing to death and would I stop behaving like a boy scout), either
end of the train could be seen only momentarily, whereas previously
there had been plenty of time to take pictures of the whole thing
as it went round the corners.

Although it was still only about 3.15 pm Moscow time, here in
the Urals, on their time and in this weather, it was already growing
dark, so dark that when we passed an extravagantly castellated little

wooden station in the woods, with a platform full of homeward-bound fishermen equipped with rods, the lights were already on. In fact, it was just like 4.45 pm on a wet November evening in England – a thought which, when I expressed it to Wanda, threw both of us into an extremity of homesickness, Wanda relapsing into a Slavonic gloom so intense that I did not even dare to ask her what she was thinking about, while I myself dreamt of crumpets and/ or buttered toast, Gentleman's Relish in a jumbo-size pot, buckets of common, sweet, orange-coloured English tea and a paperback copy of P. G. Wodehouse, any one of the Master's works provided that it was a paperback and I could make it greasy with an easy conscience, having omitted to bring any of them along with me, and now standing in desperate need of one. Instead, I was saddled with *The House of the Dead*, *Resurrection*, *Crime and Punishment* and various other five-star but equally lugubrious works, with Goncharov's *Oblomov* for light relief. This would teach me not to pose as an intellectual in future.

At 3.49 pm, having passed a large lake, and an old church, we came to the nearest thing the driver could manage to a swerving halt in the station at Sverdlovsk, the largest city in the whole region, 'the Pittsburgh of the Urals', with over a million inhabitants. From 1721, when it was founded in the reign of Catherine the Great, until 1924, when it had its name changed to Sverdlovsk (in honour of Jakob Sverdlov, first chairman of the Central Executive Committee, who died of typhus in 1919), it was called Yekaterinburg. I found it difficult to become interested in Sverdlovsk or Yekaterinburg, partly because I wished I was in England, partly because it was three-quarters dark and there was nothing to see, partly because I find it difficult to get worked up about a place that non-Communists are not allowed to visit. So after fifteen minutes, when the *Rossiya* moved out with a TAN 75 diesel engine pulling it along, as the next stretch wasn't electrified, I left with the only two vivid ideas I had had of it still intact. One of them was inspired by an old photograph, taken about a month after a White Russian army took Yekaterinburg from the Bolsheviks, towards the end of July 1918. It shows one end of a smallish room, which could be a cellar, but is, in fact, not a cellar. The walls either have battens running up and down them, which gives the impression that they are covered with striped paper, or else they have had a striped pattern stencilled on to them, as is still done in peasant houses in parts of Italy and eastern Europe, although today it is applied with a roller. The whole of one of the walls of this room, the one to the left of some double doors, is full of gaping holes which penetrate the plaster to the wattle, or whatever it is behind; and the floor is covered with debris.

The other impression is of a girl of about eighteen, sitting in a sentry box in siding 37, on the railway at Yekaterinburg wearing a blood-stained white blouse: a girl who has been trying to escape and has been wounded and taken by Red Army troops in the woods. The date was about 21 September 1918. Perhaps we shall never know if the imperial family actually died in this awful room, or whether the girl in the sentry box was Anastasia, or what then happened to her.

7

Into Siberia

No crumpets or Gentleman's Relish for the temporarily demoralized Newbys, just an excessively early dinner for two around five o'clock: the last two cans of Carlsberg, some rather soggy Moroccan sardines, another three or four gruesome inches off the Russian sausage – a feast accompanied by an extraordinary variety of bread, of all shades from off-white to black, the result of Wanda's search for the perfect Russian loaf. After this repast we sang the lyrics of a song entitled 'One Day over the Urals', but it would have sounded better if J. Garland had been belting it.

The area we were now passing through, and to the north of the line, had once been thinly populated by roaming peoples, Khanti and Mansi, whose way of life, hunting, fishing and reindeer hunting had scarcely changed from the earliest times until about 1939, when they had been 'encouraged' (the official word) to form collective farms. Until the Revolution, and probably throughout the 1920s, their way of life had probably changed little or not at all since time immemorial. In winter they wore wrapover fur coats of reindeer skin, lined with hare or squirrel fur or the down of ducks, geese or loons. Women's coats among the eastern Khanti were made of cloth-lined hare skins, squirrel paws, deer's ears, or pieces of deer fur. It took up to 800 squirrel skins to line a coat.

Each clan had its own sacred clan-site, inhabited by the spirits of its ancestors which were thought to be animals, birds, insects – butterflies were greatly esteemed – and various plants. The flesh of wild reindeer was their staple food. It was rich in protein. They ate the kidneys, liver, marrow, ears, eyes and lips raw, and drank the fresh blood immediately after the animal had been slaughtered:

any left over was used for making pancakes. The remaining meat was cooked. They extracted oil from the innards of fish and ate it mixed with crushed bird-cherries. Fish were eaten raw, boiled or dried.

At the beginning of the sixteenth century these people were over-run by Tartars, semi-nomadic cattlemen, who founded settlements on the Ob and the Irtysh and eventually became united under the Tartar Khanate of Sibir'at, on the right bank of the Irtysh near the present city of Tobolsk.

In 1552 Kazan, the great stronghold that the Tartars had founded in 1437, was captured by an army of Ivan the Terrible. Two years later Sarai (Astrakhan) also fell to the Russians. The Golden Horde of the Tartars had already been dispersed in 1478, after a strange confrontation between the Tartars and the Russians on the banks of the Oka, in the course of which both armies had retreated from one another in panic.

In 1555 the Tartar ruler of the Sibir'Khanate, Etiger, a heathen, realizing that the fall of Kazan had left the way open for a Russian invasion of his territory, began an unsolicited donation of a *yasak*, an annual tribute of furs, to Ivan the Terrible, in this instance of a thousand sables and a similar number of squirrel skins, in the hopes of mitigating his ferocity.

Three years later Ivan granted the Stroganov family a twenty-year charter to develop an area of about five and a half million acres on the Kama River. They were a family of merchant adventurers, and tne charter gave them the freedom to form what was virtually a new state.

In 1562 Kuchum Khan, son of the Khan of Bukhara, and a Muslim, invaded Etiger's khanate, captured his capital, Isker, murdered Etiger and immediately dropped the annual fur tribute. In 1573 he began sending raiding parties over the Urals into Stro-ganov territory.

Much displeased at the loss of his sables and squirrels, Ivan de-cided to strengthen the Stroganov family's position. He granted them another charter, which gave them territorial rights east of the Urals, encouraged them to wage war against Kuchum and the Khanti and Mansi whose vassals they had become, and allowed them to enlist a force of Cossacks to help defend their territory. Cossacks were freebooters, robbers and vagabonds: wanted men, beyond the law. Often they were escaped serfs. As their commander the Stroganovs chose a Don Cossack who had been a pirate on theVolga, named Yermak Timofeyevich, about whom as much is known for certain as is known about Robin Hood.

There are conflicting accounts about when the campaign against Kuchum Khan got off the ground; but it seems that Yermak left the Stroganov domains in the autumn of 1581 at the head of 800 men. These men were mostly Don Cossacks but they were reinforced by a motley collection of Russians, freebooting Livonians and Germans, three priests and a runaway monk. Having wintered either in the Urals or on the far side of the range, in Kuchum's capital, the Cossacks began the descent of the Tura River, using rafts and boats equipped with sails. Neither the Khanti nor the Mansi nor the Tartars, children of the Asian steppes, had ever seen such things and they were terrified, believing them to be great white hostile birds, and these fears contributed to the defeat of the small, mixed force of cavalry that had been sent against the Cossacks, armed with swords, lances and bows and arrows which were no match for their firearms. After this skirmish Yermak occupied the so-called 'capital' of Yepancha (the Khanti vassal prince he had just defeated), Chinga-Tura, on the site of what is now Tyumen.

Then, continuing down the river to its confluence with the Tobol, Yermak defeated Tausan, one of Kuchum's ministers. Largely composed of pagan Khanti and Mansi, his soldiers could see no point in dying for Allah, in whom they did not believe, in defence of territory of which, even to the most long-sighted of them, there was apparently more than enough for everyone.

Yermak now turned eastwards up the Irtysh and attacked Kuchum's capital at Isker, which was defended by an earth rampart with a wooden palisade on top. He took it after fierce fighting, but in doing so he lost more than a hundred men and, unfortunately for them, in doing so allowed Kuchum and the remnants of the garrison to escape. Yermak was now sitting in the terminus of a 1250-mile caravan route which led to Bukhara, and from here he sent back news of his victory, prudently choosing as a messenger and

the bearer of *yasak* one of his Cossacks who had already been con-
demned to death, for Ivan could be capricious. In fact, the Tsar
was delighted. He rewarded Yermak with rich gifts, including a
heavy armoured breastplate, and a free pardon for himself and his
men in respect of their innumerable past iniquities.

Yermak never returned to Russia. After an uneasy couple of years
taken up in collecting sables and transmitting them beyond the
Urals – uneasy because his force, like the Ten Little Nigger Boys,
was constantly being depleted in encounters with Kuchum's
Tartars and Khanti and Mansi who still lurked in the area – he
and a small reconnaissance party were surprised by a Tartar band
on a stormy night in August 1584 while asleep on an island in the
Irtysh. According to legend Yermak was wearing the heavy breastplate given him by the Tsar, and in endeavouring to swim to safety
he sank beneath the waves. Thus perished 'The Conqueror of
Siberia'.

That year Ivan the Terrible also died, and he was succeeded by
Feodor Ivanovich, twenty-seven years of age, feeble-minded and
superstitious, last of the line of Ryurik. That year, too, not before
time, another Cossack force reached the Irtysh; and the following
year (1585) Obskiy Gorodok, the first Russian town in Siberia, nothing more at this time than an *ostrog*, a wooden fort surrounded by
a stockade, was built at the confluence of the Ob with the Irtysh;
the first of a whole chain of *ostrogi*, many of which later became
towns, and which were eventually extended from the eastern slopes
of the Urals to the Sea of Okhotsk, a distance of some 2800 miles
– all in the space of little more than seventy years.

In 1590 Feodor, in whose reign peasants were deprived of the
right of free migration (one that many of them still lack nearly 400
years later), dispatched thirty families, the first Russian colonists,
to Siberia from a town called Sol'vychegodsk near Kotlas, which
for them, conceivably, coming from such a place, could have been
a change for the better.

The early Cossack explorers of Siberia were no more than leaders
of fur-gathering expeditions who moved steadily eastwards, not
overland, which would have been impossible through the forests
and swamps, but by descending one river and ascending another,

which they did with remarkable dexterity, making portages when the need arose, their tracks resembling those of a ship beating into the wind and constantly going about.

The *Rossiya* thundered on into Asia, several thousand tons or more of assorted metal, hurtling through the darkness with its corridor windows hermetically screwed up – each one with 11 screws – and with all its doors locked – all set, if anything went wrong, for a really spectacular disaster, with its 600 plus occupants like the Moroccan sardines, on the wrong side of the tins and without the key. It travelled so fast, or rather it appeared to do so, an illusion heightened by the darkness, that I was beset by the fears that have crept up on me so many times in my life on trains roaring through the night to anywhere with their whistles screaming and what always seem to me barely adequate headlights: to Krakow, Ernakulum Junction, Bodmin Road, Saskatoon, Alice Springs, Haydarpasa, Inverness, Clearwater, the Hook and now to Tyumen; fears that up to now I have confided to no one – at the thought of a lunatic painstakingly removing a section of rail, still believing that he is playing with his Meccano set (now replaced in my imagination by a less flamboyant but far more real figure, planting a bomb); the driver nodding off, or having a heart attack, or simply going too fast, '*Faster, faster, faster!*' (probably under the influence), thoughts that made me reluctant to take off whatever I happened to be wearing and put on pyjamas. Such a crash, for me, would be far worse in pyjamas, and without shoes. Wanda had always seemed impervious to such apprehensions, taking the equivalent out of herself in gruesome and protracted nightmares – big open Mercedes full of skeletons in the winter uniform of the Waffen SS – or perhaps, like me, suffering in silence.

It was only 6.35 pm (8.35 local time) when we reached Kamyshlov, the first stop, 89 miles from Sverdlovsk, which meant that we had been travelling at less than 40 miles an hour. I put on my pyjamas. Kamyshlov, source in tsarist times of the Obukhov mineral springs, 'brackish, sulphurous and chalybeate ... furnished houses and buffet for the patients ... library and band of music', a small station on the line of the Trakt, but with a pale green and cream restaurant, faintly redolent of past elegance, in which animated diners could be seen through the windows, all stuffing themselves. How nice, in spite of our sardines and sausage, which hung heavy, it would have been to join them!

Soon after leaving Kamyshlov the rain ceased and the sky became partially clear. Where we were now it had not rained. As if to prove how dry the forest through which we were passing was, a great stretch of it to the left of the line was on fire. In it the flames were racing through the tops of the pines and larches on a front that must have been the best part of a mile and a half wide, sending millions of sparks high into the sky which was a bloodstained orange. The fire had already reached the railway and any moment now it would cross it. Meanwhile, the telegraph poles were already burning and the effect was of a line of footmen holding aloft what were, with such a blaze, superfluous torches, to light the *Rossiya* on its way.

Later, somewhere out in the darkness short of Tugulym, we passed the site of what was known as the Column of Tears, the old Siberian boundary post, seen by Kennan and Frost on the second day of their journey from Yekaterinburg to Tyumen in June 1885, a journey of about 200 miles, which they accomplished in forty-eight hours.

As we were passing through a rather open forest between the villages of Márkova and Tugulimskaya' [Kennan wrote], our driver suddenly pulled up his horses, and turning to us said, 'Vot granítsa' (Here is the boundary). We sprang out of the *tárantás* and saw, standing by the road-side, a square pillar ten or twelve feet in height, of stuccoed or plastered brick, bearing on one side the coat-of-arms of the European province of Perm, and on the other that of the Asiatic province of Tobólsk. It was the boundary post of Siberia. No other spot between St Petersburg and the Pacific ... has for the traveller a more melancholy interest than the little opening in the forest. Here hundreds of thousands of exiled human beings – men, women, and children; princes, nobles and peasants – have bidden good-by forever to friends, country and home ... Until recently the Siberian boundary post was covered with brief inscriptions, good-bys, and the names of exiles ... At the time of our visit, however, most of the hard plaster had apparently been pounded off, and only a few words, names and initials remained ... In one place in a man's hand, had been written the words 'Prashchai Marya!' ('Good-by, Mary!').

At the beginning of the eighteenth century Greek engineers opened up the Nerchinsky Zavod, a smelting works by the Argun River in eastern Siberia near the Chinese frontier and two months' march beyond Irkutsk, in order to exploit the great silver deposits of the region. For these and similar projects the demand for forced labour was temporarily satisfied by shipping convicts to Siberia straight from the prisons.

In 1762 a law was passed which allowed serfs who were a nuisance to their owners to be handed over to the local authorities and shipped to Siberia; and in 1765 the death sentence was abolished. From now on, those who would previously have been executed were given the privilege of exile to Siberia with hard labour for the rest of their lives, or to the mines of the Yekaterinburg region, where gold had been worked since 1745.

As the demand for forced labour increased, so [Kennan wrote], the list of crimes and offences punishable by exile grew larger and larger. Jews were exiled for refusing or neglecting to pay their taxes for three successive years; serfs were exiled for cutting down trees without leave; non-commissioned officers of the army were exiled for second offences of various kinds, and bad conduct of almost any sort became a sufficient warrant for deportation to Siberia.

Until 1823 no accurate record of the number of exiles, or even of what they had been exiled for, was ever kept; so that often a person exiled for some trivial offence, such as losing a passport, found himself treated as a dangerous criminal, and was sent to the mines where he perished, while a criminal was set at liberty to become a Siberian colonist. In that year the distinguished Russian reformer, Count M. Speransky, established a Bureau of Exile Administration in Siberia, first at Tobolsk, later at Tyumen; and from this time onwards a careful record of the number of exiles and the reasons why they were exiled was kept. Between 1823 and 1887, the last year for which Kennan was able to give figures before the publication of his book, the total for the fifty-four years was over 700,000. In the ten years 1863–72 a further 146,380 were exiled, a figure that was exceeded in the decade 1878–87 when it rose to nearly 180,000. By 1914 the total had risen to about a million for the 114 years from 1800. No official figures are available for the period 1917–77.

As early as the seventeenth century, exile to Siberia was not thought of as a punishment but simply as a way by which those who had been mutilated, branded or flogged, as opposed to being hanged, beheaded, impaled or suspended from hooks, could be removed from the sight of their sensitive fellow men. Towards the end of the century it began to dawn on the authorities that it might pay to exile people without carrying out major amputations on them before they set out. In this way, they reasoned, a start might be made at colonizing the great, sponge-like void beyond the Urals. As a result people were exiled for the most ludicrous reasons: snuff-taking (although snuff-takers still continued to have their septums torn out), fortune telling, begging, setting fire to property accidentally, in addition to crimes previously punished by death – desertion from the Army and assault with intent to kill.

Exiles were divided into four classes. Hard labour convicts (*katorzhniki*) and penal colonists (*poselentsi*) were deprived of their civil rights and might never return. They were sent into exile wearing leg fetters, weighing 5 pounds, and with one-half of their heads shaved.

The third class was the *strelni*, persons banished without being regarded as criminals – vagrants without passports who refused to say who they were; those banished by a court of their communes, often for persistent drunkenness; and those banished by order of the Minister of the Interior. And finally there were the *dobrovolni*, the women and children of those who had been banished, who went voluntarily into exile with them.

At 9.07 pm the *Rossiya* reached Tyumen on the Tura River. It was the oldest city in Siberia, built on the site of Chinga-Tura, Yepancha's settlement, and now the sixth city in the enormous Western Siberian Economic Region, which extends from the Kara Sea in the Arctic Ocean to the borders of China and Mongolia in the south.

As the train drifted into the station, the only occupant of this great city in sight was a young girl dressed in a light cotton dress and white shoes in spite of the fact that it was getting on for midnight local time. Had she come from a party to meet someone off the train? Or had she decided that spring was here? Overhead the moon shone down from what was, apart from some infinitely remote bands of cirrus stretched across it, a clear, star-filled sky. It looked as if the long winter might really be over at last; maybe the girl was right.

Tyumen is a big supply base for the natural gas fields on the lower Ob River where it runs in towards the Urals, for the immense Medvezhiy field on the Arctic coast east of the Ob estuary, and for the equally spacious oil fields in the Vasyugan Swamp beyond Surgut on the middle Ob. The swamp is actually a floating bog in which between 50 and 60 feet of quaking, decomposed peat are covered by snow in winter and by between 3 and 6 feet of water in summer. The exploitation of this field and the construction of the railway from Tyumen to Surgut are two of the three toughest projects Soviet engineers have ever been called upon to tackle (the third is the BAM railway north of Lake Baikal).

In spite of the problems, the line is now being continued for another 300 miles or so through more of these shivering swamps to the Urengoy gas fields on the Arctic coast, east of the Ob – literally in the middle of nowhere, that is unless you count 293,000 square miles with a population of 0.2 persons to the square mile as somewhere.

The railway will reach Surgut in about 1980. Whereas in what is laughingly known as 'normal Siberian terrain', whatever that is, engineers can build 400 miles or so of line a year, up there, in the permafrost swamp they can never manage more than 180 miles, but more often only 60 miles, because, when the temperature falls below −40°F they have to stop work. When it gets down to −72°F, which it often does, steel becomes brittle and breaks, and lubricating oil freezes.

And that is not going to be the end of this fantastic and rather horrible deep-frozen train ride, on which fare-paying passengers will, presumably, be provided with foot-warmers and piped vodka in the winter months, and in the summer, when the swamp looks like a swamp, with water-wings, anti-insect cream and netting against the multitudes of gnats, mosquitoes and other insect pests which drive man and beast round the bend all over Siberia. The railway is then going to be extended for the best part of 600

miles north-eastwards to Norilsk, a great region rich in ore, including gold, nickel, copper and platinum, beyond the Yenisei, in latitude 69°N: one of the great forced labour mining areas of the Stalinist era, founded in 1935 and known as Siblag, and one of the most
deadly, of which very few of the occupants are alive to speak. One
rare survivor was the Armenian poet, Gurgen Maari, who was sent
there in 1939 and was there until 1947. Classed as an 'exile for life',
he returned to Yerevan from Siberia in 1954.

Until the Trans-Siberian Railway was completed to the Ob, in
1895, Tyumen was the place where emigrants and exiles travelling
to Tomsk and points eastwards of it waited for the horrible iron
barges, towed by paddle-steamers carrying fare-paying passengers,
which conveyed them to Tomsk, by way of the Tura, the Irtysh,
the Ob and the Tom Rivers, a journey of between seven and ten
days, according to how much water there was in the rivers. Those
bound for nearer destinations travelled on foot, or by cart. Most
of the emigrants who settled in western Siberia before 1900 came
this way. Over half a million emigrants passed through Tyumen
on their way from the west, and of these it has been estimated that
10 per cent of adult and 30 per cent of child emigrants died on the
journey.

Nevertheless, they were better off than the exiles. Those who survived at least had a degree of liberty. The exiles were kept in the
Forwarding Prison at Tyumen until the barges were ready to sail.
When they did it was with between 300 and 800 persons on board
– 800 was suffocation point on a journey in the course of which the
temperature could run up into the 100°s Fahrenheit in high summer.

Kennan and Frost visited the Forwarding Prison in 1885. While
they were there they witnessed the departure of a marching party.

The hum of conversation suddenly ceased; there was a jingling of
chains as the prisoners who had been lying on the ground sprang to their
feet; the soldiers of the guard shouldered their rifles; the exiles crossed
themselves devoutly, bowing in the direction of the prison chapel; and
at the word 'March!' the whole column was instantly in motion. Three
or four Cossacks, in dark-green uniforms and with rifles over their
shoulders, took the lead; a dense but disorderly throng of men and women

followed, marching between thin, broken lines of soldiers; next came the *telégas* with the old, the sick, and the small children, then a rear-guard of half a dozen Cossacks; and finally four or five waggons piled high with grey bags. Although the road was soft and muddy, in five minutes the party was out of sight. The last sounds I heard were the jingling of chains and the shouts of the Cossacks.

What they saw inside the prison makes gruesome reading: strangely reminiscent of similar accounts of things that happened closer to our time but never witnessed by visitors because there were no visitors.

The prisoners have neither pillows, blankets, nor bed-clothing, and must lie on these hard plank *nári* [sleeping platforms] with no covering but their overcoats. As we entered the cell, the convicts, with a sudden jingling of chains, sprang to their feet, removed their caps, and stood silently in a dense throng around the *nári*.

'*Zdrástvuitye rebiáta!*' (How do you do boys?) said the Warden. '*Zdrávie zheláiem váshe vuisóki blagaródie*' (We wish you health, your high nobility) shouted a hundred voices in a hoarse chorus. 'The prison,' said the Warden, 'is terribly overcrowded. This cell, for example, is only 35 feet long by 25 feet wide, and has air space for 35, or at most 40 men. How many men slept here last night?' he inquired, turning to the prisoners. 'A hundred and sixty, your high nobility,' shouted half a dozen hoarse voices.

In the prison hospital the most common disorders were scurvy, typhus, typhoid, acute bronchitis, rheumatism and syphilis. Only those suffering from typhus, of which there were a number when Kennan was there, were isolated in a single ward.

Never before in my life had I seen faces as white, haggard and ghastly as those that lay on the gray pillows in these hospital cells ... As I breathed that heavy, stifling atmosphere, poisoned with the breath of syphilitic and fever-ridden patients, loaded and saturated with the odor of excrement, disease germs, exhalations from unclean human bodies, and foulness inconceivable, it seemed to me that over the hospital doors should be written, 'All hope abandon, ye who enter here'.

8

The Flowery Steppe
of Ishim

At around 0.55 on the following morning, 29 May, the third day of our progression across Europe and Asia (God knows what it was locally – the time-zone map was vague about demarcations), the *Rossiya* pulled into Ishim on the Ishim River. It was pitch dark and there were no signs in sight. I only knew it was Ishim because some fellow, presumably employed to do so (usually it is done over a loudspeaker which no one can understand, even Russians), was walking past outside chanting 'Ishim ... Ishim!' reminding me of the man who plods past the Simplon Express, 288 miles from Paris at its first stop in Switzerland, groaning 'Vallorbe ... Vallorbe'. At the same time a colleague, who also meant well, was tapping the axles.

Of Ishim I knew nothing, and at 12.55 am cared less. It was not until I returned to England that I discovered that this was a place where Friedrich Heinrich Alexander, Baron von Humboldt, was very nearly shot.

In April 1829 von Humboldt, by then world-famous for his scientific explorations in South America and the sumptuous works he subsequently wrote about them, and a still active man of nearly sixty, left Berlin for St Petersburg in company with two young scientists, Gustav Rose, a professor of chemistry and mineralogy, and C. G. Ehrenberg, a zoologist. They had been invited to Russia by Tsar Nicholas I, an ardent admirer of von Humboldt, where they were to carry out studies in the mines and mineral deposits of the Urals, at the Government's expense.

From St Petersburg, where von Humboldt was fêted, taking his meals with the Imperial family – 'Wherever you go,' the Tsar told him, 'you spread a life-giving influence' – the three men set off for the Urals in what had become, thanks to the Tsar's patronage, and to von Humboldt's annoyance – who disliked the Tsar – what was practically an Imperial progression. There, on the eastern flanks of the range, he and his companions carried out various researches, particularly in the areas where gold and platinum were to be found, in which von Humboldt was convinced there were diamonds. His belief was justified: soon after his departure from the Urals the first diamond to be found there, and the first to be found outside the tropics, was discovered by a fourteen-year-old boy, Pavel Popov, who worked in a gold placer works.

On 18 July, before this exciting event took place, the three men left Yekaterinburg to go eastwards to the Ob, travelling in a recumbent posture in a convoy of *tarantassi*, their faces protected by leather and horse-hair masks against the swarms of mosquitoes, midges and biters which at this season were out in force.

They were now on the second lap of a journey which was to take them to the edge of the Dzungarian Plateau, which lies between the Altai Mountains and the Tien Shan on the present borders of China and Mongolia, then down the Irtysh, which rises in the Altai, to Omsk by boat. From Omsk they were to cross the Kazakh Steppe to the Ural River and the Volga, which they descended to the Caspian Sea, before returning to Moscow in October, having travelled some 9700 miles in under six months, with the help of 12,244 post horses.

When the cavalcade reached Ishim, the Baron, who by this time was suffering from an excess of company, went off to look at the place by himself. During his time there he was kept under constant observation by the Prefect of Police who, after a few days, felt constrained to write the following letter to the Governor-General of the Province:

Your Excellency,

A few days ago there arrived here a German of shortish stature, insignificant appearance, fussy and bearing a letter of introduction from Your Excellency to me. I accordingly received him politely; but I must say that I find him suspicious, and even dangerous. I disliked him from the first.

He talks too much and despised my hospitality. He pays no attention to the leading officials of the town and associates with Poles and other political criminals. I take the liberty of informing Your Excellency that his intercourse with political criminals does not escape my vigilance. On one occasion he proceeded with them to a hill overlooking the town. They took a box with them and got out of it a long tube which we all took for a gun. After fastening it to three feet they pointed it down on the town and one after another examined whether it was properly sighted. This was evidently a great danger for the town which is built entirely of wood; so I sent a detachment of troops with loaded rifles to watch the German on the hill. If the treacherous machinations of this man justify my suspicions, we shall be ready to give our lives for the Tsar and Holy Russia. I send this despatch to Your Excellency by special messenger.

What an escape von Humboldt had on that far-off day! Actually he was to live another thirty years, to the age of ninety. And what an escape the Prefect of Police had, too, from spending the rest of his life in the Nerchinsk silver mines, having obliterated the Tsar's protegé.

At about half past one I woke again, this time to experience a new, more gentle motion. Dawn had just broken (about four-thirty local time), and as if to show respect for it the *Rossiya* had stopped behaving like an overloaded plane trying to take off. Instead, it was drifting through a world only a fraction of which seemed to be made up of landscape, an enormous, endless prairie covered with rich, fine, gently waving grass, interspersed with fields of black earth in which crops were already sprouting, groves of silver birch and here and there, where there was a stream or marshy place, a few aspens and willows. And there were flowers, too, thousands of them: anemones, buttercups, kingcups, forget-me-nots, dandelions. The rest, about 90 per cent, was sky, still streaked with high cirrus, as it had been over Tyumen the previous evening but now, in these brief minutes before the sun would transfigure it, the colour of the lees of wine.

We were in the Steppe of Ishim, just a small part of the vast plain which, under various names, stretches out from the foot of the Urals across the Irtysh, the Ob and the Yenisei over 35 degrees of longitude and about 20 degrees of latitude before breaking at the foot of the Siberian upland in the Krasnoyarsky Kray almost 1200 miles to the east. We were in Siberia, and it was large. There was no doubt about that. Just as I had imagined it. You could put the whole of the United States into it and all of Europe except Russia and still have several hundred thousand square miles to spare. And apparently it was empty, this bit of Siberia between the Urals and the Yenisei and the Altai Mountains to the south, although statistics show that more than 13 million people live in it.

The *Rossiya* stole on to the south-east with her living cargo, most of whom were asleep, as if she was under sail, a ship moving through a Sargasso Sea of grass, so quietly that, as in a sailing ship, I could hear the creaking of tackle and her rivets working: a ship in which, ever since it had been towed by a diesel, the cabins had been covered with a fine layer of metallic dust which smudged like grated carbon when it was touched. The only other passenger on view was the boy with the Ronald Coleman moustache, coming off shift after another night of lipstick with his conductress.

And now, from the general direction of the Pacific on which it had been shining for a good five hours, the sun came shooting up over an horizon that looked as if it had been ruled with one of my H pencils, into a sky that turned first an improbable shade of puce then a fiery red, as if someone was stoking a furnace. Soon it was a great, bloody sphere, sometimes over the *Rossiya*'s port bow, then, as the line wove its way among some sunken, half-dry watercourses, over the port quarter. Then for a while it was invisible while we ran past a halted freight train that must have been more than half a mile long, made up of sealed vans and flat cars loaded with secret-looking objects covered with tarpaulins, and hauled by four giant diesel locomotives. After that we halted at a little station for a rare, non-scheduled stop. As if by magic Lilya appeared from her little boudoir, looking remarkably spruce, and let down the steps to the line. We were on the frontiers of the second and third time-zones and it was either 3.30 or 4.30 am local time.

There was not a soul in sight, not even a male or female station-master. Except for a disembodied voice coming from a crackly loudspeaker stuck up on an iron pole, addressing a world that was still asleep, the place might have been deserted. Then that too ceased. The silence was uncanny.

Beyond the station there was a village of low log houses with iron roofs, now shining in the light of a sun that looked as if it was on a collision course with the earth with about five minutes to go. The only living things on view were half a dozen magpies which were using a telephone wire as a trampoline. Ahead, the track, two parallel but apparently converging lines (something about which I had learned in the chapter on perspective in the *Wonder Book of Why and What* when I was small), stretched away into Siberia. A light, warm breeze was blowing up from the south, bringing with it the smell of earth, grass, a whiff of wood smoke and a feeling that it emanated from vast, nomadic spaces.

'Good place,' said Lilya, giving me one of her golden smiles that to me, any day, were worth about double whatever was the current price of a fine ounce of the product, and were more bracing than a whole bottle of Wincarnis tonic wine. 'No pipple.'

It was Sunday morning.

Another snooze. Then, at 2.45 (5.45 am local time) I woke again. The sun was a more normal size but dropsical behind an elongated bubble of cloud that looked like a schoolboy's drawing of a 1916 gas attack. We were still in the Ishim Steppe but according to my reading of the map were just coming into the Omsk *oblast*. The *Rossiya* was running straight as an arrow through a swampy region of weed-fringed ponds topped up with yellowish water in which wild duck upended themselves in a rather pointed way as we passed. Languidly I reached for my copy of *The Guide to the Great Siberian Railway* which, with Mischa lurking behind every corner, I kept under my pillow, in the faint hope of finding out why the water was yellow. Page 130 read like something out of a horror novel:

The majority of the fresh-water lakes situated in the southern steppes of the government have sloping reed-covered shores and an oozy and limey bottom; the water is yellow and seems to be covered with slime, which comes partly from the mud at the bottom, partly from the stagnancy of the water heated by the sun, and also from the guano of the birds, building their nests on the shores of the lakes ...

There was another interesting bit in the guide, about these creepy steppes:

The rise and fall of the water-level observed in many swamps and lakes is a characteristic and as yet insufficiently explained phenomenon. Water systems sometimes disappear altogether, and again fill with water and fish after a lapse of many years.

Which would certainly give any duck a headache.

The earth was black *chernozem* and the spring wheat looked like cress sprouting in it; there was also what was probably corn and what might conceivably, if the *Rossiya* had stopped, have been identified by an expert with a big magnifying glass to hand as flax and hemp. We were running down a 200-mile-wide band of this black earth which extends from the Ukraine, over the Urals and through these low latitudes of western Siberia to the Altai Mountains. Low or not, here in about 55°N among the sparse birches of the forest steppe, we were on the frontiers of agriculture. One would only have to move two or three degrees north of the railway to be in the *taiga*, among trappers, lumberjacks and herds of reindeer. A hundred and fifty years ago here, along the line of the railway, what is now forest steppe with a thin covering of silver birch was forest. By the 1870s, because of the enormous influx of emigrants and exiles into western Siberia, the forests had been decimated by indiscriminate felling and huge fires caused by peasants burning off the stubble. By the time a Forest Department had been established in Russia, which was not until 1884, it was too late to save it. Then, in the years when the Trans-Siberian Railway was being built, all the forest areas along the line suffered similarly; millions of trees were cut down to make sleepers, build bridges, stations and settlements and provide fuel. In 1896 the Chelyabinsk–Omsk section of the Trans-Siberian was opened up, and more than half a million colonists passed through Chelyabinsk in the next five years. By 1897 western Siberia's population was about one and a half million.

We passed a small town with dense forest looming up behind it like a cliff. The whole place was covered by a tangle of overhead cables and telephone wires, so that it looked rather like a badly done up parcel. Outside one of the houses a yellow motorcycle with an old-fashioned looking Zeppelin-shaped sidecar to match was jumping up and down excitedly, awaiting its owner, anxious to be off; at another a door opened and some hens emerged and began scratching the earth; a woman appeared, carrying a wooden yoke with two buckets suspended from it, and went off to a well for water. The world was waking up.

We were in country in which, besides Russians, who form the majority of the inhabitants of Western Siberia, there were also pocketsful of Ukrainians, Tartars, Kazakhs, Estonians and Germans – some of the 400,000 Germans, many of them Red Army officers and their men, who were deported to Siberia by Stalin during the war from the Volga German Autonomous Republic, where their ancestors had lived since Catherine the Great had invited them to settle there and in other areas of Russia in 1762.

That is to say, this is where those people were if the Ethnographic Map in the *Atlas of the USSR*, which was tough going to decipher, was to be believed: tough because it indicated in Cyrillic, with the help of a wealth of different colours, triangles, circles and blobs of various kinds, the whereabouts of the peoples who make up the population. Thus, for example, around Omsk I was never sure whether the triangles there indicated the existence of an enclave of Tungans, who are Chinese Tibetans, which seemed rather improbable, or a colony of Evenks, who are Tungu-Manchus, in which case whoever drew the map had got his triangles upside down.

Both the Ishim and the Barabinskaya Steppes, which we would be crossing after we reached Omsk, are tough places to live in. Here in the Ishim Steppe there is snow on the ground for 150 days a year; in winter temperatures of $-15°F$ are common and exceptionally it can go down to $-56°F$; while in June and July, the only months in which killing frosts do not occur, it can go up to $104°F$, but this is exceptional, too. In spite of these handicaps, in tsarist times before the railway came these steppes produced immense quantities of butter, which was melted down and exported to Scandinavia, Germany and Turkey. Today milk and meat are produced as well as butter, most of which is now tinned.

Certainly, in spite of the cold, and the dangers of travel in Siberia,

Chekhov seems to have enjoyed his long and bumpy journey by *tarantass* across the Steppes. In a letter to his mother on 14 May 1890, after twelve days on the Trakt, he wrote about the *brodyági* (tramps), who were mostly escaped convicts:

> Well, you ride and ride. Mileposts flash by, puddles, birch groves. We pass tramping settlers, a file of convicts under guard. We have met vagabonds with pots on their backs; these gents [the *brodyági*] roam the Siberian highway freely. On occasion they will do in an old woman in order to use her skirt for puttees, or they'll remove from a milepost a metal sign with a number on it, just on the chance it may come in handy. Again they will bash in the head of a beggar they meet or gouge out the eyes of their fellow deportee, but they won't touch a traveller.

About the people he met on his way through the steppes, colonists mostly, he was enthusiastic.

> Generally speaking, people here are good, kindly, and with pleasing ways. The rooms are tidy and the furniture simple, with some pretensions to luxury; the sleeping accommodations are soft, with feather beds and big pillows; the floors are painted or covered with home-made linen rugs. All this is due to the general prosperity, to the fact that a family has an allowance of 43 acres of excellent black earth which produces rich crops of wheat ... On entering a Siberian bedroom at night you are not assailed by the peculiar Russian stench. True, handing me a teaspoon, an old woman wiped it on her behind, but then they will not serve you tea without a tablecloth, people don't belch in your presence, don't search for insects in their hair; when they hand you water or milk, they don't put their fingers in the glass; the plates and dishes are clean, *kvass* is as transparent as beer ...

At 3.15 am we came into a place in the Omsk *oblast* called Nadivyeskaya. There we spent fifteen minutes sandwiched between the Moscow–Irkutsk Express, or it may have been the Irkutsk–Moscow Express – and a two-diesel load of dark red freight cars. Here we lost our diesel and got in exchange another CHS electric model. This was the place where Vladimir, the pop-eyed superman, decided to put in a second appearance, or more likely his parents decided for him. Whoever decided, with only a couple of trains to look at from point-blank range he soon ceased to be Vladimir the inscrutable superman and reverted instead to being an inscrutable small boy watching Wanda folding her nightdress and picking his nose at the same time.

To take his mind off these matters Wanda gave him an effigy of a London policeman about six inches high, recommended by the Design Centre, Haymarket, as suitable for purchase by law-abiding foreigners, and he regarded this for some time with interest, holding it in one hand at arm's length in case it blew up, while still continuing to dig away at his hooter with the second finger of the other. I wondered what was the Russian for nose bogeys.

'*Shto takoye?*' ('What is it?') he said eventually, the first interrogative he had so far come out with in the course of our long relationship.

'*Angliski Politsia, Militsia,*' Wanda said, upon which Vladimir trotted off to his compartment clutching it, but still digging away, without another word.

'*Thank you very much!*' Wanda shouted after him. She can never get over the fact that for the last couple of decades in Britain the giving of presents doesn't necessarily mean you get thanked.

'Well,' I said, seizing the opportunity to get my own back on her for having 'tol' me never to go on conducted tours in the Soviet Union'. 'If you gave him your policeman because you think you're going to get a clockwork model of a KGB agent in a mohair pullover with a detachable trench coat for rainy days, as approved by the Committee for Public Recreation, you'd better think again.'

The *Rossiya* clonked on at the sort of speed that makes the maximum amount of noise with a corresponding lack of velocity, rather like a paddle-steamer in a heavy swell. Here the huge fields in which more earth than wheat was showing were like enormous black shadows on the green, flower-strewn grass of the steppe. It was here that Kennan and his companion were so tormented by huge grey mosquitoes that they had to put on thick gloves, cover their heads with calico hoods, mask their faces with horse-hair and whirl leafy branches around their heads to stop themselves going insane, while on the 420-mile journey from Tyumen to Omsk in a *tarantass* which took them four days and four nights with eleven hours' sleep.

As in Kennan's time here the Trakt was a dust road with farms and villages spread out along it. The rows of log houses with gated courtyards could have been standing for ten years or a century, there was no way of knowing. The style of architecture had frozen immutably long ago, long before the Revolution. Their principal occupants this Sunday morning were geese, although a few men and women, mostly old, were already out in the common land on the outskirts, keeping an eye on a few cows and calves.

At around 8.30 am local time, the *Rossiya* made the equivalent of a landfall in what was under water anyway for a bit during the Ice Age. From here we could see, far off, a sort of yellow island in the midst of the steppe away to the north-east, with what looked like a number of matchsticks rising from it. In a matter of minutes, not hours, this amorphous mass was a few miles away on the port beam. It now revealed itself as an unearthly looking city, the colour of bones in the morning sun, composed of petrochemical plants, cooling towers which looked like vastly inflated Parsee Towers of Silence, storage tanks, factories and enormous, hive-like apartment blocks built to accommodate the workers, all wreathed in dust from the construction works which were still going on. The longest of the matchsticks turned out to be a tower, probably part of a microwave communication system, and certainly on the list of things not-to-be-photographed in the Soviet Union; the lesser ones were chimneys. Overhead a big jet was coming in to land at Omsk airport.

Neither Mischa nor Lilya knew the name of this strange place. It was an Omsk satellite, built on the line of the big, 40-inch oil pipe which runs for more than 600 miles from the Ust–Balyk field south-west of Surgut to Omsk, where the refinery is also picking up the oil from the Lake Samotlor line in the Vasyugan Swamp. Looking at it I wondered how anyone could endure to spend their time off in such a place for the rest of their lives, having spent each day working in it. Half an hour later the *Rossiya* crossed the Irtysh by a six-span bridge. At exactly six o'clock Moscow time it came to rest in Omsk, the second largest city in Siberia, with almost a million people living in it, 1837 miles from Moscow.

While crossing the Irtysh river I had tried to interest Mischa, who was back in circulation having had a shave, in the fact, recorded in the imperial railway guide, that the bridge girders were of welding iron produced by the Vótkin works and made in the temporary shops of Engineer Berézin in Ufá, but he pretended not to be interested.

Omsk was founded as an *ostrog* in 1717, one of a line of fortresses garrisoned by Cossacks intended to keep out the nomads who occupied most of the territory on the borders of the Siberian steppe. A new, polygonal Vaubanesque fortress was built in 1765 and it was in a stockaded wooden prison attached to this fortress that Dostoyevsky suffered four years of hard labour, together with the poet Durov: the House of the Dead, in which he was subjected to appalling floggings. After the second such beating Dostoyevsky spent six weeks in the prison hospital, and when he emerged from it he found that his fellow prisoners, who were surprised to see him alive, had given him the nickname '*pokoinik*', the deceased.

Very few people have had a good word to say for Omsk. It was windy, cold, dusty (according to the seasons) and always dirty. Chekhov ignored or bypassed it completely (at least in the *Letters* I had with me). When he got to Tomsk he didn't describe it either, only, with an excess of detail, a sausage he bought: 'But what a sausage! When you put a piece in your mouth it's filled with a stench as though you had entered a stable at the very moment when the drivers are removing their footcloths ...'

That was Tomsk. Mrs Atkinson and her husband arrived at Omsk on 27 March 1849. She was cool about it in *Recollections of Tartar Steppes and their Inhabitants* after she and her husband had had a disagreeable encounter with the police-master whose Cossack servant told them they would have to wait for two hours in the street until he was ready to receive them. One simply did not say things like that to travelling Englishmen in the nineteenth century. Atkinson sent the Cossack to rout the police-master out, but he had a hideous revenge on them.

The Cossack now had us driven to the outskirts of the town, to a most horrible place – we had to pass through a room on the floor of which men were lying stretched out in all directions, some smoking, and others talking at the utmost pitch of their voices; it was not pleasant, and, moreover, the room we entered was cold. It was now near ten o'clock, so we were glad to spread the bear-skins on which to stretch our cramped and bruised limbs; for six nights I had not had my clothing off.

Omsk looked better seen through the eyes of the Italian journalist Luigi Barzini of the *Corriere della Sera*, who entered it in a 35–40 hp Ital motorcar *en route* for Paris on 14 July 1907.*

At 4 pm we reached Omsk, lying in a sandy plain, interspersed with tufts of rushes. Just outside the city rose great and curious windmills, with their many wings standing out like spokes in gigantic wheels; and they made one think of some strange, unknown engine of war.

Considerable changes had taken place at Omsk since the Trans-Siberian Railway had arrived there in 1896. The Atkinsons would probably not have recognized it. It had succumbed, as had Alfred Doolittle, to Middle Class Morality.

We happened to enter Omsk at the hour of the people's Sunday airing [Barzini continued]. Along the wooden pavements moved the peaceful crowd of the citizens, walking with the peculiar gait of people wearing their best clothes and anxious not to spoil them. Officers and people in brilliant uniforms passed by with their families, holding their children by the hand. There was the quiet atmosphere of a provincial town taking its rest. From the churches, with their many coloured cupolas, came the sound of bells ...

Barzini was one of an Italian team of three – the leader was Prince Scipione Borghese; the third and probably the most important man was Ettore Guizzardi, driver and mechanic of genius – taking part in the Great Trans-Continental Automobile Race from Peking to Paris. The Prince, an austere, rich and extremely able man who had already explored in central Asia and descended some of the Siberian rivers, had entered the car for the race at his own expense and Barzini had been sent to join him by the editor of the Milan newspaper, *Corriere della Sera*.

The competitors, or those whose motorcars could be made to function on that date, left Peking on 10 June 1907. The route, for there was no other, was that which had always been followed by caravans. First, they crossed the Gobi Desert to Kyakhta, which the Italian team reached on 24 June. From there they travelled along the southern shores of Lake Baikal, sometimes literally on the railway

---

* *Pekin to Paris* by Luigi Barzini (London 1907).

line, to reach Irkutsk on 1 July. From there they followed the line of the Trakt and railway to Krasnoyarsk, Tomsk, Omsk and Perm which took them three weeks. On 21 July, while in the foothills of the Urals, a wheel collapsed, but a village wheelwright built them a new one in a matter of hours. On 27 July they were in Moscow and on 1 August they reached St Petersburg. The rest of the journey was plain sailing, through Kovno to Berlin, which they passed through on 5 August. On 10 August 1907 they swept into Paris, preceded by a charabanc loaded with musicians armed with trombones and trumpets all playing the triumphal march from *Aida*, and at around 4.30 pm they drew up outside the offices of *Le Matin*, the sponsors of the race in the Boulevard Poissonière, sixty days and more than 8000 miles from Peking.

While we were in Omsk the usual one-reel comedy was made under Russian direction. This time it starred Otto, The Photographer. The big scene, which should have been played in bathing costumes with horizontal stripes, was with what was, presumably, the deputy female station-master, a person of uncertain age who was wearing a truly terrible grey skirt which made her look as if she was embedded in a block of concrete. She managed to get one hand over the front of his 28 mm, Perspective Control Lens, the whole point of which was to exclude undesirable objects, and the other under his chin, shoving his head back for the final neck-break – what she was doing with her knee was not clear – all of which, presumably, was to stop him photographing the place where the front of the station building would have been if someone hadn't taken it away and replaced it with scaffolding and lots of plastic sheeting.

At 6.31 am we left Omsk.

9

Across the Barabinskaya Steppe

THE *Rossiya* ran out along the left bank of the Om, a river that rises in an appalling swamp about 75 miles north-east of Omsk, where it joins with the Irtysh. By now the sun was well up and with the windows in the corridor hermetically sealed it was both hot and smelly. The Australian with whom I had passed the time of day on several occasions arguing about whether Foster's or Swan was the better beer (he shared the next compartment with Ronald Coleman), a bearded, reticent, gentlemanly fellow from Western Australia, shed his reticence and began comparing the atmosphere to a vulture's crutch. He was on his way non-stop to Khabarovsk and therefore had even stronger reasons for getting the window open than we had, as we would be getting off the *Rossiya* at Novosibirsk.

I must say there was a pong, and it was impossible to have the windows in the compartments and the doors open at the same time, except for a few moments, because if one did all one's possessions blew away. In fact it was almost as awful as Chekhov's sausage (or could it be our sausage, we'd had it for ages?). All the rest of the compartments, the ones occupied entirely by Russians, had their doors firmly shut.

'Why don't we ask the conductress to open one or two?' I said to the Australian. 'Would you believe it, but she can't. These jokers have only got two window keys for the whole damn railway. One's in Moscow, the other's in Vladivostok. Or that's what they say. The trouble is they're such bloody liars.'

He went on like this for a bit, incited by me who wanted them open as much as he did, swinging on the handles of the window outside his compartment like some great, hairy primate, but without any visible success – not surprisingly as each window had eleven triangular-headed sunk screws keeping it shut. Dostoevsky was not the only joker to be buried alive in Siberia. I took a rubbing of the end of one of them so that I could order a key from Chubb in St James's Street if I decided to pass this way again.

Eventually the Australian woke the boy with the Ronald Coleman moustache, whose real name was Ivan. When Ivan wasn't stuffing the conductress, or re-charging his batteries with sleep, they played chess together, and sometimes he played chess with Mischa too. The Australian communicated his feelings about windows to him, presumably using the language of the birds, as neither spoke the other's language; but whatever he used, Ivan got the message and went off down the corridor, hauling up the trousers of his track suit which had been cut too high in the rise, an ineradicable tailoring defect.

Soon he was back, whistling and swinging a curious, stubby, jointed key on his finger. He was closely followed by the conductress. She was *en déshabillé*, with her hair half up and half down, and moaning 'Nyet, Ivan! Nyet!', at the same time making ineffectual little fluttering gestures, the antithesis of a determined Trans-Siberian Railway conductress, trained to beat off packs of wolves. Ivan ignored her, and eventually she retreated to her nest.

He had a hell of a job on his hands. It wasn't the right key; it had a triangular hole in it, but the hole was too big. In spite of this, by holding it at an angle, after about twenty minutes he succeeded in withdrawing all eleven screws. Still it wouldn't open. Finally with Ivan and the Australian hanging on one handle and Otto and myself on the other, like men on a staysail downhaul, the thing suddenly shot open, expelling some dead insects and about two years' supply of black *chernozem* dust from the steppes into our faces.

Afterwards Ivan opened two more windows, but more quickly now that he had the hang of it. When he had finished and we had cleaned ourselves up a large lady emerged from her compartment and shut two of the three windows before flouncing back into it and slamming the door. Even at this comparatively early hour by Trans-Siberian standards she was all dressed up, in the big cabbage print and with the bouffant hair, just as if she was about to start playing the piano at a children's dancing class in some far-out London suburb.

Ms Cabbage was shacked up with the member of the *apparat* who had only just made the train at Moscow. As Intourist had told me, with its habitual delicacy, 'In making reservations for sleeping accommodation, no account is taken of sex.' It was difficult not to speculate on what was going on in there between them. I had not seen him since he left Moscow, when he hadn't been looking so good. Perhaps he had died and Ms Cabbage had decided that it was better to go on sharing with a corpse she had got used to, rather than get issued with something a bit more fresh but possibly less agreeable. How on earth did she keep her hair looking like that? Did she have a harness, like guys on a rock wall, so that she could hang herself up behind the door for the night? Just another question that was to remain forever unanswered.

'You should screw her, too,' said the Australian to Ivan, thoughtfully translating from his native tongue into English, 'You've still got plenty of time.'

The *Rossiya* was running due east now towards the Barabinskaya Steppe, which fills what would otherwise be a rather large hole between the 53rd and 57th parallels of north latitude and between the Irtysh and the Ob.

Since leaving Omsk we had been travelling on the second section of the railway to be built from the European end. The line the *Rossiya* had followed through the Urals to Omsk had been a much more recent addition, built far to the north of the original line through Chelyabinsk, in the eastern foothills of the southern Urals. On 19 July 1892 work began on this West Siberian Railway to link Chelyabinsk with what was at that time a small settlement on the right bank of the river Ob, called Gusevka, now the city of Novosibirsk, about 900 miles to the east. Work on the Ussuri section of the line from Vladivostok had begun soon after the inauguration of the work at Vladivostok in May 1891.

Because of the shortage of money in Imperial Russia, where conspicuous consumption went hand-in-hand with an equally conspicuous lack of the necessary when it came to doing anything moderately useful with it, it had been decided to build a single-track railway to the wide Russian gauge of 5 feet, 3½ inches wider than the standard European gauge of 4 feet 8½ inches, and also to use light rails of a sort that were suitable only for branch lines, certainly not for a trans-continental railway. It was also decided to cut down on sidings and marshalling yards and to lay the rails on a far less substantial foundation than would have been permissible west of the Urals.

In fact, the orders were to build the railway as cheaply as possible, a decision that could only have been come to by a bunch of people who were completely ignorant of the nature of the country through which the railway would have to pass. The stupidity of these economies became apparent soon after the various sections were completed, when large parts of them had to be reconstructed. It became even more apparent when the Russo-Japanese War broke out in 1904 and it took between five or six weeks for Russian reinforcements to reach the Far East, partly because of the lack of passing places and sidings along the line and partly because there was no line around Lake Baikal. On the other hand, if there had been no railway at all there would probably have been no war.

The steppe country of western Siberia was difficult country for railway-builders. It was liable to flooding when the snow melted in the spring, and for this reason the entire line had to be laid on a five-feet-high embankment. Yet in spite of this superfluity of water none of it was drinkable, and so artesian wells had to be drilled; but even *this* water was undrinkable until filtration plants were built. With the exception of one forest on the Tobol River, there was no timber anywhere in the steppes between Chelyabinsk and the river Ob suitable for bridge-building or even for making sleepers. What few trees there were were too small. All the timber to build the trestle bridges and for sleepers (each of which had to be cut on site by teams of two men using cross-cut saws) had to be brought from Ufa, nearly 300 miles to the west of Chelyabinsk. Furthermore, there was no local stone with which to build culverts, abutments, piers for the big girder bridges over the Tobol, the Ishim and the Irtysh, or even to make ballast. The nearest quarries were in the Urals or 600 miles to the south of the railway, on the River Irtysh.

There was also an acute shortage of every sort of transport, from horse-drawn waggons to river barges.

Only about a third of the total work force were Siberians, and most of them disappeared in spring and autumn in order to sow and harvest their crops. The rest came from European Russia, Persia, Turkey and Italy. The Italians mostly worked as stone-masons, building culverts and bridge abutments. The life of these railway-builders was very hard, but not half as hard or as nasty as it was for the slaves working on the BAM, the Baikal–Amur–Magistral (Mainline) Railway, before and during the last war and in double-tracking the Trans-Siberian in the late 1930s, or working on the south Siberian line between Pavlodar on the Irtysh and Tselinograd in the virgin lands of Kazakhstan, which was not completed until 1953.

The pre-revolutionary workers building the first part of the Western Siberian line across the steppe slept in the open in summer. Work on the line was possible for only about 120 days a year between April and September because in winter the ground froze solid. In winter, when it was impossible to work on the line, they lived either in portable huts or in dens made with sleepers covered over with earth. This was the time of year when station houses and bridges were built and when supplies were brought in by sledge, for it was easier to bring raw materials in over the ice than to do this in summer by cart when much of the country was reduced to a morass. The construction gangs that used to work high up on the girders of the big steel bridges over the rivers east of Chelyabinsk suffered the most. Riveters were often overcome by the cold and fell to their deaths on the ice below. It was rare for one of the bigger bridges to be built without several fatal accidents.

The tools were very primitive. The navvies' shovels were entirely of wood, without even a metal tip to the blade. The only mechanical aids were a number of American-made excavators worked by horse power. Rock used to make coarse ballast was first dynamited, then broken up with picks and hammers.

Wages were between 45 kopecks and 2 rubles a day, although some skilled workers such as masons, most of whom were Italian, earned up to 100 rubles a month. (At that time a ruble equalled

2s 1¼d, or 51¼ US cents.) In summer the workers were almost eaten alive by insects (they were not issued with mosquito netting to protect their faces until they were beyond the Irtysh, far into the Barabinsk Steppe). Nevertheless, they very often succeeded in laying track at a rate of 2½ miles a day, and working at this rate, on 11 September 1894 they completed the section from Chelyabinsk to the west bank of the Irtysh. In just over two years they had built nearly 500 miles of line. Eighteen months later, in March 1896, the Irtysh was finally spanned and from that time onwards the whole of the West Siberian section from Chelyabinsk to the west bank of the Ob (the line from the Irtysh to the Ob had already been completed) was open to traffic.

Around 8 am (11 am local time,) the *Rossiya* entered the Barabinsk Steppe, a vast expanse inhabited by Russians, Estonians, Latvians, Germans and, well over the horizon to the north, some Chuvash. Until far into the second half of the nineteenth century, what was to be the line of the Trans-Siberian Railway in western Siberia formed the frontier between the Russian colonists who pursued an agricultural way of life and the nomadic Kirghiz to the south. The Kirghiz lived in *kibitkas*, otherwise yurts: circular tents of grey felt set up on a wooden framework. They valued their livestock far more highly than their women. A wife had the equivalent value to four sheep or one very inferior cow. Convention demanded that a visitor to their encampments in the treeless steppes should ask first after the health of the animals. Kirghiz men lived an expansive life. They drank enormous quantities of *kumiss*, fermented mares' milk, of which any guest was obliged to empty a vessel containing a minimum of three pints, to be followed by a second dose, and they enjoyed wrestling.

To keep the Kirghiz out of the northern steppes, the Russian government forcibly colonized this frontier with thousands of armed Cossacks and their families. But in spite of these precautions they were not always successful; many Kirghiz settled on the line of the Trakt and some intermarried with the colonists. Alexander Michie, a Scottish merchant who made the arduous journey between Peking and St Petersburg in 1863, wrote that 'the Kirghiz women are physically superior to the Russian women of the same class – cleaner, better dressed, and handsomer. They have, in many instances, blue eyes and fair complexions, in marked contrast to the Kalmuks and Mongols. In manners they are more cheerful than the Russians.'

Here, beyond Kalachinskaya, where the line ran close to the Trakt, the steppe was a great, open grass plain full of buttercups, with birches, aspens and willows growing in it. Some of these birches were so small that at first I thought that they were bushes of some other species. Sometimes they formed great groves, with long, enchanting vistas of green grass and meadowsweet running through them which led to other groves and other vistas, so beautifully disposed that they looked as if they had been planted by some eight-eenth-century landscape gardener in a nobleman's park, except that such vistas probably went on for hundreds of miles. Everywhere there were big herds of black and white and brown cattle either in the common land on the edges of villages or else out on the steppe itself; but wherever they were they always had a herdsman or herds-woman watching over them.

This was what I could see of the Barabinskaya Steppe from the window – when I *could* see it. We were now in the section of the Trans-Siberian Railway, between the Urals and the Kuznetsk coal basin, east of Novosibirsk, which not only has more freight traffic on it than any other line in the USSR, but more than any other railway line in the world. All through that Sunday the freight trains to the west were so frequent – approximately one every two minutes, each of which took about fifty seconds to pass the *Rossiya* – that for much of the time everything north of the line was blotted out.

Around 9.30 am, having crossed the 75th meridian, we passed through Tatarsk, a small town of low-built houses that looked far older than they probably were. There was no sign of what had been, according to the photograph in the 1900 imperial railway guide, the rather attractive wooden church, built near the station in 1897 in honour of the Archistragus Michael and paid for by the Alexander III Fund, which provided money for the building of dozens of similar churches along the line. It had probably been used for firewood by the soldiers, Czechoslovaks, White Russians and Bolsheviks, who careered up and down the line just after the

Revolution. At one time there were up to 10,000 Czechoslovakians in Siberia. What they were doing there is too complicated to explain here, except to say that for some months, at the height of the Civil War in which they had played a crucial part, they controlled – in fact practically owned – most of the Trans-Siberian.

Tatarsk stood in a swampy plain, with what looked like plantations of birches stretching away beyond it to east and west but which were natural growth. Out in this expanse a big herd of horses was cropping away, watched over by a man on horseback who was standing in his stirrups with his back to us as we went past. He wasn't interested in trains. According to the Russian railway map we were now entering the fourth time zone beyond Moscow. The sun was high now as it was 1.45 pm local time and the light was brilliant, almost incandescent, although it was soon after breakfast from our point of view. This was the moment when Irina came zooming into our compartment, armed with her leaky old vacuum cleaner which took ages to pick anything up, and began the daily ritual of sucking up breadcrumbs and broken bits of honey biscuit, while we held our feet in the air and made feeble jokes which she couldn't understand.

Now the steppe became more and more swampy and there were many lakes. At a place called Chany, workers on a nearby building site were living in a siding in what looked like pre-revolutionary passenger cars painted an astonishing, acidulous shade of green. Somewhere near here, south of the line, was Lake Chany which covered over a thousand square miles and was full of fish. What we were now passing through was a waterscape rather than a landscape, in which farms and entire villages were sometimes almost entirely surrounded by water: country that produced enormous quantities of domestic geese and duck. Even the grassland on which the cattle grazed, unimpressed by the apparitions of the mirage, which were now in operation, was full of what looked like waterlogged shell holes, and some of them had springs bubbling up in them. In fact, under the Barabinskaya Steppe, at a depth of between 3000 and 10,000 feet, there is a huge lake of hot water, some of it boiling.

At times the mirage made even the lakes with their fringes of tall

yellow grass seem illusory; but the most spectacular effects were
further off, out on the horizon that wobbled like a jelly. There, it
might have been a mile or many miles away, lines of willows and
aspen hung upside down on top of their true selves, top to top, so
that each tree looked as if it had been halved down the middle, joined
with hinges at the top and then opened out like a child's toy or a
book.

In May 1893 work began on the construction of the railway
through this strange country from Omsk to the River Ob. The fresh-
water lakes, as they still do, attracted hundreds of thousands of
migrant geese, duck and other water birds, but otherwise it was a
hell of a place to build a railway. Many of the lakes were either brackish or sour. In some places they had evaporated altogether, leaving
salt marshes on the edge of which rotting vegetation gave off a terrible stench of sulphuretted hydrogen. In summer whole jungles
of nettles grew anything up to eight feet high and the workers had
to hack their way through them. The country was fever-ridden and,
like everywhere else in Siberia, an inferno of insect life.

It took twenty-seven months to build the railway to the left bank
of the Ob across the Barabinskaya Steppe, which was finally reached
in August 1895. The great seven-span bridge over the Ob was not
completed for another two years. Yet the cost, including the bridge,
was only about £4 million, which was well below estimate.

From then on what had been a journey from Osmk to Ob by
tarantass of three days and the best part of three nights, driving
more or less without intermission alongside the Trakt, became a
twenty-four-hour journey by fast train, with stops at fifteen stations.
Today the 391 miles from Omsk to Novosibirsk take about nine hours.

It was about this time, while the mirage was producing spectacular effects, that I realized that I hadn't seen Wanda for some time.
Just as I was beginning to think of asking the radio operator to send
out an SOS she came back wearing a slightly unctuous expression.

'Where have you been?' I inquired. 'I thought you must have
got off somewhere.'

'Talking to the conductress Mischa had the row with yesterday.
She's really very nice. She let me take pictures of the people in her
open coaches.'

'Did they mind?'

'No, they loved it. I took her picture, too.'

'How did you manage that?' I tried to sound disinterested but it was difficult to keep envy out of my voice.

'I lent her that Silver Jubilee *Vogue* with all those pictures of Royalty in it. I said that she reminded me of Queen Victoria, and I gave her a pair of tights.'

'Not Queen Victoria at *her* Silver Jubilee?'

'No, when she was younger.'

'I've got an idea,' I said. 'Why don't you suggest to Mischa that he makes it up with her by telling her she reminds him of Kruschev when *he* was younger.'

'*You* suggest it to Mischa,' she said. 'It's you he's really fond of.'

At midday train time, 4 o'clock in the afternoon in the steppe, we reached Barabinsk, a town about midway between Omsk and Novosibirsk, originally a place of exile for Polish Jews and now, according to the Soviet Atlas, a big dairy and fishing centre on the Omsk–Novosibirsk oil pipeline. The station was a pleasant place. There was an old-fashioned wooden station house, and there were fruit trees in blossom on the platform. I was just about to photograph a middle-aged couple from the window, in black and white using a 300 mm lens as they were so far away – they were holding hands and, at least, they looked happy – when Mischa, whom I thought had taken the Sunday off, appeared in the doorway. 'Please do not photograph the station,' he said.

'Why not?'

'It is too old.'

'Well, what about Omsk? Omsk wasn't all that old!'

'Omsk station was not yet ready to be photographed.'

'Anyway,' I said, 'I'm not photographing the station, I'm photographing a happy-looking, middle-aged couple holding hands under a tree.'

'I am afraid I must ask you not to take this picture,' he said, zooming off to tell Otto not to photograph them either.

So I didn't.

Lunch, eaten around 4.30 pm local time, was not so hot. In fact it was cold and the sausage had to be thrown overboard. It had gone green since we last saw it, and was beginning to show the same symptoms as Chekhov's disgusting Tomskian sausage, so we made do with bread and cheese. The booze was finished long ago. Unless we reached Novosibirsk, pretty soon, Fabled City and the Chicago of Siberia, whatever that meant (presumably St Valentine's Day Massacres and hooch made in bathtubs), we would be like Magellan's men, cutting the rawhide chafing gear off the yards and boiling it up for *Mittagessen*. We were certainly both losing weight at a remarkable rate.

After this banquet I tried to sleep; but it was impossible. I was hypnotized by the Barabinskaya Steppe. All of what was left of this now golden afternoon I goggled out of the window at it, to the left for the two minutes between freight trains, to the right for the fifty seconds or so that it took them to pass, hooked on the enchanted birch groves. How wonderful it would have been, I thought, to wander off into them, on and on northwards through one dreamy clearing to another, until I met my first reindeer and knew that it was time to turn back.

It was not only an enchanting afternoon for me: it was also a lovely one for the inhabitants, in these fleeting weeks before the insects arrived on the scene.

On the outskirts of one village what appeared to be the majority of the inhabitants, apart from the aged – men, women and children – were bathing together in a little river at a place where it wound through some meadows and under a wooden footbridge. In another, where a troop of horses was being taken home down the main street at a canter, people were drawing water from a group of wells; but instead of using windlasses to wind up the buckets they were employing the oldest form of water-raising mechanism known to man, next to dipping it out with half a coconut: a counter-balanced bailing bucket, in this case a long pole with an axle driven through it with a bucket suspended from one end and a counterbalance weight on the other, which they hauled down into the well by a rope attached to the top end. There were half a dozen of these machines, alternately dipping their buckets into the water and then lifting them in the air, and from a distance they looked like a flock of long-legged, long-beaked birds drinking. How beautiful the steppe was in this long evening. My impression of the steppes had been a bit different from Lenin's, on his way into exile in the winter of 1897:

The landscape along the road through Western Siberia, which I have just travelled from end to end (three days and 1,300 versts from Chelyabinsk to Krivoshchenkova) are extraordinarily featureless [he wrote, while waiting at the station of Novosibirsk, which was then called Novonikolaevsk]: a bare and empty steppe, snow and sky . . . Not a house, not a town: an occasional village, sometimes a stretch of forest, but mostly steppe.

Soon a factory loomed up against a vast horizon to the north, and, just as another had done that morning west of Omsk, which now seemed a world away, a jet was screaming in to land at Novosibirsk airport. Yet in spite of modern intrusions we were still very much in rural Russia.

In the villages, where the line ran close to the Trakt, little bands of young men in white shirts and girls in print dresses were slowly going home together, some of them hand-in-hand, carrying bunches of wild flowers which they had picked in the steppe. In the West, dressed in much the same way, they would have been doing the same thing – back in the 1920s.

Then, quite suddenly, the steppe was finished and the *Rossiya* was running down through an escarpment, past *dachas* and factories with tall chimneys to the bridge over the Ob River which had cost a million dollars in 1897 and was built with steel from the Urals on steel bearings from Poland and with stone abutments and piers stuck together with cement that came from St Petersburg. Then it came to a halt in the biggest station in the biggest city in Siberia, 2089 miles from Moscow and 2721 miles from Vladivostok. It was 5.06 pm Moscow time, 9.06 pm at Novosibirsk.

10

The Chicago of Siberia

WE stood on the platform at Novosibirsk while two drivers tried to cram our luggage into the boots of their beat-up taxis. The *Rossiya* had already left for Krasnoyarsk, Irkutsk and points east with Lilya and Irina waving madly from the doorway of their car. It had been a sad moment. We would never see each other again and Lilya had shed some tears and given Wanda a leaving present, a set of picture postcards of the Trans-Siberian Railway. Even the Australian and Ivan, the Cannibal of the Sleeping Cars, had been there to see us off. All we needed was a hidden choir singing 'Lord Dismiss Us With Thy Blessing', and it would have been just like the end of one's last term at school.

The infant Vladimir had also left the train, prosperous in a big topcoat which made him look like a dark blue balloon. 'Where's the cigar?' I asked him. 'I hope you didn't leave it burning in the compartment.' But, as usual, he wasn't giving anything away. Instead, he allowed his grandmother, who was part of the welcoming committee, to kiss him. I bet it cost her a ruble or two.

At last the long Sunday was almost over – or rather, it ought to have been over. At present it showed no signs of coming to an abrupt end. Here it was, half-past nine at night and the sun was still up. Nevertheless, it was coming to an end for the Novosibirskians who had travelled out into the country for the day by train in thousands to gather wild flowers. They had found out where to go, and on which trains to travel, by pressing buttons on a board in the ticket hall, as demonstrated, later, by the station-master. In autumn they would press another set and would be told where fungi were sprouting. I forgot to ask him what happened in winter. Did they go out after ice?

Now they were pouring out of the station, contented but a little limp, like the bunches of flowers they had picked, most of which, apart from being bright orange, looked like buttercups.

'What are dose flowers?' Wanda asked Mischa, who was becoming impatient with the taximen – he, too, had had enough of today.

'Snowdrops.'

On the other hand the day was just beginning for a little squad of teenage girls from the Siberian School of Choreography, waiting to welcome someone off a train. Dressed in mini-skirts, white knee-length socks or tights, some of them in the top halves of sailor suits, with their right feet turned out as if they were about to break into *Swan Lake*, they stood on the platform as immobile as porcelain statues of ballet dancers and as self-consciously aloof as real ones. Then, just as I thought that one or other of them must change position, scratch herself, yawn or even speak, the train they were waiting for came in and disgorged a whole troupe of expensive-looking theatrical but otherwise genuine gypsies, the sort who live in huge trailer caravans surrounded by acres of polished brass, some of them clutching accordions inlaid with mother-of-pearl and unidentifiable stringed instruments, and all uttering outlandish cries.

It was the moment the dancers had been waiting for. A grim-looking duenna handed the tallest and grumpiest-looking girl (grumpy probably because she was already too tall and too big to make the grade) a bunch of bright red carnations entombed in plastic, the little troupe switched on smiles like laser beams, and to an unspoken one, two, three . . . took off with the right foot in the direction of the leader of the gypsies, an astonishingly *mondaine* figure wearing a silver grey suede coat with a white fox collar and brilliant, white-capped teeth which must have cost her a bundle west of the Elbe, who was now moving towards them in a cloud of Diorissimo. In a few moments the welcome was over; the little girls and the gypsies were loaded into a fleet of shiny black motorcars and driven away, leaving a bunch of porters to load quantities of Vuitton-type trunks into a truck. The next time we saw the gypsies was in *Carmen* at the Opera House.

All the improving books I had with me said that Novosibirsk was enormous – the third largest city in the USSR after Moscow and Leningrad. Its machine construction, metalworking, metallurgical and chemical industries were flourishing, and so was its trade in grain, meat, butter and so on. It was also the regional centre for Kuzbas, the huge coal-, coke-, chemical- and mineral-producing complex in the Kuznetsk Basin away to the east and south-east, the presumed source of the little nugget of coal which had blown in on the table of our sleeping compartment, while we were still well west of the Urals.

But in spite of all this, it was somehow unimpressive. Its tree-lined streets were pleasant enough, and its citizens on the whole looked well-hipped, but what it notably lacked was a horizon – at least, from wherever we were taken to admire it, and if there were more grand ones it was the business of the boys from The Agency to unveil them for our benefit. Whoever gallantly compared it to Chicago had, presumably, never seen that draughty but unforgettable dump on the western shores of Lake Michigan; and a night out at the Ob Hotel, which was presumably considered one of the better sorts of place – otherwise what were we doing there paying good money for first-class accommodation? – was more like a gathering of the clans at Stoke-on-Trent than a night out at Drake's in the Loop.

But in spite of its shortcomings, Novosibirsk had certainly come on since its foundation in 1893, when its population was 3000. By 1900, by which time it had been named Novonikolayevsk, the population was 15,000. By 1908 it had doubled. By 1914 it had doubled again. Thereafter, many years passed before anyone could be sure how many people lived there. Certainly a lot died, both Bolsheviks and White Russians, during the Civil War, and the town changed hands many times. When the Bolsheviks succeeded in crossing the Ob and entered the city in December 1919, at a time when Newby was living in the lap of luxury in Barnes, SW13, tucked up in a bassinet shrouded in voile to keep off any draughts that might conceivably find their way into his coal-fire-heated nursery, they found more than 30,000 people dead in its streets and houses, most of them victims of typhus.

Its really spectacular growth began with the initiation of the First Five-Year Plan in 1928. In that year the construction was begun, by slave labour, of the Turksib, the Turkestan-Siberian Railway, which was completed in 1931. The Turksib was built to carry grain and timber by way of Novosibirsk to the cotton-growing areas of central Asia.

In 1930 the first factory producing agricultural machinery for the black-earth steppes of southern Siberia was built at Novosibirsk, and at more or less the same time the Ural–Kuznetsk Combine was set up. This provided heavy two-way traffic for the Trans-Siberian Railway, which nearly overtaxed its capacity. The railway carried iron ore from Magnitogorsk in the Urals, which had huge quantities of the ore but no coal, eastwards to the blast furnaces in the Kuznetsk Basin, which had huge deposits of coal but at that time no ore. The return journey to the west was made with waggons loaded with coking coal for the foundries and steel mills at Magnitogorsk, a round trip of 2200 miles. It was the existence of these two huge arsenals, known collectively as the Second Metallurgical Base, which, thanks to Stalin's foresight in setting them up, saved Russia when the arsenals in the Leningrad area and what was known as the First Metallurgical Base in the Donetsk Basin, in the Ukraine, were both overrun by the Germans.

The setting up of the Ural Base was attended with great difficulty and privation. As John Scott wrote in his book, *Behind the Urals*:

A quarter of a million souls – Communists, Kulaks, foreigners, Tartars, convicted saboteurs and a mass of blue-eyed Russian peasants – made the biggest steel combination in Europe in the middle of the barren Urals steppe. Money was spent like water, men froze, hungered and suffered, but the construction went on with a disregard for individuals and a mass heroism seldom paralleled in history.

The Ob Hotel, a multi-storey matchbox on the right bank of the Ob, was not one to which non-fellow travellers from capitalist countries generally have access as it is not an Intourist hotel. When we were there a large proportion of the guests were of Mongolian origin, many of them wearing good conduct badges and medals. Others could have been East Germans, Poles, Lithuanians, Czechs on a pat-on-the-back trip, or even Russians. All were clad from head to toe (the men that is – the women were slightly more adventurous) in subfusc grey synthetics, and in the lifts, which was the only time one got close to them, they never spoke, even among themselves.

There were two good things about the Ob Hotel: the view from our bedroom, and the female staff who looked after us, who were kindly, in contrast to the restaurant staff (who were also women). In their restaurant beer and vodka were invariably 'off' and they treated us in a very offhand manner, unless Mischa or some other member of The Agency was present, when they were all smiles. Certainly there was nothing good about the loathsome bathroom and lavatory, which various maids tried hard to brighten up without any visible effect; with its floor covered with enough loose tiles to play dominoes; its lavatory seat covered with sinister and irremovable stains which some maniac had wrenched from its hinges and which, if either of us had dared to sit on it, would have taken us on a skateboard ride to eternity, and what would have been its plugless washbasin if we hadn't still had our rubber ball. As we worked our way across the USSR I often wondered why there was such a shortage of waste plugs. Either there had never been any, or people stole them. If they stole them, once they had plugged their own basins, what did they need more for, unless they sold them, gave them away as presents or hoarded them away and occasionally had them out to gloat over, as a form of undebasable currency? Or did they eventually ransom them back to the original owners?

However, the view from our room – when we finally reached it, after a mad interlude in which the luggage of all four of us was taken to the eighth floor and deposited in the room of a guest from some part of central Asia who was lying on his bed, having just taken his socks off – was terrific. Below us the Ob, here about half a mile wide – flowed down on its 2625-mile course from north-western Mongolia to the Gulf of Ob in the Arctic, into which, in flood, it ran out at a rate fourteen times the annual discharge of the Don, having drained a million square miles of Asia.

It was a splendid and lively scene that presented itself. Big white excursion steamers loaded with people, some of whom were also clutching limp bunches of orange-coloured snowdrops, were coming up under the bridges towards the landing stages, past the dredgers moored off-shore whose crews were also having a day off, passing under an unfinished concrete bridge, which still had one span missing, under the seven-span cantilever bridge, the master-piece of Professor N. A. Byeleloubsky who designed all the bridges on the West Siberian section and which carries the railway over its first really major crossing east of the Urals and under the big road bridge. Between the two downstream bridges were the cranes and grain silos in the Novosibirsk port area, now bathed in the last of the sun which was disappearing behind the big apartment blocks in Kirov on the escarpment of the Barabinskaya Steppe.

Down on the foreshore, between the landing stages and the road bridge, hundreds of people – black matchstick figures against the shimmering water – were fishing, bathing, contemplating the river or congregating in little groups around the fires over which fisher-men were grilling their catch; and as the light waned more and more fires began to flare up.

It was a scene more Asian than Russian, in spite of the western attributes, the shipping, the cranes, the bridges, the monolithic buildings on the horizon – which was not surprising, as we were in Asia, in the same longitude as Benares on the Ganges; and indeed the whole scene was reminiscent of a reach of the Hooghly near Calcutta, except that there the bathing would have had a religious significance. Neither was the noise really European in its abundance and variety: the continuous roar of heavy traffic, the rumblings of the trains on the bridge which were accompanied by the dismal mooing sounds that engine drivers always wring from their loco-motives when crossing bridges, the sounds of the ships' sirens and the shouts and cries produced by a horde of human beings – all this pandemonium reminded us both vividly of a day, now long ago, when we had gone down in our rowing boat under the Howrah Bridge at Calcutta to the landing place at the Armenian Ghat after descending the Ganges.

In and around Novosibirsk we found ourselves traversing a well-worn trail which had been followed God knows how many times by other Agency 'guests', as its representatives quaintly insisted on calling us (presumably because a guest is expected ultimately to defer to the wishes of his hosts). In doing this they conveniently forgot that every movement we made from one place to another – they were not great walkers – every tip that Mischa dispensed with what seemed unnecessary liberality in a country that still attempts in the presence of foreigners to keep up a pretence of equality, and every minute of time was being paid for with large sums of foreign currency.

Here, and in the rest of Siberia traversed by the railway, apart from the vast and splendid landscapes which we saw from the windows of the *Rossiya*, I had the uncanny sensation of having seen it all before. In a sense I *had* seen it all before, either in the innumerable illustrated handouts produced by Intourist and Soviet Railways, or else in old, germ-laden copies of the *National Geographic Magazine* which I used to leaf through in doctors' waiting rooms, with all those breezy cross-heads in the text which made me feel that they had been written by The Agency rather than by men and women down on 17th and M Streets NW in Washington DC. WARM HOSPITALITY IN A FRIGID LAND. ONE-TIME LIMBO FOR POLITICAL EXILES, SIBERIA TODAY WEARS A NEW IMAGE. . . . THE WORLD'S GREATEST STOREHOUSE OF UNTAPPED MINERAL WEALTH. TIGERS ROAM WHERE REINDEERS GRAZE.

Not only had a lot of it happened before; as we proceeded across Siberia it became increasingly obvious that a lot of happenings didn't happen until we actually appeared; like the children all dressed up, who just happened to come into the hall of their school down on the Mongolian border, although the holidays had begun; the cowboy herding cattle across what I recognized as a well photographed bit of landscape, just as we passed; the fishermen on the eastern shore of Lake Baikal suddenly beginning to unload the catch (which they had brought into harbour hours before) when we appeared, hours late because our jeep had broken down. The only unrehearsed act while we were at Novosibirsk was that some organization sent Otto a woman. It was obvious that this was a mistake and that she was intended for someone else, probably a librarian, as she was apparently in business not for money but for books written in English. It was certainly an official mistake, though nothing to do with The Agency, as there was no way in which an unofficial woman, or anyone else, could get past the concierges who sat opposite the lifts on every floor day and night and who would hand over the room key only on production of a special card.

Although, on that exciting evening at Novosibirsk when we first saw the Ob, three days seemed too little time to spend in such a city, they in fact passed with almost painful slowness, thanks to our hosts' inability to be ready to set off anywhere at the advertised time. At first we were puzzled by this, but eventually we put it down partly to the fact that they had an incomplete knowledge of the nature of time and partly because they consumed so much of it in interminable telephone calls across the Urals to Agency Headquarters.

On the third morning we waited for two and a half hours outside the hotel for something to happen, in the meantime watching a little band of boys and girls, aged about eight or nine, who were devoting the first days of the summer holidays to cleaning up the grounds after the long winter, under the command of a dishy looking redheaded mistress in a yellow shirt and a plastic mini-skirt. They were armed with rakes and brooms and from time to time the boys pretended to machine-gun one another with them; and when Wanda and I got fed up waiting and set off in a huff downstream in the direction of the not-to-be photographed bridges they mowed us down too.

It was a brilliant morning, with a strong wind raising clouds of sand on the foreshore. At one of the landing stages a big doubledecker paddle-steamer had just tied up, having made the five-day journey from a port upstream of the Gulf of Ob, a journey that we were unlikely ever to make. Downstream the cranes on the big dredgers were dipping over the water, scooping up ballast which would be used to fill in the ravines with which the older part of the city was intersected, giant versions of the bird-like water-raising mechanisms we had passed in the Barabinskaya Steppe, and there were slim little boats from which men were fishing with nets stretched on metal frames.

Down here on the foreshore it was very different from that first calm evening. Now, in the screaming wind that was blowing, there were only about half a dozen heroes dressed in quilted black cotton coats. One of them, what Wanda described as 'an olderly man', had,

for additional protection against the elements, inserted himself up
to the neck in a plastic bag. They were fishing with rods with little
brass bells on them and lots of hooks baited with maggots for silvery
little fish with sandy-coloured backs called *sodak*, and those who
had been lucky enough to catch any were grilling them over a fire
which was throwing out long trains of sparks downwind. When they
saw that we were interested they grinned, displaying mouthfuls of
fish and black bread.

On the way back from the railway bridge to the hotel, where our
hosts were by now impatiently awaiting *us*, we passed through a
public park. In it, hidden away behind some trees, there was a little
pavilion from which draught beer was being dispensed to a queue
of men. Leaving Wanda to return to the hotel, anxious not to miss
any experience that showed signs of not having been organized for
our benefit, I joined the queue, which turned out to be composed
of unshaven, bad-tempered alcoholics. How they contrived to
remain alcoholics while drinking this watery-looking beverage
remained a mystery until I realized that each one of them was
equipped with an enormous pot, or some similar receptacle, some
of which must have held as much as 6 or 7 litres. When I finally
reached the head of the queue I discovered that I only had 30
kopecks in change, the rest of my money being in 100 ruble notes,
which the white-coated barman refused to change, and I was forced
to give up my place in the queue to the accompaniment of a certain
amount of jeering from these gruesome looking individuals and slake
my thirst with a drink of *kvass*, – a dark, moderately alcoholic
beverage, made from black bread and yeast – which was being drawn
off by a hygienic-looking girl in a white coat and wearing a sort
of white coif on her head, from a white tank on wheels, down by
the landing stages.

'You are late,' they told me severely, when I got back to the hotel.
'We have been waiting for you.'

EXTRACTS FROM MY DIARY AT NOVOSIBIRSK

30 May. Discuss programme. Can we talk to signal men at Novosibirsk Station, find out what happens to the points when it's − 40°F

and below, go into the *taiga*, visit a village along the railway, or at least a station? The answer to all these requests is 'No', except the last – we do actually get to a small station on the Turksib Railway. We even fail to see the *taiga*.

Think up dedications for my book, if a book emerges. Finally settle for

To The Agency, without whose help this book would have been written more cheaply and at least a year earlier.

Driven in the car to Akademgorodok, the great Siberian scientific centre, conceived in 1957. It is hidden among conifers, its tree-lined avenues as deadly as Canberra or New Delhi, but one hopes with more exciting things going on behind the bland facades.

'The Agency has written that you are coming; but you are writing about the railway. What is the purpose of your visit here?' asks an intelligent female in Administration. I tell her I don't know. She smiles and sends us out to look at the Ob Sea while she gets down to some brisk telephoning.

The Ob Sea is the Ob pent up by a hydroelectric scheme. There is a sand beach, warm, dry and dirty, and there are many bathers from Akademgorodok, some beautiful, a few fat, none of them members of the labouring classes – you can tell this even better with their clothes off. Winter being only just over, the water of the Sea is filthy inshore, like mulligatawny soup, and bulldozers are removing debris from the beach.

After lunch in the academics' club, which is clean and elegant, taken to a board room where we are closeted with the Professor of Mediaeval Siberian History and several colleagues, one of whom is a lady of Mongolian extraction, probably Buryat, who is engaged on a thesis entitled 'Capitalism and its Relation to the Trans-Siberian Railway'. All except the Professor, including Otto, who is nearly driven insane by the long speeches and wishes he was outside (as I do), look as if they would like to rush away and get on with their jobs. It is difficult to know what to ask a mob of assorted savants, especially arriving on their doorstep out of the blue.

We discuss Trans-Siberian roads. Why, I ask, up to now has no trans-continental road been built? One is actually in construction but they do not tell me this. Too long, too expensive to maintain and to keep open, they tell me.

I go to work on the Buryat lady. All I get out of her is that relatively few convicts were employed on the construction of the railway. She is keeping the rest for her thesis. What is the strategic importance of the railway to the USSR today, and is it not a rather tenuous link with the Far East? Answer: This is not our business. All this time Mischa is scribbling away. I suddenly realize that The Agency are employing him to get material for pieces for them, at our expense. The room is terribly hot. Altogether, we drink about eight bottles of mineral water of which there are stacks on the table.

'Your book will be a milestone,' says the Professor in an interminable peroration. 'More like a tombstone,' I reply in my vote of thanks, which brings some laughs, but not many. The Professor ends up with a little joke about the attitude of Siberians to Siberia (which I hear subsequently in similar boardrooms, and from other Boss Men, no less than six times): 'A place where 100 rubles is not money; 1000 kilometres is no distance and half a litre of vodka is not a drink.' I could have done with a shot myself.

Then shown a small but very interesting collection of artefacts, some of them prehistoric. The most impressive exhibit, to me, is a collection of clay pots decorated with women's faces from the Pacific seaboard. We also visit the Mineral Museum in which we are shown 20,000 Siberian minerals.

Rush back 20 miles or so to Novosibirsk just in time to miss steamer trip on Ob. Otto discovers pretty girl on the landing stage who has also missed it and photographs her thirty-five times, which cheers him up. He deserves her. He had a lousy time at Akademgorodok.

Gala Night at the Ob Hotel. Photography frowned on. Local girls in long dresses. One outstanding male-type Lesbian clad with splendid simplicity in a white shirt with her white butch underwear showing through and white pants that look as if she had been melted down and poured into them before being allowed to grow firm. She kisses while she dances and generally takes a lot of risks for someone in about 55°N, 83°E, but she appreciates our applause and comes over to our table to tell us so – Mischa distressed. We could have danced all night, to a pretty noisy group which dispensed rock, tangoes, waltzes and fox-trots, except that a Militiaman with a sweeping moustache named Sasha closed everything down at 11.30, having previously ejected all drunks and all persons without seats. Temperature 86°F. Dinner, fish from Ob with egg, cucumber, radishes and cream, Ukrainian wine (poor). Restaurant loos are filthiest we have so far seen – not only no plugs but no taps and no seats! Do people use them as picture frames?

31 May. Trip into city with Agency man at Novosibirsk whose father had been station-master here. In spite of having lost both legs in the battle before Moscow in 1940 he is an immensely powerful man with arms like tree trunks, and he emanates an aura of barely pent-up energy of a kind I have never before come across. This is the only man I have encountered so far in the USSR who has really put the wind up me, and Wanda is also terrified. His spell began to work when we passed the Church of St Alexander Nevsky, one of the original churches of the settlement, and he quoted the medieval Prince Nevsky's words to a number of German knights he had taken prisoner and whom he now set free: 'Go now, and tell everybody to come to our country as guests without fear. But he who comes with a sword will perish by the sword.' Even swordless, I felt cold shudders going up and down my spine. I suppose we would say things like this to visitors to England if we had been invaded by Mongols and Germans.

. . . While we are in Lenin Square admiring the Opera House and Ballet Theatre (started as a Palace of Science and Culture in 1931 and finally completed in 1943 as an Opera House when the battle for Stalingrad was at its height, largely by women and children) and listening to our man from The Agency droning on, telling the story about the rubles and the kilometres and the vodka, Otto gets out of the car to take some pictures. While he is looking at a young girl in a turquoise moss crêpe day dress crying her heart out on the shoulder of a young man on a park bench and wondering whether he dare photograph them, a boy of about seventeen comes up and asks him in excellent English for some late news on the Beatles.

Immediately, without being told to do so, our driver, who is not a taximan and who is also very powerful (everyone is powerful here), leaps out, seizes the boy by the collar and literally frog-marches him away, in spite of his protests that he means no harm. I ask Mischa, who is interpreter for Agency man as he speaks no English, what on earth the driver is doing. 'He is a no-good fellow,' he replies. I try to imagine a similar happening in Trafalgar Square with a no-good fellow approaching a foreigner who has been taken there by a member of the British Tourist Authority, but fail.

1 pm. Drive into a police roadblock close to a military airfield, which even our legless friend has difficulty in getting through, then into pine woods full of marguerites, what look like giant blue sweet-peas and something they call a bluebell which isn't – Siberian spring is mid-March to mid-April in these latitudes; summer ends 25 September. The snow comes end of October; December is the coldest; February has the heaviest snow with blizzards.

Eventually arrive, at the end of a long ride through woods, at a Pioneer Camp for Children called 'Green Republic', in which the little darlings elect their own president or whatever and organize their own sentries. Mercifully, it is empty, the camping season not having begun. It is however carpeted with the most beautiful flowers, which Otto begins to photograph but is forced to give up as he is holding up the programme. He was furious.

On the way back into the city, on the six- or seven-mile-long Krasny Prospekt we cross a ravine full of old wooden houses, pleasantly disposed. The ravine is being filled in, the houses demolished, we are told with relish. The same goes for some really beautiful houses and fine old trees by the main road, all of which are getting the chop simultaneously. I tell Mischa to tell our friend that if he comes anywhere near my old house in England he will be met with barbed wire and with machine-guns firing on fixed lines. He enjoys this militant reaction.

2 pm. You would think it would be food time but now we are at Novosibirsk Station, being given the red carpet treatment by Station-master Alexander Butkayev, twenty years in the business, whose station copes with millions of passengers a year, 75,000 a day and sixty-five passenger trains each way a day. About 5 pm, after having seen all his crèches and waiting rooms but nothing really appertaining to the railway – the frequency of goods trains, for instance, is a close secret – we drive off all the way back to the Ob Sea to a suburban station called Rechkunovka, where nothing is happening. Then, God help us! We all take off for the second act of *Carmen*! Audience cool, collected, well-dressed, little girls on this big night out with flowers worked into their hair and all those gypsies from the station now on stage. This long day ends watching mad Georgian guests gyrating in the restaurant of the Ob Hotel, which we reach more dead than alive. This is the night, or rather the early hours of the following morning, when Otto is sent his book-lover.

1 June. The day no one turns up until 12.30 pm. Across the river to the Monument to the Fallen, colossal monoliths covered with thousands upon thousands of names, all in bronze, like a huge telephone directory for the dead. These, and a sacred flame, are guarded by child sentries who change guard every fifteen minutes, marching to their posts with a ridiculous and extremely unpleasant form of goosestep. Strange how the USSR should wish to perpetuate in this way the memory of Hitler's storm troops, who used to strut about in a similar fashion, as do the troops of some emergent African nations. In the pm, still lunchless, to Sibirgy Protrans, the Siberian Railway Construction Institute, the head of which is an extremely handsome black moustached, black-haired Georgian, Ali Jalijanov, who I swear (having been in the garment business) is wearing a suit of real Scotch tweed. We are taken to the inevitable, huge boardroom. These boardrooms have long, glass-covered tables, or else they are glassless, in which case the table tops look as if they have been flooded with molten chocolate which has been allowed to set. Other obligatory equipment is a picture of Lenin (busts appear to be kept, on the whole, for the lower orders who are presumed not to be *au fait* with dimensions) and long rows of never-to-be-opened books, lots of tall chairs and clusters of mineral bottles and glasses. In fact, they are just like boardrooms anywhere.

The meeting with Jalijanov is the best I have in Siberia, or in Russia for that matter. For an hour or more he gives us, with the aid of very large-scale wall maps which foreign intelligence services would like to see, a brilliant exposition of the difficulties of building the line across what is virtually minestrone from Tyumen to Norilsk, illustrating what he says with remarkably vivid drawings which he makes with a felt pen. When we leave I ask him to give me them as a leaving present, but once his magical presence is withdrawn they no longer make any sense. He invites me to travel on his railway, north of Tyumen. It is strange and fearful to think that such an able, splendid-looking man should, by the nature of his job, just as does the station-master, know the whereabouts of those who are sent away, and almost certainly be involved in arrangements for them to be transported with the least possible fuss.

Last dinner at the Ob Hotel: soup with bits of meat in it and sour cream and a very nasty minced meat 'steak'. After the excesses at the gala dance the previous night, beer is 'off'. To the station in two taxis at 8.30 pm local time to catch the *Rossiya* to Irkutsk.

11

The Taiga

As soon as we entered the station it was four hours earlier and time for tea, in spite of the fact that we had already had dinner. At 5.06 pm another *Rossiya*, of which the Russians have inexhaustible supplies, rolled into Novosibirsk and was besieged by a horde of potential passengers, none of whom were acquainted with the Russian equivalents of 'Excuse Me!' or 'Sorry!' And worse, some of them were serious offenders so far as personal daintiness was concerned. I was glad that the girls from the Ballet School had been persuaded not to see us off. They would have found the whole thing utterly tiresome.

When we finally did get aboard with our luggage, which had increased, thanks to the amount of unreadable literature with which we had been issued, but which we did not yet dare throw away, and our individual cardboard food-and-drink boxes, which we had recharged, I could not help noticing that we were not given much of a welcome by our two 'soft-class' conductresses. In fact we were not given any welcome at all. One was fiftyish with her hair in a bun, a couple of bosoms that looked as if they had been caught in the wringer about 1951 and an air of indifference to other people's sufferings, bravely borne. In Britain I would have identified her either as the head of a couture workroom or else as a wardress at the Central Criminal Court.

The other was about thirty, blonde, very white-skinned, wearing a very white shirt. She was about 4 foot 9 and must have weighed in at around 168 pounds – but all muscle. She reminded me of an igloo with someone frozen inside it. It was difficult to take much of a shine to either of them.

It was a warm evening in Novosibirsk, and what with the train's heating, the smells of parts, some more public than others, which hung over the carriage like a pall, and the memory of the grey dinner flavoured with onions we had recently eaten, it was a bit too much. A few more minutes and we would either faint or be sick. I tugged at the window in the compartment. Eleven triangular-headed screws winked back at me. It had been given the treatment, as had those in the corridor. A night in this car would mean a lingering death.

'Get the conductresses!' Wanda said. She was already turning green. The dinner, with which something as well as the taste had been wrong, was beginning to work in her. 'Get *zem* to open it!'

'Listen,' I said, as she tottered out of the compartment in search of a car with open windows. 'If you think I'm going to do it twenty-two times with these conductresses at my age just to get eleven screws out of a window, you've got it all wrong. I'm writing a book about a train ride, not *The Confessions of a Window Screwer*.'

Nevertheless, because of the love I bore for her, and because I was feeling pretty green myself, as soon as the *Rossiya* pulled out of the station I set about getting 'zem' to open it.

First, I made sure that there were other compartments in the car with windows that were open, or would open. This included the one occupied by Otto and Mischa. Then I practised what I hoped was an ingratiating smile in the mirror but what I saw reflected was the face of a corpse in *rigor mortis*. Smiling would get me nowhere. Picking up my phrase book, I inserted markers at the appropriate pages – as if I was going to read the lesson in a parish church, rather than do battle with a Rosa Kleb – and rang for room service.

My call was promptly answered by the Wardress. I was glad that she was still in full uniform and hadn't stopped to slip into something loose. We greeted one another, each in our own dissimilar fashions, she by raising her eyebrows, I by reading from pages 36 and 192, verses 9 and 10, as follows: 'Aknno eesporchyehno. Pah-magheetyeh mnyeh pazhahloosta': which, if you get it right, is the Russian for, 'The window is jammed. Help me, please!'

'*Nyet*,' she said, and went away.

I had got it right.

Like a small boy who has been bullied, running off to tell his older brother, I scuttled off to fetch Mischa and a terrific scene developed between him and the Wardress, while I looked on aghast, like a necromancer who has actually succeeded in raising the horrors he has invoked. In the course of it the Igloo appeared and so did Mischa's Red Pass, which I was beginning to think, for all the good it did, he had been given with a Special Trial Price packet of Surf as part of an Introductory Offer.

This time, however, it raised a third character, supplied by courtesy of Chekhov, the Ticket Inspector, a small, kindly man with wispy hair and the expression of one who had been crucified, but always taken down at the last moment.

'*Pozvoltsye*,' he said ('Allow me'), taking the Wardress's hinged key from her.

Eventually he got all eleven screws out; but as I expected it wouldn't open, even with the Igloo hanging on the handle.

'*Né horosho*' ('No good'). '*Nelzia*' ('It cannot be done'). And went off. We thought he had given up (by this time Wanda was back, a pale ghost, having been sick); but soon he returned, bearing a huge axe – presumably part of the *Rossiya's* rescue gear, as it was too big for any kitchen.

'*Topor*,' he said ('Axe'), and inserted the blade between the window and the frame. There was a horrible crackling of woodwork.

'Now we pull,' he indicated, making pulling signs.

Three of us hung on it, he himself, the Igloo and me. All there was room for, even with the table folded.

As we took the strain I suddenly recalled the words of a poem about a windjammer off Cape Horn swept by a mighty sea which I had been trying to remember when we had hauled down the window on the other *Rossiya*, 'ten men hauling on the lee fore brace . . . seven when she rose at last'. Just then it came down with a rush.

'*Horosho!*' ('Good!') he said. It turned out that he wasn't a ticket inspector. He was much more important, the Brigadier in charge of the train. There was a lot of laughter and shaking of hands. These were the sort of Russians I had hoped to meet in Russia. Wanda dished out packets of cigarettes. Mischa in my eyes, at least for the time being, was now a Knight in Shining Armour, and his pass *did* work. The two conductresses, whom I now thought of as Madonnas of the Sleeping Cars – I had Maurice Dekobra's *La Madone des Sleepings* in my bag, unopened – rather than bosses of SMERSH, got out some damp cloths and gave the compartment a going over; a girl appeared from the direction of the restaurant car selling the sort of sausages that explode and squirt when you bite into them. We ordered a round. Soon the walls of the compartment were covered with little spots of pig fat. The conductress went to work on them, too. Wanda reeled off for a second time to be sick. When she came back she felt so ghastly that we had to keep the window shut for the rest of the night. It was too cold to keep it open, anyway.

All that night under a huge moon, while Wanda shivered under a pile of coats with a Boots hot water bottle on her tum in the intervals between making numberless excursions down the corridor, the *Rossiya* thundered first north-east and then east on its thirty-four-hour journey to Irkutsk in eastern Siberia: at first through rolling country in which the enormous ploughed fields looked like a sea after a storm in which a heavy swell is still running; then up to the watershed between the Ob and the Tom and across the northernmost part of the Kuzbas; then through what had been part of the *taiga*, the great boreal forest, when the line was built. The real *taiga* would not be on view until we were east of the Yenisei, which we should cross around seven the following morning. All through the night, too, the blonde conductress, who had come out of her igloo and was called Galina, brought glasses of boiling tea to Wanda and re-charged her hot water bottle, as if fearful that she might expire – usually just as she was dozing off.

At about half past eight she sat up in her bunk, looking, if possible, more miserable than she had previously.

'Hurruck,' she said, which is what she makes my name sound like when she is feeling emotional and her English is on the retreat. 'Hurruck, it's half past one in England. I wish we could be at the place we sometimes are on this day at half past one. Sitting on a rug in the car park, drinking our wine and having our fortunes told by a gypsy.'

'My God!' I said. 'I'd forgotten. It's Derby Day. Never mind, there's plenty of time to get down to the Paddock before the first race. I wish we were there, too' – and I really meant it.

At around 9.30 pm, we crossed the Tom by a big girder bridge. The moon was south of the railway now and the sky up towards the Arctic Circle was an astonishing apple green. Under it the un-ruffled river, seen between the girders, was the colour and con-sistency of olive oil.

The station building at Taiga, the junction for Tomsk which lay about 50 miles down the Tom to the north, looked enormous; but it was not exactly loaded with people at 9.36 pm Moscow time. I got down and crossed the platform to the waiting room under the menacing gaze of the station-mistress who had a red hat, a big bottom and development up front like an overhang on Annapurna. Outside a crapulous looking man was sitting on a bench with a bottle. The waiting room was large and empty – not surprising, as it was 1.40 in the morning at Taiga – and decorated with palms; it was like being in a theatre at the moment when the curtain rises but none of the actors have appeared.

One way and another it was a relief to be back on board the *Rossiya*; to talk to Galina, the conductress, who spoke a little English. She told me that the previous September she had been on the Moscow–Peking run. During the Cultural Revolution, she said, Soviet trains had been smeared with filth. When she was there, in 1976, she had found the Chinese hungry and suspicious and she and all the rest of the crew were locked in a hostel until it was time to return to Moscow. If anyone waved to them he or she was taken away. She went on with this tale of woe for some time, criticizing China and the Chinese for much the same eccentricities that Russia and Russians seemed to share.

At 4 am Moscow time Wanda sat up, full of fight. 'I am feeling better,' she announced. She looked as if she had done a ten-day crash diet twice over. 'I would like some bread and jam.'

I was more than glad. I had been wondering for some time where I could summon a hospital train from. 'I bet they haven't got any jam in the restaurant car,' I said. 'We're just coming into Achinsk. I'll try there.'

Meanwhile I looked up Achinsk in the Imperial Railway Guide.

Back in 1900 there was a stone cathedral and three other churches, one of them attached to a notorious prison which must have been a ghastly place. In 1885 the correspondant for the local *Sibir* newspaper wrote: 'The Achinsk prison is a *cloaca*, where human beings perish like flies. Typhus, diphtheria and other epidemic diseases prevail there constantly, and infect all who have the misfortune to get into that awful place. Not long ago a young girl, a political exile, died there of typhus fever.' A few months later one of *Sibir*'s correspondents was arrested, kept two days in prison without food, flogged, put into leg-fetters, and sent back to his place of residence in a temperature of −47°F. He was not charged with any crime other than furnishing his paper with news.

Achinsk was an eight-minute halt for the *Rossiya*, so when the Wardress let down the steps I zoomed out through the station, which was not selling jam just then, into Siberia, which stretched away in all directions. The town centre was not on the doorstep. By a miracle, round the corner there was a wooden construction with a window full of pots and bottles and inside, at the receipt of custom, a very old lady.

The only reference in my phrase book to 'jam' was as a stuffing for pancakes. I tried this on her and she gave me a small packet of flour and what looked like a glass bottle of lower-fruit-standard plum jam. I gave her back the packet and two rubles and took the bottle, and she gave me one ruble back and a quantity of dull-looking change. By now the *Rossiya*'s hooter was raising the dead. Then I rushed back to the platform where it and the Wardress were both jumping up and down with excitement, anxious to be off, like part of an animated cartoon.

'I've been to the restaurant car,' Wanda said. 'There's no jam.'

'It's all right,' I said, 'I've got enough here to last all the way to Vladivostok and back.'

When she opened it she found that it wasn't jam; but something sour, the sort of thing some misguided people eat with pork chops under the impression that it brings out the flavour.

'You're som shopper!' she said, 'my husband.'

And so, we left Achinsk where the jams are made from manglewurzels or even more exotic roots, the most northerly station on the Trans-Siberian in the whole of Siberia, drinking tea and eating honey cakes of which Wanda had bought a further supply at Novosibirsk. Pretty dangerous fare for someone just snatched from the grave, but then she enjoys living dangerously.

We settled back to watch Siberia rushing past in the opposite direction. The mist lifted to show forests filled with tall beeches, poplars and a few firs, interspersed with green valleys alive with big yellow kingcups, the brilliant orange flowers that Mischa called snowdrops and wild cherries in full white blossom. Slowly as we watched, the scenery changed and we entered the *taiga* for the first time, the primeval uncut virgin forest. Gloomy country, sunk in swamp and shadow and very cold, where the trees are all firs and men and women clustered round fires in small clearings. Settlements were few and far between, with small houses built of grey, unpainted wood. All the way, rising and falling beside the line, rutted and muddy, crossing streams where abutments were all that was left of the bridges that had once been, was the Trakt. Tough going for any traveller now, but no more tough than it had been for Kennan and Frost:

It was all that five powerful horses could do to drag our heavy *tárantáss* up the steep hills and through the abysses of tenacious semi-liquid clay in the intervening valleys. Even where the road was comparatively hard, it had been cut into deep ruts by thousands of freight wagons; the attempts that had been made here and there to improve it by throwing tree-trunks helter-skelter into the sloughs and quagmires had only rendered it worse; and the swaying, banging, and plunging of the *tárantáss* were something frightful. An American stage-coach would have gone to pieces on such a road before it made a single station ...

Tough, too for Prince Borghese, Luigi Barzini, their driver Ettore and their Itala motorcar, twenty-eight days out from Peking on the Great Peking to Paris Race of 1907:

About nine o'clock we reached the bank of a river, the Kemtschug near a small village, which is called *Great*: 'Bolshaya'. We asked for the ferry-boat, the usual *paravieda* which takes *telegas* across.

'It was here', answered the peasants who had gathered round us, 'but the flood overturned it and it sank ...'

'There was a bridge', they said to us, 'but the flood has pulled it down.'
'Perhaps you can tell us of a ford?'

'No, the river is deeper than a man's height in the middle, and there is no ford across it....'

... We sent for the *starosta*. He was an old, white bearded *mujik* dressed in an *armiak* of embroidered velvet, which gave him an appearance as of an old *Boyar,* or Russian nobleman, come down in life ... A short discussion took place among the *mujiks*, and after this the old man declared with a polite bow that he hoped to let us cross the Kemtschug in a few hours ...

In a moment Bolshaya was up in arms: the peasants, armed with hatchets, ropes, spades, and pails, gathered on the banks of the river ... The *starosta* was in command of the manoeuvre ...

Some men went into the river, tied stout ropes round the boat, and by these ropes pulled it up close to the bank, then with their pails they emptied it, and set it afloat again; this work lasted several hours. Then some planks and beams were quickly carried to the bank, and with the extraordinary cleverness in timber-building always exhibited by the *mujiks*, a solid landing stage was built in a very short time.

When everything was ready, we came down, our car was got up, hoisted on to the still moored boat, and the boat drawn, pushed, accompanied by men through the water, began its journey across. The rope which moored it was now thrown to the other bank, where a long chain of men started pulling it. The actual landing was easy to manage. The car came on to the bank like a triumphal chariot, drawn by a multitude streaming with water and perspiration but aglow with the joy of success.

Tough going; but not so tough as that encountered by the builders of the railway on this stretch of the Mid-Siberian Railway when, under the command of Chief Engineer Nicholas P. Mezheninov, they began work on the Tomsk–Irkutsk section of the railway on 16 May 1893.

As on other sections of the line workers were organized in gangs by contractors who made the wage agreements with them. These were based on 'norms' set up by the strongest workers who were bribed to do what an ordinary worker found impossible. Those who failed to carry out the task in the 'normal' time were fined. There were dozens of other fines for everything from damage to tools to alleged disrespect. And this was only the beginning. 'There were deductions for real and fictitious "advances" made, for transport to the construction site, for food, clothing and tools received from state warehouses, and for "rent",' the historian Hilda Hookham wrote.

One group on the Mid-Siberian line reported: 'They tipped us out of the carts. We looked around and there was nothing to be seen. They hadn't even built any barracks for us. The foreman said 'Fend for yourselves, boys'. We put our knapsacks down on the snow ... we dug some sort of pit, built a framework with poles over it and covered it with earth and turfs. The den was ready. 'Rents' for such accommodation normally accounted for thirty to forty per cent of the wages.

What little money they did receive on Saturdays went in the officially recognized spirit shops set up along the line which sold vodka spliced with raw spirit. But in spite of this unfriendly treatment they carried out their task, cutting a path more than 250 feet wide through mile after mile of virgin *taiga* – in order to lessen the danger of forest fires from the sparks emitted by engines – before beginning to level and grade the track, sinking in the great swamps, which had to be filled with tree trunks and drained, cutting through belts of hard stone at the Kemchug River, building enormous embankments instead of cuttings and tunnels, which the Government had decreed were too costly, and innumerable culverts and wood and masonry bridges.

Some of the rails were brought all the way from Tyneside. In 1887 Captain Joseph Wiggins, a native of Sunderland, succeeded in penetrating the Kara Sea and sailing up the Yenisei. In 1893 he made another voyage with a cargo of 6000 rails for the railway in the S.S. *Orestes* and was able to tranship them into barges at the mouth of the river. Wiggins was honoured by the Russians for this and subsequent voyages by having his memory enshrined at Mys Vigginsa, a point on the desolate shore of the Kara Sea.

By 1894 the railway was so short of labourers, in spite of having nearly 30,000 men in the field, that 1500 convicts and exiles from a prison near Irkutsk were pressed into service. By offering the convicts a remission of one year's sentence for eight months' work on the railway and a daily wage equal to about 6d before the First

World War, and by granting two years' remission to other exiles, spectacular results were achieved. The criminals committed no serious crimes while working on the railway and only a few ran away.

On 13 December 1895 a train carrying passengers, most of whom were construction workers, made the first journey over this 475 mile section of the line from the Ob to Krasnoyarsk; and as they trundled past the shrines that were eventually set up at the approaches to every major bridge on the Trans-Siberian Railway along its entire length, the passengers and drivers crossed themselves – a sensible precaution: the first test locomotive to travel over the stretch west of Achinsk fell through the ballast into the river.

The next great obstacle was the Yenisei River, which at Krasnoyarsk required the building of a six-span bridge more than 1000 yards long, and this was not completed until 1898, again using stone brought all the way from St Petersburg. Because of the intense cold on this and every other bridge with stone abutments, the stonemasons had to protect the unset concrete and mortar with wooden sheaths. When the cold was especially intense the sheathing had to be warmed with fires.

The next section, the 679 miles from Krasnoyarsk to Irkutsk, was even more difficult. There was more *taiga* and more mountain spurs to cross, and it was very nearly twice as long as the Ob–Krasnoyarsk section; and there were many more rivers. In January 1899 the first regular train steamed into Irkutsk, which was soon to become a riproaring metropolis. That same year, with the completion of a further 40 miles of line, the Trans-Siberian Railway was open to traffic from Europe to the shores of Lake Baikal.

Just before 7 am Moscow time we were in the outskirts of Krasnoyarsk and my first impression was of an old, pleasantly ramshackle shanty town, a blown-up version of the stockaded fort built in 1628 to keep the natives in order, which seemed odd for a city of more than half a million people, producing every conceivable thing from gold ingots to double beds. At that moment I did not know that a large, modern city lurked on the heights above the river. At 7.01 the *Rossiya* groaned to a halt, as if the marshes had given it rheumatism, in the station of the biggest city in eastern

Siberia, 2565 miles from Moscow, which the station, as large stations always do everywhere in the world, effectively blocked from view.

Krasnoyarsk was a fifteen-minute stop. On the platform a man with a nasty-looking muzzled thing, which I bet was a wolf, was chatting up a couple of those midget, 44-hip female railway workers, while two lovely long-waisted, junoesque girls in identical roses on black background print dresses (the sort of garments I used to buy for the elderly provincial trade back in the late fifties) were giving one another what looked like a pretty extensive going over, in spite of the drizzle, spreading lipstick all over the place and releasing great gusts of Moscow Nights, which costs a few rubles, I can tell you. In fact, so heady did the air become that I forgot to go off and ask the station-master if there was any beer on his station.

All too soon, as they say, we were off again; but not before I ascertained that we had been given yet another engine some 240 miles back down the line, another electrified CHS. We seemed to be getting through a hell of a lot of engines on this route. Just before the wardress shot the steps up one of the two girls in the black background prints, the pair of whom I was beginning to think were Siamese twins, relaxed her grip on the other, skipped aboard and vanished into a 'soft-class' compartment occupied by a young, beautifully brought up Swiss girl who was going round the world in three years and looked like the 'before' part of a before-and-after going-round-the-world ad. Among others currently in 'soft class', besides ourselves and Mischa and Otto (who was giving Mischa grounds for divorce with his tripod and big lens), were a female Russian schoolteacher, thirtyish, personable, chatty and travelling alone on the way back to her home at Chita on the far side of Lake Baikal; and two anxious East German gynaecologists bound for Irkutsk, who looked as if they had been hunted by Goering in some game reserve but had managed to get away, on account of his having run out of ammunition.

We crossed the Yenisei by Professor L. D. Proskuriakov's great, six-span bridge. Some river! It is between 2300 and 2400 miles from its source in Mongolia to its estuary on the Kara Sea.

Sitting in it were strings of barges with so much timber on deck that they looked ripe for capsizal. The west bank was lined with cranes, with the modern city on the heights above; the far bank was an immense factory area, rather like Dagenham in the Thames Estuary, and about as attractive. No sign of the splendid villa erected by Gennadius V. Yudin, an enormous, grey-bearded, millionaire distiller and book collector who in 1907 sold his entire library of 80,000 books to the Library of Congress, 'with the sole idea of establishing closer relations between the two nations', charging them a derisory $40,000 for what was even then worth $100,000 and which gave the Library's Slavonic Section a unique start. No sign either of the big nucleus of labour camps for which Krasnoyarsk was infamous well into the fifties.

Once over the river the *Rossiya* started to climb up a series of long, rocky valleys. Up and up. If we went on like this we were going to need oxygen apparatus. Then we began to descend a long, wooded valley full of brightly coloured houses. They could scarcely have been the *dachas* of the Krasnoyarskians – too far off: bright blue houses, brighter because the weather was once again blooming gloomy, green houses, yellow houses. But no red houses. Each one with its immaculate private plot which looked as if it had been cultivated by a fatigue party, with chicken and geese in pens, all expecting us to stop and give them nourishment. We were in dark- but not black-earth country which was being ploughed with horses. Some of the fields had only recently been cleared of trees and they had heaps of newly bulldozed roots all over them.

Up over another watershed – all these watersheds were making me thirsty – then through Uyar, formerly Olginsk, named after the Grand Duchess Olga Nikolayevna, which had been established by colonists from Poltava and Kharkov. When it comes to changing the names of the places you love, you can't beat the Russians. Then down again; soon we should be needing lifebelts. I'd always imagined Siberia to be flat. Here the land sloped away from north to south with wide-angle views over steppe, wider even than Otto could encompass with his widest-angle lens without producing something that looked like a baked apple. Another quarter of an hour and it was sloping the other way, from south to north, like the Haunted House in a fun fair.

At 11 am all four of us set off for the restaurant car, ostensibly for a beer but really for the exercise – we all knew that there wouldn't be any. We were right; but although there was no beer, or semblance of service, either, we sat there and soon we began to look like all the other people in the car, who look like Intourist photographs of people in restaurant cars on the Trans-Siberian Railway, who all look as if they were suddenly going to offer one another chocolates with violets on top out of boxes with caballeros and señoritas on the lids.

'Lissun, Mischa,' Wanda said in that special voice which told me that my little helpmeet was finally out of danger in spite of the honey cakes, 'Why is it that whenever we went into a shop at Novosibirsk there were enormous queues?'

'Because there are not enough assistants.'

'Why aren't there enough?'

'Because Russian women are too proud to serve in shops.'

'Well, there are thousands of women assisting in the GUM in Moscow, and there were still queues. You know why? Because there were lots of departments selling nothing, and others selling a lot. In summer they should send the assistants in winter coats to the fresh fruit department.'

The GUM, otherwise the *Gosudarstvenny Universalny Magazin*, otherwise the State Universal Store, is a short sprint across the Red Square from Lenin's Tomb. It was built in 1894, as the result of a big property deal between the Tsar and a developer, and it covers 26,500 square yards, with a 274-yard frontage on Red Square. It is as if King George v had provided Selfridge with the site for an emporium facing Buckingham Palace on condition that he got a slice of the action.

What is even more strange is the attitude of the post-Revolution occupants of the Kremlin to it. For years, until 1935, the buildings were empty. The leaders could easily have used them to house a quite substantial part of their pullulating bureaucracy. Yet sausages, vodka and articles of clothing, some of them of an intimate nature, are still on sale facing the Tomb, and within view of the upper parts of the Praesidium of the Supreme Soviet. GUM has 130 departments and 4000 employees, and long queues wind down narrow staircases and all over the vast building for oranges, meat and other foodstuffs, as well as for any other scarce commodities.

'No Moscow people use the GUM,' said Mischa. I must say I admired his effrontery. 'They're all visitors. Russian tourists.'

'It can't be true. About the customers being tourists. Some of them were wearing bedroom slippers. Besides, you don't come all the way from Kiev to buy 25 grammes of butter or a great hunk of stewing meat.'

He didn't answer and, sensibly, Wanda did not pursue the matter. We might have more important things to argue about later. But I wondered why Russians who are forced into contact with foreigners in an official capacity always deal with any questions that seem to display a too zealous spirit of inquiry, or even to imply the smallest criticism of either the regime or their way of life, by answering them in a manner that is so manifestly untrue that the questioners feel it to be an affront to their intelligence and end up by being as irritated as the Russians already are by having had to make up their untruths on the spur of the moment, knowing that they are feeble and totally unconvincing. This predilection for outrageous lies is not a product of communism. It even antedates the rule of the tsars. Its origins are hidden somewhere in the mists of antiquity and are probably found in the innate love of secrecy inherent in the Slavonic soul.

Now the *Rossiya* was traversing a stretch of eroded steppe which resembled an enormous golf course with twice the normal quota of bunkers in it. For more than 400 miles we had been running through another coalhole, the Kansk–Achinsk Basin. Although there were no pitheads in sight it was running over untold millions of tons of brown coal, here so near the surface that you could practically dig it out with a bucket and spade. No bird life around either. All day I had counted only two crows, two magpies and two unidentifiable ones. Where were they all? Where were all the coalmines?

For the first time in daylight on the voyage I gave up and began to read, from a copy that looked as if it had been thrown out of a fever hospital, Maurice Dekobra's, *La Madone des Sleepings*, a title of genius which, in the year of its publication, sold more than half a million copies and was later translated into twenty-seven languages, which put the author well to the fore of other contenders in the *wagons-lits* field of literature for some time to come.

At 2.30 pm Moscow time, when evening was coming on locally, the *Rossiya* drew into Tayshet, a waterlogged place hidden under a forest of electric pylons, with a station house that looked like some loony château on the Franco-Belgian frontier. Tayshet is the junction for the western end of the BAM Railway, which will eventually link the Trans-Siberian Railway with Sovetskaya Gavan, a port on the Tatar Strait opposite Sakhalin Island, by way of Komsomolsk-on-Amur, about 1800 miles from Tayshet.

Work was begun on this enormously difficult project in 1938, with a labour force that eventually involved the use of about half a million slave workers, from the Pacific end and from Tayshet. Work on it was abandoned at some time during the war and the track already laid was torn up and transported to the west, where it was used to repair the heavily war-damaged railway systems. By this time, at the western end it extended as far as Ust-Kut on the Lena River from Tayshet. Work on the eastern end, as far as Komsomolsk-on-Amur, was completed in 1945 by slaves who had previously worked on BELOMOR, the White Sea Canal project. Nothing more was done, ostensibly, until 1974, when Brezhnev announced that one of the great works of the 1976–90 Fifteen-Year Plan would be its completion.

Eastwards of Ust-Kut the railway traverses some of the wildest, most difficult terrain for railway-builders in the whole of Asia. It is being driven across the northern end of Lake Baikal, where there are huge deposits of asbestos, and then through the Stanovoy Highlands. The first great river obstacle is the Vitim, a river three times more powerful than the Ob at Novosibirsk. Hereabouts, in the Ugakan fields there is so much copper lying about that a female Soviet scientist thought it was fungus. By the time it reaches Komsomolsk, where the Amur has long since been bridged, it will have traversed an earthquake zone, seven mountain ranges and five rivers, including the Lena, no small stream. One of its principal uses will be to carry oil from the West Siberian pipeline to the Pacific coast. By the time it is completed it will have given employment to about 100,000 (one hopes, voluntary) workers.

Enormous efforts are being made to attract youthful workers to this project, which has the same romantic associations and challenge for the more elderly members of the Soviet administration as the building of the Dnieper and Bratsk Dams and the Magnitogorsk Steel plant. Everywhere in European Russia and Siberia the Komsomol, the Young Communist League, is urging young people to take up the challenge, and in every city we visited photographs were prominently displayed showing enthusiastic volunteers, who had just been given a short-back-and-sides, setting off for the construction camps wearing smart, new green combat suits with 'BAM' embroidered on the shoulders and brandishing mandolines.

At 5.34 pm, Moscow time, by which time it had been dark for some considerable time, we reached Nizhneudinsk – not even the Imperial Guide could summon up much enthusiasm for it – and entered the fifth time zone from Moscow, which made it ten-thirty at night.

Here I finished *La Madone des Sleepings*. It was a let-down; the very, very faintly erotic story of 'Lady Diana-Mary-Dorothea Wynham, *née* à Glensloy Castle (Écosse), le 24 Avril, 1897, fille unique du Duc d'Inverness. Education sportive au College de Salisbury'. Last seen by me on page 301, before I fell asleep, boarding the Orient Express at the Gare de l'Est with two valises and a mauve crocodile overnight bag. And that is all the 'sleepings' railway enthusiasts get. On page 307 the book ends. Dekobra should have taken a trip on the Trans-Siberian and asked for his window to be opened.

After having spent 307 pages with Lady Diana-Mary-Dorothea Wynham I was a wreck. I went to bed and slept through mile upon mile of wet *taiga* and steppe and through innumerable crossings of watersheds in the Sayan Range while Wanda, who couldn't sleep, kept count of the stations, grappling with the Cyrillic.

When I awoke day was breaking. We were in a great open steppe with patches of snow and here and there a village with a light or two burning at a street corner. It was cold and a strong wind was blowing. The sky was like porridge. As the *Rossiya* roared past great clouds of pigeons zoomed up into it.

I went to wash. The water was hot for the first time since Novosibirsk. Perhaps I should have run it longer.

'You are fine man,' said Galina, when I emerged. 'So are you,' I just stopped myself from saying. 'No hair on my head – well not much.'

'No hair, no matter,' she said, making my day. If I had had some armour-plated extensions to my arms I would have squeezed her.

Now the sun was dazzling over the steppe – which was being dug up for coal – we were in the Cheremkhovo coalfields – and there were vistas, punctuated by tall chimneys, all the way down the valley south to the great forests around Lake Baikal. Then the refineries and the factories and the freight trains hemmed us in, and the *Rossiya* was sliding into the station at Irkutsk, 3244 miles from Moscow. It was 3.06 am Moscow time. When we did get off, to a warm farewell, the wardress kissed Wanda.

'What have you been doing to her?' I said. 'It looked pretty kinky to me.'

'I lent her that *Vogue* ...'

'...and told her she looked like Queen Victoria. I should have called her Auntie Vicky,' I said.

I was glad we were getting off. I was saddle-sore.

12

The Paris of Siberia

The sun shone brightly on the domes and cupolas of Irkutsk when they burst in the view; the effect of the dazzling ... white walls and bright green roofs of the churches was strikingly beautiful.

> Alexander Michie. *The Siberian Overland*
> *Route from Peking to Petersburg,*
> *through the Deserts and Steppes of Mongolia,*
> *Tartary, &c.* (1864)

OUTSIDE the station I just failed to fall down an unfenced rectangular hole in the road about five feet long and six feet deep with a sewer at the bottom of it, which looked as if it had been dug as a grave for Vice-Admiral Alexander Kolchak, head of the White Russian forces, who was here taken off a six-train convoy on which he was travelling to Vladivostok by the Bolsheviks, together with the larger part of the Imperial State Bank's reserves, which amounted to over 663 million gold rubles. Kolchak, courageous, irascible and tragically (for himself and thousands of ordinary Russians) ineffectual, was shot by a Red Army squad, who said that he died 'like an Englishman'.

Then we piled into a bright green Czechoslovakian Intourist minibus and crossed the River Angara to Irkutsk which is on the right bank, to Kirov Square, in which lady street-cleaners, head-scarved and bundled up against the cold morning air, were sweeping the pathways around the ornamental fountains in the park that occupies the greater part of it, using long, witch-type brooms.

The Angara Hotel (how one longs in Russia for some hostelry with a name like the Dog and Duck or *Au Pied de Cochon*) was modern with large plate glass windows on the ground floor in which the curtains had shrunk – in my experience usually a warning sign to sleep elsewhere – and through them the lower parts of which people could be seen moving about the public rooms.

After the usual interminable businesses that take place in all Soviet hotels and which make getting to the room as difficult for visitors as if they were waiting outside the walled monastery at Mount Sinai for the monks to let down a rope, we went aloft in a lift that made a whirring noise like a pheasant taking off and emitted electric flashes like death ray guns in a *War of the Worlds*.

The suite was clean, reasonably spacious; the sitting room had a glass-fronted cabinet full of the sort of thin-stemmed glasses embellished with gold designs you drink drinks with maraschino cherries on sticks from; the mattress was free of rocks and the bed-room was furnished with a dressing table with a narrow mirror six feet high, all ready for some Siberian giantess to preen herself in; there was a refrigerator in the vestibule; the bath was commodious, the plumbing worked, there were plugs, and the lavatory seat was anchored to the receptacle. There was even a bidet which didn't hit you between the eyes with a jet of water when you turned it on. In short, it was a lap of luxury, although in summer it would have been an oven.

By hanging out of the window, with Wanda grasping the waist-band of my trousers, I could see the spot where the Cathedral of Kazan should have been standing; but all that was now visible was a large official building of the Stalinist era with a massive portico, which entirely filled the north end of the square. The cathedral with its five domes and detached belfry had been almost totally destroyed by artillery fire in the Civil War. However it was just possible to see to the right of this big block the Cathedral of the Epiphany, built in 1747 and part of another church, the Spasskaya.

Irkutsk was founded on an island in the Angara in 1652, when a nobleman named Ivan Pokhobov arrived there with a band of Cos-sacks to collect the *yasak*, the fur tribute, from the Buryats who inhabited the country to the west and east of Lake Baikal. He built an *ostrog* on an island at the confluence of the Angara and Irkut Rivers. Nine years later the settlement was moved to the right bank of the Angara, more or less at the point where stood the two churches that I could see from the bedroom window.

The Cossacks were late in arriving at this point on the Angara. Principally because of the resistance offered by the Buryats and the Tungus who lived in this region, they directed their voyages to the north of Lake Baikal, leaving what is now Irkutsk more or less out on a limb.

After Yermak's death by drowning in 1584 the opening up of Siberia proceeded with amazing rapidity.

By 1619 some *pomori*, peoples of the sea, in search of whalebone, walrus tusks and tusks of frozen mammoths, of which more than 20,000 were found in the space of 200 years, had succeeded in doubling Cape Chelyuskin, the most northerly point of mainland Asia, leaving coins to prove it. These men probably came from Mangazeya, the so-called polar Baghdad, which had been founded in 1601 in an incredibly remote situation on the River Taz at the head of an inlet from the Gulf of Ob. Mangazeya had trade links with the caravan routes from China and central Asia by way of the Yenisei, and with Archangel by a secret route along the coast of the Kara and Barents Seas, crossing isthmuses and following rivers known only to the *pomori* who used them to carry tusks, bones and sables to the west. In 1619 this trade was forbidden by Tsar Mikhail, the first Romanov, who feared that some foreign power, either England or Holland, might seize Mangazeya and put trading posts such as Tyumen and Tobolsk, six months' journey up river from it, out of business. It was a slow sentence of death for the town, and when it was accidentally burned to the ground in 1678 it was already moribund.

In 1620 the Cossacks, who pursued furs with the same ruthlessness as the Conquistadors went after gold and silver, reached the Lena, the longest river in the USSR. Twelve years later Peter Beketov sailed down its middle reaches with thirty men and built an *ostrog* on what would later be the site of the city of Yakutsk.

Most of these seventeenth-century voyages were made in fragile, flat-bottomed, 30-foot long boats equipped with oars and a single sail known as *kochi*, which were light enough to be carried over portages. Being keelless, they could only run before the wind. There were also seagoing versions up to 60 feet long.

It was from the Yakutsk *ostrog* on the Lena that Vasily Poyarkov, a man too cruel even for the Cossacks, set off in 1643 with 130 men and succeeded in reaching the Amur River by crossing the Stanovoy Range, north of the present line of the Trans-Siberian. There, after eking out their winter rations by eating specimens of the local Daurs (Mongolian-speaking dwellers on the river bank) from which their leader abstained, they sailed down the river to the estuary, the first men to reach the Pacific, finally returning to Yakutsk, loaded with furs, by crossing the river systems inland from the Sea of Okhotsk, in 1646.

It was from this *ostrog*, too, that in 1649 the Ataman Khabarov led a heavily armed expedition to the Amur by way of the Olekma River, which he then descended as far as its junction with the Ussuri, blowing the river peoples – Daurs, Nanays, Horse Evenks and Birars – to smithereens with cannon, pillaging villages and committing fearful atrocities. This senseless carnage provoked a strong reaction from the Chinese on whose borders these peoples lived, and led in 1689 to the Treaty of Nerchinsk, which forced the Russians off the Amur and from the adjacent territory for 200 years.

Meanwhile, in 1648, from an *ostrog* on the Kolyma, which subsequently became the settlement of Nizhnekolymsk, a band under the command of Semen Deznev succeeded in sailing eastwards from the mouth of the river to the extreme north-eastern point of Asia, Cape Deznev, on the Bering Strait, meeting the Chukchis, people who traded across the strait with the Red Indians for beaver skins; he eventually made a landfall, after having lost a number of the party in the Gulf of Anadyr. They had discovered the Bering Strait eighty years before Bering himself sailed through it: the first Europeans to sail from the Arctic into the Pacific. Unfortunately, the report that Deznev wrote and forwarded to Yakutsk from his *ostrog* on the Anadyr River, which shows that he realized that the continents of North America and Asia were separated, was pigeon-holed, and was not discovered until ninety years later.

In the course of these voyages the Cossacks followed rivers that contained so many sturgeon, sterlet, pike and salmon trout, to name a few of the sorts that inhabited them, that the fish were sometimes forced bodily out of the water by their sheer weight of numbers. The Cossacks committed ghastly atrocities among the local inhabitants, though no worse than those committed at that time by explorers in other parts of the world. In return they were often ambushed, hit on the head with clubs and killed with poisoned arrows. On the other hand, sometimes they got on very well with the people they encountered. It is difficult to comprehend the distances over which they operated. Of the men who were to follow them at a much later stage, Terence Armstrong, the author of *Russian Settlement in the North*, wrote:

It was not uncommon for a group of Russian pioneers to set up their small headquarters 800 km from anywhere that could be called a town, and for individuals to be out in the forest another 500 km beyond that. This was as if they had started out from Calais (but their town would have been very much smaller), trekked through almost unknown and uninhabited country, built a hut or two to operate from near Turin, and had struck off in ones and twos as far as Rome – the whole of this in country without roads of any kind.

These were small distances, compared with those that the Cossacks covered in the seventeenth century.

Throughout the eighteenth and nineteenth centuries Irkutsk increased in importance. It was the centre to which furs and ivory were sent from all over eastern Siberia, and it also became the forwarding place for merchandise brought from China along the great caravan route that extended from Peking across the Gobi Desert to Kyakhta on the Russian–Chinese border. Outward-bound from China, the caravans carried tea, of which the Russians consumed prodigious quantities, silk and porcelain. On the return journey they took hay for the inhabitants of the Gobi, black sables and black fox, which were used in China for trimming the robes of Mandarins, and the tusks of mammoths from the shores of the Arctic, which, the explorer Nordenskiöld wrote, 'they believed to be the tusks of the giant rat *tien-shu* ... [which] lives in dark holes in the interior of the earth', and which some Chinese *savants* believed might be the origin of earthquakes.

As a result of the establishment of this thriving trade, numbers of Chinese merchants took up residence at Irkutsk; and when they eventually died and their compatriots sent their embalmed remains back to the land of their ancestors for burial, they often filled the dead one's skull with gold dust, by the expedient of blowing it through a tube into the especially excavated brain cavity by way of the nostrils.

In the nineteenth century Irkutsk became a place of political exile. The most important group to be exiled there, and one that was to bring intellectual distinction and a certain elegance to the life of the city, was that of the Decembrists. In 1825 the Decembrists, who included among their number rich noblemen, officers of the Imperial Guard and men of good family, as well as men of letters, had been about to seize the opportunity presented by the three-week interregnum between the death of Alexander I and the accession of Nicholas I to bring about a *coup d'état*. The leaders were sentenced to death and the remainder were sentenced to exile in Siberia, with hard labour in the mines for periods of anything from ten years to life. The wives of these men, some of whom were princes and counts, almost all of them persons of taste, fortune and refinement, were allowed to follow them into exile on condition that they never returned to Russia, and many availed themselves of the opportunity.

In fact, very few of the Decembrists carried out the full sentences of hard labour that had been handed down to them. After a comparatively short time had elapsed they were allowed to take up residence in such towns as Irkutsk, Yeniseisk and Krasnoyarsk, where they built houses and created a social and intellectual life for themselves.

Perhaps the greatest burden the Decembrists had to bear was that any children born to them in Siberia were declared illegitimate, and could inherit neither their parents' names nor their titles. Nor could they ever return to Russia or claim any political rights in their place of exile. These harsh conditions prevailed for thirty years until the accession of Alexander II in 1855, when all the surviving Decembrists and their children were pardoned and allowed to return to Russia if they wished to do so. Many stayed on however.

There was a further influx of exiles into Irkutsk when a number of the 18,600 Poles arrived there upon being exiled to Siberia after they had risen against their Russian masters in 1863. Many of them, too, were members of the intelligentsia. The next wave of exiles were anarchists, nihilists and other terrorists who arrived in eastern Siberia in the second half of the nineteenth century.

The conditions of exile were much relaxed in the twentieth century when Stalin, Dzerzhinsky, Kirov, Frunze and Molotov, to name a few of the more notable protagonists of Marxism, were exiled to the Irkutsk area, from which none of them had much difficulty in escaping when they made up their minds to do so.

By the mid-nineteenth century gold had been discovered to the north and east of Irkutsk, and after a few years the place became a boom town. Fortunes were made by the owners and managers and sometimes even by single prospectors, mostly peasants and ex-convicts, who often lost them again almost instantly. The principal benefactors were the vodka distillers, owners of places of entertainment and such ancillary industries. At this time Irkutsk was a place of such conspicuous consumption that even Veblen, the inventor of the phrase, might have spared it a footnote in his book on the subject. Some citizens sent their dirty washing to London to be laundered, a round trip for it before the railway was built of a year.

Kennan met a man at Irkutsk, a Mr Butin, who had bought the largest pier glass in the world at the Great Paris Exhibition of 1878. He had eventually taken delivery of it after it had travelled halfway round the world to Nikolayevsk-on-Amur, from which port it had been taken in a specially chartered barge up the Amur and the Shilka to Nerchinsk, from where it had been taken overland to Irkutsk. This gave birth to a more entertaining version of the event. In this one a man orders a sheet of plate glass, also from the Great Paris Exhibition but one that took place ten years earlier, and had it carried all the way to Irkutsk across Europe and Asia by relays of men. When it finally arrives at the man's residence he discovers that it has been cut to the wrong size, and smashes it.

All these delightful extravagances were brought to a temporary
halt in a nice, warm day in July 1879 (by which time the population
had risen to more than 30,000) when three-quarters of the city was
burned to the ground, with the loss of 100 stone buildings and 3500
wooden ones, including eight churches of various denominations,
two synagogues, five bazaars, the customs house and the meat
market, leaving 24,000 people homeless.

But in spite of this setback, the city soon rose again, phoenix-
like from its ashes, with a far larger quota of splendid buildings,
this time built of brick and stone, and the conspicuous consumption was continued with renewed gusto.

We all liked Irkutsk, including Mischa. He seemed happy there,
almost relaxed. To me its inhabitants had a more insouciant, less
purposeful air than those of Novosibirsk, and certainly they were
more relaxed than the Muscovites. It was as if their sheer physical
distance from the capital, more than 3200 miles away to the west,
had, figuratively speaking, enabled them to break the shackles that
bound them to Mother Russia in Europe: shackles in which so
many of their forefathers had actually arrived there and which, again
figuratively speaking, were still so palpable in Moscow that often
I was surprised not to hear clanking sounds as its citizens moved
through the streets. At Irkutsk even the man from the local branch
of The Agency was fun and as we walked through the streets
together, lugging Otto's tripod, he used to utter strange ventriloquial
noises which caused the Irkutskians, who included large numbers
of Buryats, to brake suddenly in their tracks and wheel round like
London taxis in order to see what monstrous thing was pursuing
them.

And there were to be, I was glad to find, none of those long ses-
sions round the boardroom tables with the *mineralnye vodi* (mineral
water), which we were soon to discover was not a drink at all but
a diabolical secret weapon, infinitely more evil in its intention and
consequences than any nerve gas.

On our first night in Irkutsk, having grown tired of vodka, and
anyway with no way of acquiring a bottle, I chose to open our one
and only bottle of Scotch malt whisky, a half litre of Grant's Glen-

fiddich. After having a shot of this delectable drink we decided to
replace what we had drunk with a small quantity of the *mineralnye
vodi*, in order to eke out the supply. Later that evening when I decided to have another shot I found that the entire contents of the
bottle had turned into a jet black, undrinkable fluid, of use possibly
to embalmers in pursuit of their craft, but to no one else.

Instead of boardrooms we were taken to some museums and to
the Irkutsk Fur Base, which handles the furs trapped in an area
of eastern Siberia measuring three and a half million square miles.
Of the museums one of the best was at the Institute of Agriculture.
The exhibits included a gigantic black bear which had been shot
by our guide, who was the resident taxidermist, examples of *Cervus
elephus siberius* and *Moshus moshiferus*, large and small sorts of
Siberian deer, and a bird said to be of the chicken family which
was more like an over-inflated turkey and of which I failed to catch
the name. Perhaps I dreamt it. There was even a stuffed wolf, the
only wolf I saw in the whole of Siberia.

We also saw the School of Trapping, where Yuri Glinsky, who
taught this art, was instructing a band of men who were learning
to be professional hunters in the setting of traps and snares and in
the use of the 28 calibre micro-rifle, the weapon preferred by the
hunters as the projectiles make only small holes in the skins. There
were cages with portcullises which fell when the animals entered
them, traps made with logs of wood which clonked them on the
head, others that were nothing more than egg-shaped holes in the
earth baited with live mice (not available for demonstration pur-
poses), traps equipped with cross-bows which drove bolts through
them, and multiple snares. With all this lethal apparatus lying
around unsprung in the *taiga* it was little wonder that The Agency
was reluctant to let us loose in it, and they never did.

The Fur Base was situated in a dreary-looking grey building out
on the road to Lake Baikal. It turned over 800,000 skins a year. The
skins were inside out and looked like date boxes, and they were
sorted into six categories of excellence by calm-looking females. It
was not exciting work but it was quiet, rather like the workroom
of a couture house, and better than working in the Shelekhov
Aluminium Plant which we saw later and which stretches for

miles along the bank of the Angara, southwards of Irkutsk, where the workers were covered from head to foot in alumina (oxide of aluminium).

There were forty sorts of sable at the Fur Base, and the best of all were very dark with flecks of black in them. There were also silver and red sables. The finest of all were from Barguzin, a closely guarded, one-time Imperial reserve on the north-east shores of Lake Baikal, which cost 100 rubles a skin (the prices quoted being those paid by the Base to the trapper, augmented by a 10 per cent handling charge). A full length coat of Barguzin sables cost £100,000, and one of the few examples in existence is owned by Queen Elizabeth who got it from Russia with love. Another is the property of Valentina Tereshkova, the first woman cosmonaut, who must find it a nice change from a space suit. The lowest priced sables were 40 rubles.

There were mounds of skins: wild dog from the Amur at 15 rubles a skin, and water rat, warm and weatherproof, the favourite among the local Siberians, of which 200 skins were needed to make a coat. There were squirrel (80 skins to a coat) at between 3 and 4 rubles a skin, ermine and fox (10–15 and 40–46 rubles), arctic wolf (25 rubles), ranch and wild mink (the wild variety 36 rubles), arctic fox (75–100 rubles), prairie fox, (6 rubles) and, at the bottom of the scale, white hare, used for children's coats (half a ruble a skin). A lot of these skins would be sold at the Leningrad and London auctions.

As we were leaving, Chief Engineer Alexander Komov, who was in charge of the base, presented Wanda with the extreme tip of the tail of one of the half-ruble white hare skins. 'Ask him if he can spare it,' Wanda said to Mischa. 'I would hate him to be short for London and Leningrad.'

I liked Irkutsk best in the early morning. I used to go out around five-thirty when the air was still so cold that my breath smoked like a steam engine. At this hour the city was deserted, and it would remain so for another hour and a half, except for the lady sweepers wielding their brooms and chewing gum, a few athletes jogging along the embankment of the Angara, one or two rude looking little dogs and swarms of small birds which chattered away to one another

among the branches of the poplar and maple trees which gave a
sylvan air to the streets. And when the sun came up behind the
spire of the Roman Catholic church, whose only support now that
it was closed was a scaffolding of timber, and shone down on to
the domes of the Spasskaya, the Church of the Saviour, the Cathedral of the Epiphany in what had formerly been Gorodsk Square,
and the Znamensky Convent, they looked like golden fungi growing
in the springtime of the world. Next to the cathedral was what
had been, until the Revolution, the Nicholas I High School for
Young Ladies. If Baedeker had got its location right it was now a
bakery.

On a Sunday morning we visited the convent. The church was
dedicated to the Apparition of Our Lady. Ladders had been erected
and men were high up on the roofs whitewashing the walls of the
tower and the belfry while one was at a dizzy height on a long ladder
which had been erected against the spire, cleaning the cross while
clouds of swifts whirled about him.

Inside the porch there was an old lady asking alms and a formidable one was guarding the door. The church was crowded with
people of all ages. The officiating prelate was a youngish man
dressed in gold brocade and a pearl grey mitre studded with bril-
liants. His assistants were in bronze coloured satin. The singing was
impressive. Ikons were on sale, some of them quite costly, and
Wanda bought the most expensive one, a mass-produced item with a
printed image of Christ in a tin frame. It cost five rubles, and was
Russian-made. The mind boggled at the thought of an ikon factory
run by Communists. Yet there undoubtedly was one. Truly, this
was a remarkable country.

Near the church were the tombs of Princess Yekaterina Trubetskaya, wife of an exiled Decembrist, the first wife of a conspirator
to accompany her husband into exile, and those of her three children; and behind the apse, crowned by an obelisk with his likeness
carved on a marble medallion, was the tomb of the redoubtable but
cruel merchant-explorer Grigory Shelekhov, who in 1784 established a fur-trading post on Kodiak Island off Alaska, the coasts
of which Bering had discovered forty-three years earlier. Shelekhov,
who often on his journeys used a skin canoe which is preserved in

the Museum of History and Ethnography, was one of the pro-
ponents of the Russian-American Company, founded by Paul I in
1799, who gave it the monopoly of hunting and mining on the North
American seaboard north of latitude 55°.

I discovered that behind the brick and stone buildings put up
before and after the great fire, which embraced an astonishing
variety of architectural styles from the cool, neoclassical splendour
of the White House – the residence of the tsarist governors of eastern
Siberia – to the dignified dottiness of what had been the premises
of the Russo-Asiatic Bank, there were whole networks of streets of
chocolate-coloured single- and two-storey wooden houses, a few
with their original raised sidewalks of wooden planks. Some of the
two-storey houses with their carriage gates and courtyards were like
little palaces, and had been built with such delicacy that all that
seemed to be needed was one good gust of wind to carry them away.
Others, with walls built with what appeared to be whole trunks of
trees, resembled the *izbas* of the Siberian countryside and were so
heavy that one end or the other had sunk into the earth giving them
the appearance of sinking ships. Nearly all of them, large and small,
had beautifully carved baroque window frames. Most fantastic of
all were the houses built with shingles. On these, the eaves, the
barge-boards, the porches and every other imaginable appendage
that could be decorated, all of which were of Siberian cedar, had
been so extravagantly fretworked that some of them were more air
than timber.

Looking at these houses with their window frames outlined in
green and white or blue, colours that the Russians use with genius,
it was difficult to know in the early morning whether the single-
storey ones, which had their heavy shutters closed and barred, were
occupied or evacuated and waiting for the demolishers to move in.
One either had to wait until later, around seven o'clock, when the
chimneys of the wood stoves began to belch smoke and the occupants came out wearing black felt slippers to let down the iron bars,
or go round the back where, if anyone was still in residence, there
would usually be a well-tended vegetable plot. Even when the shutters were folded back these houses were still secretive, their windows
so crammed with pots of geraniums and begonias that however hard

THE PARIS OF SIBERIA

I tried I could never see much more than the top of a cupboard and an old fashioned fringed lampshade sheltering a 40-watt bulb.

The demolishers were everywhere at work and in some places entire streets of houses were in process of destruction, either by being knocked down and the timbers burnt or by being set on fire while still standing, which could be done quite easily if they were sufficiently isolated from all houses that were not yet scheduled for destruction. Soon they would be replaced, as they had been in many other parts of the city, by apartment blocks.

I asked the chief of The Agency at Irkutsk why the authorities were destroying these beautiful and apparently sound buildings. 'Because', he said, 'they are full of bed-bugs; because they cannot be adapted for steam central heating and because they are not appropriate for modern, Soviet citizens.' And he went on to try to distract my attention from this subject, about which he knew that I felt strongly, by uttering some of his ventriloquial calls. 'Listen Ivan,' I said, 'when I was a sailor before the war I fed more bed-bugs than you will ever see in your life; but that was nearly forty years ago. There's been a lot of progress in the anti-bed-bug field. If you Russians are too busy fooling about in outer space to order up some bug killer why don't you ask the World Health Organization to do posterity a favour by presenting you with a few hundred thousand tons of the stuff. Don't you ever think of your patrimony?' 'We think of our patrimony,' Ivan said, 'but we don't think of it in the same way that you do.'

'Well, you'd better start thinking in the same way,' I said, 'or we'll have bed-bugs on the moon.'

13

A Short Trip
to a Sanatorium

We have really beautiful and effective hydroelectric stations in Sweden
but we willingly recognize that Bratsk Hydroelectric Station is grand in
every respect.

> Group of tourists from Sweden
> Per Bergmak
> Straffak Scott (head)

We arrived with the idea to visit your hydroelectric station and were very
much astounded to see that this huge structure combines the might of
a giant industrial plant with the splendour of a palace.

> Yves de Coque
> Professor, Belgium

From the visitors' book in the hydroelectric station at the Bratsk High
Dam, printed in the Official Guide.

'TOMORROW', Mischa announced in the special voice reserved for
good news, 'we shall go to Bratsk, to see the High Dam.'

None of us really wanted to go to Bratsk, except Mischa, who
presumably wanted it for the piece he was writing and because for
any good Communist the sight of this phenomenon locked away
in the *taiga* 300 miles north of Irkutsk induces a state of ecstasy
similar to that produced by the first sight of Mecca on a Muslim.

To me dams are impressive while they are being built and the
workers are still ramming the piles in. They are also memorable
when they burst, when they constitute 'a story'. When they are finally finished, after all the trials and tribulations, and when the turbines begin to turn, they tend to look rather small – that is, unless

they are 550 feet high, like the Grand Coulee on the Columbia River, in which case they just look dangerous. Worst of all, they form what are to me hideous lakes behind them.

'The trouble with dams', Otto said, 'is that for a photographer they're so self-conscious.'

'Did you know', I said, opening the *Guinness Book of Records*, which I had brought with me for just such a crisis as this, 'that the world's largest concrete dam, and the largest concrete structure in the world, is the Grand Coulee Dam on the Columbia River, Washington State, USA?'

'Did *you* know,' said Mischa, quoting from memory with the effortless ease with which any Soviet citizen worth his salt can recall the superlatives of his country and even the figures down to the last digit without recourse to the *Guinness Book of Records*, 'that the four largest hydroelectric plants in the world are in the Soviet Union and that the largest of these are at Krasnoyarsk and Bratsk, and that Bratsk has more than double the kilowattage of Grand Coulee, and Krasnoyarsk has more than three times the kilowattage of Grand Coulee, which is only the world's fifth largest plant? And did you know that when the plant at Sayano–Shushensk on the Yenisei goes into operation it will produce 6,400,000 kilowatts which will be 304,000 kilowatts more than Krasnoyarsk and 4,375,000 kilowatts more than the Grand Coulee?'

'Did *you* know,' I said, having found what I thought was a face-saver on page 158, 'that "the ultimate long-term planned kilowattage of the Grand Coulee will be 9,771,000 kW with the completion of the 'Third Powerplant' (capacity 7,200,000 kW)"?'

'Your book doesn't say when that will be,' said Mischa.

'Well, it doesn't say when the Sayano–Shushensk plant is going to be working either,' I said, but I knew I'd lost.

'You should have a more up-to-date book of records. This one is of 1973. Besides, you should also visit the Bratsk Sea, the biggest man-made sea in the world, the city of Bratsk, which has 184,000 inhabitants, the aluminium plant, the wood-chemical cellulose complex which produces the largest amount of wood pulp in the Soviet Union and one-sixth of all the cellulose, and the Cossack town built there in 1631.'

We went to Bratsk. I only hope that The Agency appreciates what a treasure it has in Mischa.

We flew there in a TU 104A which had a lavatory with a sofa in it on the starboard side, after waiting around in a weird, ochrous airport building with corridors full of nickel-plated hat stands for long enough to order some runny fried eggs which we were unable to eat because as soon as they arrived the flight was announced – the best way to precipitate a journey is to order food.

The weather was bad, with ragged streamers of smoking cloud spread across the horizon where violent rain squalls were taking place and clouds overhead like porridge. Below us was some evil-looking *taiga* with the long rides made by the lumbermen stretching away through it as if for ever, interspersed with green and ploughed fields and an occasional lake. Soon we climbed through the cloud and there was nothing to be seen except for an apple-green sky banded with cirrus.

In an hour we came down through the murk over the Bratsk Sea and landed on an airfield hacked out of endless forests of pine and larch, a tree that can grow 65 feet in 85 years to a foot in diameter, live for 600 years, is resistant to rot, and in the USSR is used for making everything from coffins to houses: forests so full of furry creatures, including bears, that when the Bratskians enter them they usually take a gun.

It was cold for the time of year, 23°F, with a nasty wind. In England by this time, if it was a normal summer, women would be out in their bikinis.

As soon as we got to the airport building Mischa announced that we would have to go back to Irkutsk. Apparently the weather was worsening (which seemed a good reason for *not* flying), and if we were held up in Bratsk for the night we would miss the *Rossiya*, which we were due to board the following morning. We refused to leave, having been brought here more or less against our wills, and one of those scenes followed over which I draw a veil. We stayed on at Bratsk.

Whoever chose the site for the Bratsk High Dam was some picker. It stands in the rapids of the Padun Gorge at a point where the gorge is 500 yards wide and flanked by cliffs nearly 300 feet high, between which the Angara races down towards the Yenisei and the Kara Sea. In winter the gorge is choked with ice. There were no roads to the outside world through the *taiga* and the only amenities were provided by a small hamlet, isolated from the outside world except by water, which was all that remained of the *ostrog* founded by the Cossack hetman, Maxim Perfiliev, when he and his band reached this point, also by water, in 1631.

There are only eighty days in the whole year when the temperature rises above freezing; while in summer it shoots up to 95°F (35°C), and then the *taiga* becomes an inferno swarming with midges, mosquitoes and the deadly *clesh*, whose bite causes encephalitis and against which the present inhabitants are inoculated. In summer it is impossible to enter the *taiga* without wearing protective netting and to have even a snack in the open air means ingesting a main course of insects.

Before work could begin on this ambitious and seemingly crazy project it was first necessary to build a hydroelectric plant at Irkutsk. The power station came into operation in 1966, some years after the scheduled date; but it was not until three years later that all its turbines came into full operation, during which time it was working at 25 per cent of its capacity, a delay that caused great financial loss. This was because there were not enough industrial plants in the region to make use of its potential and because it had not been possible to link the station with any outlets to the west. Even when the trunk transmission line to Krasnoyarsk was completed it used only half of its capability.

These setbacks gave rise to serious criticism among members of the *apparat*, which revolved around the question of whether the complex should have been built at the Padun Rapids at all, a question to which Khruschev, who had been one of the principal advocates of the site, referred in a speech that he made in 1961 after a visit to it, many years before it was completed.

'We built it quickly but the electric power consumers that the station will require do not exist on the spot,' he said. 'The construction of this station will give us the possibility of processing timber here and constructing chemical and aluminium plants. But all that would also have been possible in Uzbekistan and Tadzhikistan. Moreover, the climatic conditions are better there....'

It was not until about 1971, after the aluminium plant had been built, that Bratsk really began to give value for money. Today it also provides the energy for a smelting works which uses iron ore mined in the area and at Zheleznogorsk, east of Bratsk and the Ilim River, where the mountains are solid iron, with which it is linked by the BAM Railway from Taishet on the Trans-Siberian line. It also powers a wood-chemical plant which produces sulphate, cellulose, newsprint, paperboard, rosin and industrial yeast from what is virtually an inexhaustible source of timber.

We stood on a platform at the foot of the intake dam. It rose from the rock floor of what had been the Padun Rapids, 400 feet above it, half a mile of pale concrete with the power house below, the most vital part of the three-mile-long retaining walls. Along the top of it, invisible from where we stood, there was a highway and the BAM Railway from Taishet which would eventually be connected with the Pacific.

There was not a human being in sight, which was not surprising as at any one time there are not more than ten persons on duty. The only sounds were those made by the waters of the Angara as they seethed out through the turbine exits on their way from their sources, the 300 or more streams and rivers that feed Lake Baikal, some humming noises and the wind in the trees. Behind us on an artificial plateau a couple of big diesel engines were moving a 300-ton transformer on a 16-axle carriage out of the electric switch-yards and on to the Taishet spur for an overhaul.

At the foot of the dam was the generating station, as lofty inside as the nave of a cathedral, if one could imagine a cathedral that long with a floor clean enough to eat breakfast off if we had been offered one. In it an electric counter decorated with a plaque of Lenin announced that up to this time, around 11 am on 6 June 1977, the power house had produced 290,908 million kilowatts of electricity, all of which had been consumed.

Behind this fragile barrier was the largest and deepest artificially impounded reservoir in the world, the filling of which had sunk an unspecified number of dwellings and displaced 70,000 people from

Outing on Lake Baikal. Wanda, wearing loaned 'outing' hat, is second from left in front row

The house of a forest guard and his wife near the Angara River

Village boy,
Listvyanka

Bratsk

Siberian baby on a
station awaiting
onward
transportation

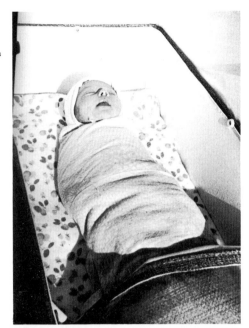

Exponents of free
enterprise on a
station

Rossiya entering guarded tunnel in the Primorskiy Range south of Irkutsk

Girls in Ulan Ude

Village boys in
Transbaikalia

Backyard in the
Selenga Delta

Fishermen at Oymur, Lake Baikal

Nikolay Tserendashyev, Chairman of the Banner of Lenin Collective Farm

The *Rossiya* east of the Yablonovyy Range

A church in the wilderness on the bank of the Ingoda River

Tikhookeanskaya (Pacific Ocean) Station, Nakhodka. End of the line for a loot-laden Japanese struggling to join the good ship *Baikal* about to sail for Yokohama

their homes, none of whom had had the opportunity of writing to *Pravda* about it. Upstream was Lake Baikal, a great volcanic rift in the earth's surface which was only awaiting an appropriate moment to blow its cork out and sweep away Irkutsk, and the dam, the end product of the labours of 54,000 heroic men and women: a capacity it had demonstrated on the last day of December 1861, when a comparatively minor tremor had shaken samovars, rung church bells over a wide area on the shores of the lake and drowned 1300 people. It didn't look particularly big, the dam, but it was holding up a lot of water in a land where man-made objects look like the work of pygmies.

'I still don't think it's anything photographically,' Otto said. 'It's just like the dining car of the *Rossiya*. However hard you try you end up with a set of pictures for a hand-out by Intourist.' He was dead right, and leaving it more or less unphotographed we went away.

Time was short, as Mischa assured us, and it continued to be short during our entire time in Siberia, whenever we were off the train; so we set off at a crazy speed along the top of the dam, across a stretch of road that was being done up, full of lorries loaded with muck, and past a highly photographable colony of little wooden *dachas*, some of them with wood stoves in their gardens, which Otto clicked away at through the window, cursing the driver who betrayed a disinclination to stop.

Both to Otto and myself, two men with a highly developed sense of direction, it was obvious that we were journeying towards the east. The city of Bratsk was to the west.

'Where are you taking us, Mischa?' Otto said, once we had passed the *dachas*. 'Surely Bratsk is the other way.'

'We are going to inspect a cardio-vascular sanatorium,' he said. 'It is on the shores of the Bratsk Sea. There we shall have lunch with the director and there will be opportunities for photography and conversation with the patients. Few foreigners have been there. There is no time to go to Bratsk city. It is now 1.45 and we have to be at the airport at three.'

'Listen, Mischa,' said Otto, using the words 'Listen, Mischa' which we all used when addressing this unfortunate man if anything showed signs of beginning to go wrong. 'If you think I've come all the way into the depths of Siberia lugging all this equipment to visit a sanatorium when there's a city with 184,000 inhabitants round the corner buried in the *taiga*, you've got it all wrong. I need to get close to some human beings who are doing something – digging holes, pushing prams – not just sitting on a terrace.'

I had never seen him so angry since Mischa had needled him about the Jews.

'You will have, as I have told you already, the opportunity to photograph the patients, and the sanatorium. We cannot turn back now, all is arranged.'

It was true. As we drove up the drive we could see the patients neatly disposed on the steps, men and women who on closer inspection proved to be Russians, Ukrainians, Buryats, Evenks and others, members of tribes it has so far been impossible to identify, even with the aid of photographs – all in their best clothes and wearing badges and medals that they had been awarded in the course of a life of toil. They gave us a warm welcome. They seemed as glad to see us, as I would have been glad to see them if they had decided to visit me in a cardio-vascular sanatorium on the shores of the Bratsk Sea, coming into summer with the midges and the mosquitoes and the deadly *clesh* already warming up for take-off. I felt ashamed of the thoughts that Otto and I had harboured about visiting them.

Twenty minutes later we were on the way to the city of Bratsk, or one of them, because altogether there are a number of Bratsk satellites. We had only managed it by forgoing lunch. I must say the director looked quite pleased. If, as Mischa had said, it was rare for foreigners to visit his establishment, which in Russia always provided the excuse for a good spread, there would be no lack of other guests to replace us.

Mad with hunger, and at the disposal of what we had long ago recognized to be a mad driver, we howled westwards in the direction of Bratsk, over the dam and into the *taiga*, on a road that had cost over a million rubles a mile to build and was costing who knows how much annually to maintain. On the way we had a fleeting glimpse of the cellulose factory, smoking away on the shores of the

Bratsk Sea. I wondered what damage it was doing to its waters. Mischa said it was under control, whatever that meant. No one I ever met in Siberia seemed interested in the problems of pollution. It was something that happened to other places in other countries. In a sense I sympathized with the Siberians. Siberia was so big, nature so much in the ascendant, that it seemed impossible that there was anything man could do to harm it.

The outskirts of Bratsk was a vast hive of tall apartment blocks: concrete cells from which the workers were absent, gathering pollen elsewhere. They were uncanny, Orwellian dwellings years before their time, rising from sites hacked and bulldozed out of the *taiga*. The centre was less inhuman, the scale of the buildings more acceptable. It could have been the centre of a new town in the English Midlands. Heroic male workers wearing trilbies and car coats were pushing prams.

After five minutes in the main square of Bratsk, Mischa announced that we would have to leave instantly. At 3.15 pm we reached the airport where we waited one-and-three-quarter hours for the plane to take off for Irkutsk. It had certainly been a memorable day.

14

The Way to Transbaikalia

HAVING said goodbye to Irkutsk, the Paris or Pearl of Siberia, and having carefully avoided falling into the open grave outside the railway station, we boarded the *Rossiya*, now on the sixth morning of its journey from Moscow, and at 3.19 am, (8.19 am in Irkutsk, in the fifth time zone from Moscow) we were whirled away in the general direction of Vladivostok which was now only 2566 miles and by my reckoning fifty stops to the east.

As if to confirm that the journey was not yet over, on the outskirts of the city we passed over a level crossing where there was a kilometre post which indicated that we were now 5205 kilometres from the western extremity of the Russian railway system and exactly halfway from it to Vladivostok, 5204 kilometres down the line.

We were now travelling in what was relative and unaccustomed discomfort, owing to someone having fouled up the embarkation arrangements. As a result of this Wanda and I found that we were to share a four-berth compartment with two large, elderly Siberian ladies, while Otto and Mischa had drawn two equally extensive men. Both parties were unrouseable to discuss these problems, sunk in the sort of sleep that comes of believing that it is 3.19 in the morning and not 8.19, so we decided to take over a four-berth compartment in the next car – on the Trans-Siberian Railway, as in war, it is better to be with people one knows – and this we did, in spite of the conductress who told Mischa it was against the regulations and got huffy. In it we played an unrehearsed vaudeville act, entitled 'Fun in a Sleeping Car', which lasted for 8 hours and 13 minutes, the time it took to reach our next stopping-off point, Ulan-Ude, using props that included every piece of luggage we possessed and Otto's tripod, which he insisted on erecting on the grounds that he might not be passing this way again.

The *Rossiya* was heading into the Primorskiy Range, which here separates Irkutsk from the western end of Lake Baikal, at first running close to the River Irkut as it wound down to join the Angara from its source near the Mongolian border, and for a short while following the main road into Transbaikalia. Then it turned up a small tributary of the Irkut, here running through meadows in which birch trees were rippling in the breeze and where there were large villages with big stacks of timber in them, brought down from the forests of pine and fir and Siberian cedar high above this winding valley, which grew progressively wilder with patches of old snow among the outcrops of rock. Meanwhile we nibbled at delicious little cakes covered with sugar and raisins, sold to us by the conductress who had suddenly thawed out, called *romavaya baba* (Roman woman).

In the early days of the Trans-Siberian rolling stock had crossed Lake Baikal on ferries; then in 1900 a railroad had been built round the southern edge of the lake. But this 80-mile long section on which we were travelling between Irkutsk and Slyudyanka was completed only in 1956. It was built to replace the Circumbaikal Loop which followed the left bank of the Angara to Port Baikal, at the point where the river flowed out of the lake. This line to Port Baikal became unusable when the building of the Irkutsk Hydroelectric Plant raised the water level.

The Circumbaikal Loop was begun in 1900. It was the work of thousands of Russian, Italian, Turkish and Persian labourers who were kept in order by Circassian guards. The Loop line continued for 50 miles along the side of sheer cliffs above the lake to Kultuk at its south-western end. In the space of three years they cut thirty-three tunnels through the cliffs and built more than 200 bridges and innumerable embankments – all this on a coast exposed to fearful storms and blizzards.

Only slightly less difficult to build than the cliff section was the first 42 miles along the left bank of the Angara River, which was inaccessible from the landward side, where gorges, rock falls, bays and tributary rivers were some of the obstacles. This 42-mile section took four years to build. Meanwhile other gangs constructed the easier section between the ferry port of Mysovaya and Tankhoy on the far side of the lake.

Until the completion of the Circumbaikal Loop, Port Baikal on the north-west shore was the terminus of a ferry which carried the rolling stock across the lake to Mysovaya on the far shore. The contract for the first of these train ferries, which also had to be an ice-breaker, had been signed by Prince Khilkov, the then Minister of Ways and Communications, at the end of December 1895. The contractors were a British firm, Sir W. G. Armstrong, Mitchell and Company.

The *Baikal*, as she was later named, was a four-funnelled vessel, 290 feet long, with a beam of 57 feet. The hull was constructed with inch-thick steel plating, reinforced internally with two-foot thick timber sheathing. Propulsion was provided by three triple expansion steam engines, developing 3750 horse power, which drove two steel propellers and a bronze forescrew in the bows capable of breaking through ice up to four feet thick, and it had fifteen boilers which burned wood fuel. The engines, boilers, water-pumping machinery and some other items were made at St Petersburg.

The work of building the *Baikal* at Newcastle-upon-Tyne took a year and every part was stamped with an identifying number. When it was finally completed it was taken to pieces, packed up and sent to St Petersburg where all the components were again divided up, this time into 7000 separate packages, for the immense journey across European Russia and Siberia to the lake.

At Krasnoyarsk the great bridge over the Yenisei had not yet been completed and there the whole consignment had to be offloaded and shipped down the Yenisei and up the Angara by barge and sledge, a distance of well over 1000 miles, which involved unloading everything at the rapids and making portages.

The first parcels began to arrive at Listvyanka, a small port across the Angara from Port Baikal, towards the end of 1897, but piecemeal, so that parts of engines turned up before the keel. It was a miracle that nothing of importance was lost *en route*.

At Listvyanka a marine engineer and four foremen from the Tyne were waiting to rebuild the ship, together with a force of Russian workmen, some of whom had been sent from St Petersburg.

The *Baikal* was finally launched at the end of July 1899, almost four years after her keel was first laid at the British yard. Even then she still lacked her fifteen wood-burning boilers, which had been held up at Krasnoyarsk for two years awaiting the completion of the bridge. When she finally went into service, in April 1900, she had a displacement of 4250 tons and drew 20 feet. Meanwhile dock facilities had been built for her at Port Baikal and Mysovaya.

No one in Siberia had seen anything like this huge, slab-sided, gleaming white vessel. Three lines of track were laid on her main deck to accommodate the carriages of an entire train, or 25 loaded flat cars. There were staterooms, first- and second-class cabins, deck accommodation for more than 600 third-class passengers, a sumptuous restaurant, crew accommodation and a chapel in which it became fashionable for Irkutskians to get married. Another, smaller, vessel, the *Angara*, had meanwhile been commissioned from the same firm and in the autumn of 1901 it too arrived at the lake in pieces and was reassembled there. Unfortunately, the experts had miscalculated the depths to which the lake was capable of freezing and it was soon discovered that the only way in which the *Angara* could operate in winter was for the *Baikal*, which had to be without a train on board, to charge the ice ahead of her and force a passage. In severe weather both vessels became ice-bound and then the train passengers had to cross the ice in sledges. Even in the summer months the ships were often immobilized for days on end by fog.

In February 1904, while both ships were ice-bound in a temperature of −40°F, the Japanese launched their surprise attack on the Russian Fleet at Port Arthur and it became imperative that the military reinforcements that were being rushed to the east, and which were piling up at Port Baikal, together with all their trains loaded with war material, should be able to continue their journey.

It was now that Prince Khilkov put into operation a plan that his Ministry had toyed with years before and then rejected, which was to lay a track across the ice, which that winter was five feet thick, using extra long sleepers to spread the load. An experiment was made using a test engine, which suddenly plunged into the depths owing to the existence of unsuspected warm springs beneath the surface. It made a hole in the ice almost five feet wide and more than 14 miles long. After this disaster engines were dismantled and, with their component parts loaded on to flat cars, were dragged across the ice by huge teams of men and horses, while the army marched, or travelled in sledges, if they were lucky – a seventeen-hour journey on foot across the ice with halts at huts set up at intervals. In this way thousands of men with their munitions, dozens of locomotives and thousands of flat cars crossed the 25-mile expanse of ice to Tankhoy on the southern shore of the lake, where they were able to resume their journey by the railway.

In the meantime the contractors and their huge, cosmopolitan labour force were working flat out in the $-40°F$ weather to complete the cliff section of the Circumbaikal Loop between Port Baikal and Kultuk; and in September 1904 they succeeded. It is true that the first test train to run over the route was derailed ten times in the 50-mile cliff section and took three days to cover the entire route, and that Prince Khilkov's inaugural train, which passed over it a week or so later, was also derailed; but the latter was only derailed once, and the whole work must be regarded as a triumph.

The only loser was Khilkov himself, the man who had not only initiated the construction of the line, but had succeeded in forwarding an entire marooned army to the Far East in impossible conditions. He was later sacked by the Finance Minister, Count Sergius Witte, on the grounds that 'he was not administrator enough to be equal to his ministerial tasks'. Perhaps Witte was disturbed by the cost of the Circumbaikal Loop and the ferries, something like fifty million pounds, out of which the ferries alone had cost about £690,000, about twice as much as had been budgeted for. The cost was not surprising. By the time the *Baikal* reached the shores of the lake, with customs duty added – a strange imposition in such circumstances – and the transportation charges to the lake, her original price had been augmented by 129 per cent.

After the completion of the Circumbaikal Loop both ships still continued in service, but as passenger steamers. The *Baikal* was destroyed during the Civil War. The *Angara* survived and we caught a fleeting glimpse of her, anchored in a bay of the river, while on our way to visit Port Baikal.

Port Baikal still continues to function as a seaport and as a terminal station on the cliff-hanging line from Kultuk. It is a ghostly place with a long, wooden station house embellished with mansard roofs, the remains of its ferry facilities and sidings, in which very ancient and austere passenger cars with wooden sleeping berths (which were nothing more than wooden planks) were decaying gently: reminders of a once-flourishing place on the shores of Lake Baikal.

At around 5 am Moscow time, the *Rossiya* panted up over the watershed of the Primorskiy Range and began running down through the forests on the Baikal side, through a series of hairpin bends round which a succession of big freight trains – one every four minutes – were being hauled and punched, each by four diesels, up what are the steepest gradients on the entire Trans-Siberian Railway, raising great clouds of dust behind them. Then the *Rossiya* roared into the first of two sets of heavily guarded tunnels, the first tunnels we had passed through since leaving Moscow, now more than 3300 miles away; and a few minutes later the snow-covered peaks of the Khamar Daban Range on the south side of the lake could be seen. Then, through the haze that shrouded everything, all of a sudden, stupendous, unearthly, ethereal like a great golden bowl with the morning mists rising from it, appeared the lake itself.

But although that morning Lake Baikal possessed an unearthly, shimmering beauty, it was not always like that. When a wind called the *sarma* blows from the north-west, which it does for almost 100 days a year, with a velocity of anything up to 80 miles an hour, it raises a nasty, short sea up to seven feet high.

Almost all that I now knew about it was the result of a fascinating morning spent at the Limnological Institute of the Siberian Academy of Science at Listvyanka. It contains within it the biggest volume of fresh water anywhere on earth, one-sixth (16 per cent) of all the fresh water in the world.

Down in its depths (the deepest of which is the 6365-foot Olkhon Crevice) at between 700 and 1600 feet, where the temperature is a comfortable 38°F – they die at around 45°F – live two varieties of fish called *golomianka*. The *dracunculus* (*Comephorus baicalensis*) is the largest of the two, being about eight inches long. These fish have pop-eyes, rather like huge car headlights, set in a head that is a third of their entire length. Being confronted by one of them for the first time, standing upright in a bottle of alcohol at the Institute and staring insanely at me, was a most disturbing experience. Each autumn the females, being viviparous, instead of laying eggs produce about 2000 ready-to-swim progeny. When they die male and female both sink to the bottom, where they add to the silt which in places is estimated to be up to 5000 feet thick, a study of which has enabled Soviet scientists to establish a claim that this tectonic depression, formed in the Tertiary era, 25 million years ago, is the oldest lake in the world.

Not all the *golomianka* end up on the bottom when they die. The females of the larger variety come to the surface where, if they are washed ashore, being nothing much more than a backbone encased in fat, designed to live at extreme pressures, they melt or burst, leaving a pool of oil rich in vitamin A, held in high esteem by the Buryats, who used it as fuel for their lamps and also medicinally.

Those that are not washed up, or taken while they are floating, are eaten by the *nerpas*, the freshwater Baikal seals (*Phoca baicalensis*) of which there are thousands upon thousands, themselves a phenomenon; although they harbour parasites of Arctic origin, no one really knows how they reached the lake. The Buryats used to catch them in winter by setting horse hair nets under the ice.

Even the Baikal sturgeon is extraordinary. It takes twenty-one years to come to maturity, by which time it weighs 500 pounds and can produce up to 20 pounds of caviar – which is why, until recently, it was threatened with extinction. And there is the *omul*, a unique variety of gwyniad (*Salmo* or *Coregonus omul*), a white fish of the salmon family which cries when it is caught. In winter it is fished for through holes in the ice. Grown-up *omul* eat their young whenever a suitable opportunity presents itself. The *omul* is delicious served up in the form of *ukha*, a fish soup, or eaten raw, lightly salted, in which state it keeps for about five months.

There are also 280 varieties of shrimp-like *amphipodae* and a unique, segmented worm (*Manayukia baicalensis*). Something like 1200 of the creatures living in the lake are unique to it; and in season there are millions of *rucheiniki*, flightless, waterborne insects, which remain in a larval state for two or three years and then suddenly hatch out to live a brief life of two or three days close in to the shore, before being eaten by the *omul* who find them an acceptable alternative item of diet to their own next-of-kin.

There is also a wealth of inanimate phenomena: *bikerit*, a sort of floating wax, found on the surface of the water, which burns like naphtha and was used by the Buryats as a cure for rheumatism and scurvy – they certainly knew how to exploit what God had put to hand – and something that they called *imusha*, a liquid substance which was identified by tsarist savants as being either a kind of mineral oil (*vitroleum unctuosum*) or a broken-down form of guano produced by cormorants, herons, seagulls and other birds; it issues from a wooded ridge on the Holy Cape in the remote Barguzin region, where the finest flecked black, silver and red sables in the whole of Siberia come from. And there are four kinds of dark emerald coloured sponges (*Spongia baicalensis*, *S. bacillifera*, *S. intermedia* and *S. papiracea*), all of which have been found useful in the past, when wet for cleaning samovars, and when dry, by silversmiths, for cleaning silver.

The lake is also subject to mirage, not only by day, which is scarcely surprising, but by night. One of the more astonishing nocturnal manifestations was that of a whole train of the Trans-Siberian Railway which was observed steaming across it with all its lights on, thirty miles from its actual position on shore. Earth tremors are also frequent, producing apocalyptic rumblings and disturbing the surface of the water.

Altogether, it is not surprising that the *shamans* of the Buryats, the sometimes possessed priests of a thoroughly ununified religio-magic cult which was embraced by most of the peoples of Siberia, whether they were aboriginals or comparative newcomers, believed that the island of Ol'khon, midway up the lake off the north-west shore, was the dwelling place of the evil spirit Begozi, whom it was necessary to propitiate, as well as the site of a camp occupied by their great hero, Genghiz Khan. They also used to ask Dianda, a sea god, who appeared to them on Cape Shaman, to stop the *sarma* blowing and also to drive the *omul* close inshore. This headland is far up the lake on the north-east side, and there the water is so cold that there is often ice floating in it in July.

As soon as the *Rossiya* emerged from the mountains on to the shore of the lake the sky, which had up to now been completely cloudless, suddenly became overcast and a cold wind began to ruffle the water. It was as if the magical effects we had seen from the heights above had never happened.

Now, for more than 100 miles the line ran along the southern shore, through Slyudyanka, Tankhoy and Mysovaya, either close to the shore, which was sand or shingle and littered with the trunks of trees thrown up by gales, or through *taiga*.

Slyudyanka is a mica mining town on the shore of the lake. Because the *taiga* behind it had been denuded of trees by over-cutting, in 1960 it was partly wiped out by an avalanche of mud. Here there was a fourteen-minute halt, possibly to allow the engine to cool off before proceeding. While waiting I got into trouble with another passenger, a young army officer travelling with his family, who looked as if he ought to start cutting down on his black bread intake, for photographing some circa 1930 steam engines in an engine cemetery. After Mischa had had a row with him he became friendly with Otto. It turned out that he was an enthusiastic amateur photographer and for the next two hours he drove Otto nearly demented by showing him hundreds of examples of his own work, over-exposed transparencies with finger marks all over them, of his family (most of whom were already on view), of ghastly sunsets and of birds, some of which had already flown away, tired of waiting for him to get them in focus. To interrupt the showing of this apparently endless collection, which promised to last all the way to Ulan-Ude, Otto demonstrated the workings of his remote control apparatus by firing off a Nikon with it.

'We would not use this in the Soviet Union,' the officer said disapprovingly, realizing what Otto was up to; and he retired, hurt, to his compartment, where he sulked. The passengers on this section of the line were the most hostile to photography by foreigners we had encountered on the entire journey and there were complaints to the conductress each time Otto appeared carrying a camera, although they themselves snapped away with impunity.

'They think you are photographing the bridges,' Mischa told him.

The *Rossiya* entered the *taiga*. It stretched away dark and dense and forbidding, full of unseen, unworked coal deposits, to the icy ridges of the Khamar Daban Range in which molybdenum and wolfram were being mined. Cold, secretive-looking rivers flowed down through it into the lake. At one place, miles from any habitation, the train stopped for some minutes at a place in the forest where a gang of men were repairing a culvert, while one of their number stirred the contents of a pot which was seething over a fire and a small, blond-haired boy with a fishing rod in one hand set out plates on some planks which had been laid on the ground, preparing for a slightly overdue midday meal, for it was now 12.45, local time.

This north-facing *taiga* with rivers that freeze to the bottom, is cruel-looking country and cruel things have happened in it, though perhaps no worse than anywhere else along the railway.

What is still the only road through it was originally built by Polish exiles who had been sent on there from Irkutsk after the insurrection of 1863. In 1866 they attempted to overpower their guards (which they did, killing an officer), hoping to escape over the mountains and cross Outer and Inner Mongolia to China, where they planned to find a British ship to take them to freedom. The attempt failed and five of them were sentenced to be shot.

This section of the line, which until the building of the Circumbaikal Loop extended from the ferry port of Mysovaya to Sretensk, 500 miles or so away on the Shilka River, was in the years of the Civil War the happy hunting ground, of the Ataman, Grigory Semyonov, a half-Russian, half-Buryat, anti-Bolshevik Cossack chieftain in the pay of the Japanese who were hoping, in the state of chaos that prevailed throughout Siberia, to annex Russia's eastern empire for themselves.

Semyonov (whose day, in his own estimation, did not begin until he had killed at least one human being with his own hands), his deputy, the equally vile General Ivan Kalymokov, and a sadistic entourage that included a Colonel Sipailov and a Captain Grant, who had Scottish antecedents, commuted up and down the railway in Transbaikalia in armoured trains, with names such as *The Destroyer* and *The Merciless*, together with their band of Cossack,

Buryat and other Mongolian ruffians, looting the villages along the line and torturing, raping and murdering. In winter they poured water over their prisoners turning them into icy statues from which limbs could be broken off, as mementoes of their visits. In January 1920, at a place near Kyakhta, the old tea caravan town on the Russian side of the Chinese border, Semyonov and his men executed 1800 prisoners in five days, shooting, decapitating, poisoning and asphyxiating them, methods that they employed on successive days to relieve the monotony of their self-appointed task. On the fifth and final day those who remained were burned alive. All this in country in which famine and typhus were already endemic; in which every station was surrounded by the unburied dead, as they were all along the railway from Irkutsk to the Urals and beyond them.

Prince Borghese, Luigi Barzini and their driver, Ettore, in the Peking to Paris Automobile Race, found that since the building of the railway the road along the lake shore had been neglected and many bridges were down. Their progress was reduced to a snail's pace, until the Prince telegraphed to the Governor-General at Irkutsk asking him for permission to drive along the railway line. After some delay permission was granted.

The sensation of this motor journey was at first delightful. That superb, even, level, clear road was full of attraction after the ruts, the woods, and the ditches of the other. Narrow and high, this road gave one the idea of a slim line stretched over the country, of an immense, always varied, ribbon-like bridge ... The sleepers, though very near each other and covered with a layer of sand, made the car sway and gave it a motion as of a slight, gentle gallop, but if we went faster the gallop became violent and ended in a terrible jarring ... We went across numerous little bridges of the same breadth as the sleepers, without parapets, slung over deep ravines, in the depths of which we could see the foaming water through the large spaces between one sleeper and another ... The car advanced with its left wheels between the rails, and the right wheels on the outside – over the few inches of sleepers ...

They continued in this way until they reached a station where they had to abandon the line temporarily as a train from Mysovaya was signalled. Impatient to get on, they decided to continue on the road for a while but while crossing a bridge it collapsed and the car fell backwards into the bed of a torrent, ten feet deep. No one was seriously hurt, the car was relatively undamaged, and with the help of twenty Siberian peasants and the station-master they soon got it out, and continued their journey along the railway, this time narrowly avoiding being run down by a goods train.

Out in the lake, near Tankhoy, a man without a boat was standing on a rock, which barely broke the surface and was just large enough to accommodate his two feet, fishing. At Mysovaya, where the ice-breakers delivering the trains had once tied up, a funeral was in progress and the body was being carried uphill to a cemetery in a red coffin, followed by a procession of black-clad mourners.

'Got it!' said Otto, having used his motor-driven Leicaflex to record this fleeting moment. I told him he was in the wrong job. He should have been a big game hunter.

Now, once more, the line ran along the shore of the lake, on the edge of swampy *taiga*, skirting the outlying ridges of the Khamar Daban, crossing a number of streams and torrents, and a couple of rivers, and finally emerging from it into a wide steppe, the delta of the Selenga River.

Then, quite suddenly, as one had learned to expect in Siberia, the weather changed and the whole vast landscape was illuminated by a pale, silvery light: the ponds and little lakes; the villages of *izbas*, which were enlivened by the same exuberantly carved and painted window frames we had seen at Irkutsk; the white-painted fences; the clusters of bird-like counter-balance buckets rising above the wells that a Russian on the train called *zhuradl*; the blossoming fruit trees which had been evolved from cold-resistant strains by the Soviet scientist, Michurin; the long earth roads, on which little flocks of boys and girls were cycling for the fun of it, with the telephone and power poles running away alongside into the distance, and it shone on the maintains across the lake on its far shore. Suddenly, everything had become wonderful and interesting again.

At Selenga, a town on the left bank of the river, a large wood pulping plant was belching smoke into the sky, one of two on the Transbaikal shore – the other is at Baikalsk at the south-western end – which are giving a headache to conservationists who have every reason to fear that the waters of the lake, still pure and drinkable in 1977, will be polluted. Already more than 50 of the 336 streams that feed it have had their fish spawning reaches ruined by detritus from wood-chemical enterprises and lumbering operations. According to an official Russian report, even in great rivers like the Volga, the Kama, the Belaya and the Irtysh, fish life is rapidly becoming extinct.

At 11.14 am Moscow time the train slid quietly into Ulan-Ude, where it was 5.14 in the evening – time for tea.

15

The Buryats

We first met with these people a few miles on the western side of Irkutsk, and their physiognomy at once told us they belonged to a different race from any we had seen. They have large skulls, square faces, low and flat foreheads; the cheek bones are high and wide apart, the nose flat, eyes elongated, the skin swarthy and yellowish, and the hair jet black.

> Rev. Henry Lansdell. *Through Siberia*. 1881

IN those far-off days when I had kept my sauna bath tryst with Mr Oblomov, I had asked if I might be allowed to visit some of the original inhabitants of Siberia. We were being allowed to descend from the train at Ulan-Ude in the land of the Buryats, which was unusual, so I allowed myself to nurse a secret hope that I might be allowed to meet some of the natives. Might my proposals, and Mr Oblomov's suggestions, have been considered at long last? Could instructions to whisk me hither and thither in Siberia have been telegraphed through?

Just in case my luck might change, I had studied some of the details about the peoples of Siberia before I came, obtaining most of my information from an interesting – but now, unfortunately, out-of-print – book, Miss Czaplickà's *Aboriginal Siberia* and another, also out of print, *magnum opus*: *The Peoples of Siberia* by M. G. Levin and L. P. Potapov. From these three erudite anthropologists I had learnt much about the Buryats.

The origins of the Buryats, who speak a Mongolian dialect, are controversial, shrouded in mystery. According to their own folklore their original homeland was around the shores of Lake Baikal. But the *Secret Tales of the Mongols*, written in 1240, records that Genghiz Khan sent a number of expeditions to subdue the native tribes in this area. As a result they became inextricably mingled with the Mongols.

After the penetration of their territory and their subjugation by the Cossacks, the tsars exempted the Buryats from the *yasak*, the fur tribute. In 1822 the administrative reforms initiated by Speransky, the humane and far-seeing governor-general of eastern Siberia, embodied in them the Statute for the Administration of Natives, intended to protect them from exploitation by Russian traders. This led, in the case of nomadic Buryats, to the setting up of what were called 'Twelve Steppe Dumas', to which they elected their own representatives. It was unfortunate that the inertia that was characteristic of the imperial administration made the practical application of the statute largely a dead letter. Nevertheless, it remained in nominal operation until 1917.

By the time the Revolution took place the western Buryats were still, as they had been for centuries, confirmed agriculturalists, whereas at the extreme eastern end of their territory, on the Onon River, on the borders of Outer Mongolia and in other areas, they were still pastoral nomads, rearing horses, cattle, sheep and camels, and still migrating, but now only twice a year, from their summer pastures to their winter camps and back again. Between these two radically different ways of life there were subdivisions of Buryats who engaged in hunting, fishing and lumber work.

Until long after they supplied themselves with firearms, the semi-nomadic and hunting Buryats employed the bow and arrow for shooting wolves from horseback. The hunting Buryats used their primitive flintlocks for hunting squirrel, sable and ermine, but only from the middle of October, when the season opened, until the snows came. Thereafter they used traps until the season ended, at the beginning of February. Bears were smoked out of their dens and then either speared or clubbed to death. They also hunted the Siberian deer, selling the antlers to the Chinese who esteemed them for their aphrodisiac properties.

They were expert artisans, blacksmiths being held in particular religious veneration. There were also jeweller blacksmiths, who produced decorative work for the embellishment of headdresses, harnesses and weapons and who were adept at inlaying base metals with silver and gold, and in making rings. And there were saddle-makers and tanners and felt-makers, a domestic industry, the felt being used to make the covers of their yurts, or circular tents, which had a lattice frame and were the habitations of the nomads and semi-nomads all over central Asia. (The western Buryats lived in wooden huts which in form were reminiscent of the yurts.)

In winter the men wore fur robes secured by belts ornamented with copper plaques, to which they secured their flints for making fires, steel plates which were stitched to a bag decorated with steel or silver spangles. These flints were highly valued and one set could be traded for a horse. In summer their outer garments were of similar shape but made from material. Both men and women also wore goatskin coats for everyday work.

The men shaved half their heads and wore pigtails. Their hats had conical crowns. Women wore headdresses adorned with silver, coral, malachite and mother-of-pearl.

Women were chattels to be used at whim. It was about as difficult for a Buryat to get rid of his wife as it was for him to swallow a horse-fly. If he didn't want her she could be given to a near relative. Nevertheless, the rules governing the deportment of the husband in his relations with his wife were very strict. He was not allowed to dress or undress before her and he was also forbidden to invade her sleeping place, or to use indecent language in her presence.

A daughter from one family was sometimes exchanged for one of another, marrying, when she became nubile, one of the sons of the family to which she had been sent. Within the female hierarchy the mother-in-law reigned supreme. In spite of all this male Buryats were complacent enough to allow their women to marry Cossacks and other Russian settlers.

The food of the pastoral Buryats was as monotonous and off-putting as that of any other Asian nomads: mutton in summer, beef in winter, both boiled in water, generally without salt; dried curds made by boiling and fermenting milk, the thick scum taken from boiled milk; and, among the western Buryats, *salamat*, flour boiled in sour cream. And they drank tea made from bricks formed from the cheapest powdered leaves, which were a currency among them, served with milk to which salt and mutton fat had been added. Their alcoholic drink was *arkha* distilled from milk, the *kumiss* of the Mongols. The cooking was done over fires fuelled with *argols*, the sundried dung which were of four degrees of excellence: *argols* made from the dung of goats and sheep, which produced the fiercest flame; *argols* of camels, which gave less intense flame; *argols* of cattle, which were smokeless; and the *argols* of horses, which were used for fire-lighting.

Some rich men among the pastoral tribes possessed enormous numbers of animals. The English missionary, A. E. Stallybrass, who spent many years among the Buryats in the 1830s and who was one of the team who translated the whole of the Old Testament into Mongolian, said that some of them possessed as many as 6000 or 7000 sheep, 2000 head of cattle and 200 horses, while a Captain J. D. Cochrane, the author of *Narrative of a Pedestrian Journey through Russia and Siberian Tartary from the Frontiers of China to the Frozen Sea and Kamchatka*, published in 1825, wrote of a Buryat chief who owned 40,000 sheep, 10,000 horses and 3000 head of cattle, which sounds as if it might be an exaggeration.

The favourite pastimes of the Buryat men, which formed part of the spring festivals and attracted great crowds of onlookers, were archery, wrestling and horse-trotting races. Their famous dance was the *yokhor*, which they still perform. It entails forming a circle with linked arms and then moving round in it, at the same time swaying from side to side and raising the feet alternately, and chanting.

In 1920 a Far Eastern Republic was set up beyond Lake Baikal with the approval of the Japanese and with the tacit approval of the Bolsheviks, who were not in a position at that time to prevent it even if they had wanted to. This resulted in the formation of the Central-Buryat Committee of Eastern Siberia, a communist–bourgeois administration. It persisted until 1922, when it was incorporated into the RFSR as an autonomous republic, the Buryat–Mongol ASSR. In 1958 it became the Buryat ASSR. At the 1926 census the number of Buryats was 238,000. At the 1974 census, out of a total population of 834,000, the Buryats accounted for 27 per cent (225,180).

The bedroom of the Selenga Hotel at Ulan-Ude, a city that is – or was when we were there – off the Intourist route for foreigners from the West, had walls that smothered us with cream-coloured powder if we happened to brush against them. On the other hand, it had an enormous television set which produced programmes in both Russian and Buryat.

The bathroom was gruesome. The bath had deep scars on it and equally ineradicable greasy stains. The hot water tap was connected with the cold water supply and the cold tap with what would have been the hot water, which didn't matter as there was no hot water for us or anyone else in Ulan-Ude during most of the time we spent there. I asked Mischa why the local newspapers failed to report this fact, which I would have thought would have been front page news, but failed to get a satisfactory reply. There was no plug to the wash-basin, which didn't matter either, as we still had our rubber ball; and there were no taps. You filled the washbasin with water, which was extraordinarily cold, by swivelling the shower over it, which didn't work either, unless you shook it violently, when it suddenly belched water and soaked you to the skin if you didn't watch out. But the most awful feature of this terrible little room was the seat of the lavatory basin, which looked as if it had been left to decay in a damp cellar for years and years.

To make up for these shortcomings, the staff on our floor were fat and jolly. A plaque on the door of a little room at the end of the corridor announced 'The Lady on the Third Floor'. Here whichever of them who was on duty made tea for us in an electric samovar. On the night of our arrival, we sighted a dissolute-looking blonde wearing a white, moss crepe mini-dress and carrying a large teddy bear on her way to a party in someone's room. The room was next to Otto's, and the party went on into the small hours and continued, unabated, throughout the second night. He spent both nights, uninvited to it, sleepless, banging either on the wall or the door, and by the end of the second night he looked a wreck.

Downstairs, the vestibule, which had a fully grown stuffed bear in it, covered with dust sheets because the room was being done up by female Buryat house painters, was separated from the buffet on the ground floor and the restaurant on the first floor (both of which were excellent) by a metal grille. This grille had a self-locking door in it and was guarded, day and night, either by a female janitor or by a militia man. Their job was to prevent the wilder, non-card-carrying citizens of Ulan-Ude, some of whom were already drunk and banging on the grille, demanding admittance at 8.30 am, from getting into these dainty, civilized places. In spite of looking grim and efficient, these gate-keepers adopted a rather empirical method of choosing whom they should or should not admit, and quite soon, from breakfast time onwards, there were drunken persons on the inside of the grille too.

Here at the Selenga, our double bedroom, exiguous sitting room and minute, chamber-of-horrors bathroom cost 25 rubles a night, more or less the same as it had for similar but much better accommo-dation at the Intourist Hotel at Irkutsk, and for a double bedroom with bathroom at Novosibirsk: not cheap, but cheaper than the double bedroom and bathroom at the (Intourist) Ukraina Hotel in Moscow which cost 42 rubles, about £35 a night at the prevailing rate of exchange (about 1.20 rubles to the pound). In addition, pay-ing these rates at the Intourist hotels, we got the use of a car for three hours a day, which made them seem more reasonable.

Ulan-Ude is situated on an old Cossack site in the basin of the Selenga at its confluence with the River Uda, between the Ulan-Burgasy and the Yablonovyy Range of mountains, which is about 700 miles long, rising to a height of over 5000 feet and forming part of the watershed between the rivers that flow to the Arctic and those that flow east into the Pacific. It has the biggest plant east of the Urals for building and repairing diesel engines and rolling stock, set up in the 1930s by Commissar Lazar Kaganovich, an old-guard Stalinist and one of the ablest Soviet administrators of the time. Kaganovich was a cruel, pitiless man, who during the Great Terror drew up his own lists of railwaymen who should be purged, and whose comment on its all-embracing nature was, 'When the forest is cut down the chips fly.' He himself was eventually purged; but not until 1957. That year Khruschev, who at one time had been

Kaganovich's protégé, expelled him from the Praesidium, of which he was the only Jewish member, and from the Central Committee, for having mismanaged the Soviet railway system. Molotov and Malenkov were also dismissed at the same time, and all three of them were treated with a clemency that neither Kaganovich nor Malenkov had ever shown to others. According to Khruschev, or so he said, while addressing the XXII Party Congress, Kaganovich had telephoned him, begging him to spare his life, imploring him 'not to allow them to deal with me as they dealt with people under Stalin' – 'them' and 'they' having had Kaganovich as one of their more enthusiastic associates. He then disappeared from public view and it was said at the time that he had been sent as manager to a cement factory in the Urals.

It was in the thirties, too, that 1802 miles of the Trans-Siberian, between Ulan-Ude and Khabarovsk, were converted to double-track by slave labour, as part of the Second Five-Year Plan which lasted from 1933 to 1937. A completely new line was also built during this period, also by slave labour, from Ulan-Ude to Naushki on the Mongolian border, which linked the Trans-Siberian with the Trans-Mongolian Railway to Ulan-Bator and Peking.

Ulan-Ude was quite a pleasant city and still had a distinctly frontier air. The streets in the older part of it were laid out on a gridiron pattern and in them most of the houses were still wooden ones, although there were a lot of apartment blocks behind them and in other parts of the city. Through the middle of it ran the Leninskaya Ulitsa, the principal shopping street, in which the majority of the buildings looked as though they had been built before the Revolution, although this is something that is difficult to determine in the Soviet Union where buildings with many of the attributes of pre-revolutionary ones continued to be built long after it had taken place. It was lined with poplars and trees called *cheromka*, which had green berries, and it was an animated street, full of button-nosed, slant-eyed Buryats, most of whom seemed to have enormous foreheads, peoples of mixed blood, and European Russians, all nattering away to one another in queues for desirable commodities in the shops, some of which extended out into the street, and all seeming to be getting on extremely well with one another. Here, for the first time since leaving Moscow, we all went shopping for things other than food and drink. Otto bought a workers' jacket made of shiny, black quilted cotton for 10 rubles, 30 kopecks; and Wanda bought two for our grown-up children. (They looked fine on the Russians, but when the children put them on later on they looked like a couple of armadilloes and they never wore them again.) The shops were full of goods and Mischa was able to buy all sorts of small things that he said were difficult, or impossible, to find in Moscow. He was particularly pleased to discover a sovereign remedy for stomachache and disorders of the liver, a herbal medicine made from a bush called *oblepikha*, and some spares for his electric razor.

There seemed to be plenty of money about, and it was interesting to speculate on what the prices of the things in the shops really meant to the Russians, when all we knew was that for us the exchange rate of the ruble was around one ruble, 20 kopecks to the pound. A hideous nylon jersey dress decorated with horizontal green and white stripes, of a sort sold in London street markets for £5 or £6, here cost 70 rubles (later we saw several people in the streets actually wearing it). A subfusc, grey suit of questionable cut and quality cost 92 rubles; a pair of plastic woman's shoes, 25 rubles; a roll-neck pullover 54 rubles; a cotton jacket lined throughout with wolf fur, 70 rubles; and a fur-lined corduroy waistcoat, which seemed cheap at the price, 25 rubles. Many of the men wore oatmeal-coloured caps of ribbed material and these cost 3 rubles. A synthetic tie was 4 rubles.

In the YAKHA, which was the largest department store in the city, a very tinny, non-automatic washing machine was 145 rubles; a fridge with a freezing unit that looked as if it had been designed forty years back was 105 rubles; a television was anything up to 350 rubles for a big-screen model; and an electric iron was 6 rubles, cheap even to us. A nickel-plated, electric samovar, an article as indispensable to a Russian as a hearing aid to a deaf person, cost 28.50 rubles.

In the Music Department an upright piano was 650 rubles; a violin, which looked as if it could be played by someone who knew his or her business on the bow end, was 20 rubles; and if any one

of us had wanted a piano accordion, perhaps the last thing, apart
from an upright piano costing 650 rubles, that any of us really
needed on the *Rossiya*, it would have cost between 120 and 360
rubles. Plastic dolls were 16 rubles in the toy department, where
almost everything was plastic apart from some ingenuous, country-
made wooden toys which would be found only in the most sophisti-
cated shops in the West, and then not intended to be played with
by children; these cost next to nothing, but seemed to have been
in stock for a long time.

The best buy, with almost transparent aluminium cooking pots
selling at 1 ruble 50, was a consignment of pots made of solid iron
and enamelled on the inside which, judging by the rust on them,
must have been made at the time when Ulan-Ude was still called
Verkhneudinsk. They were difficult to lift unaided, and about as
much use as an upright piano on a Trans-Siberian train; but Wanda,
who has a good eye for a bargain, bought one at a knock-down 1
ruble and 20 kopecks and stowed it in her head-hunter's bag. From
now on, whenever she had to carry it anywhere she walked as if
she had one leg shorter than the other.

Walking the side streets of old Ulan-Ude, in which the women
used buckets to draw water from the cast-iron standpipes at the
corners, carrying them home on wooden yokes, and the merry children, home from school, played hopscotch, could be a dangerous
business especially at night. There were manholes from which the
covers had been removed by sewermen who had omitted to put them
back, and clusters of twisted steel rods protruding from the pavements, the remains of some uncompleted resurfacing scheme.
Equally dangerous were the mounds of concrete that the workers
had mixed to make these reinforced foundations and, having used
what they required for the job in hand, had left on the sidewalks
to become solid.

On the hill above the old town, up which tramcars driven by
peroxided lady drivers groaned, was modern Ulan-Ude, where
there was a large opera house of the Stalin era with a team of bronze
horses and riders poised above the pediment, apparently bent on
suicide. Between this building and the Broadcasting Station a road
led into the main square, where there was a bronze head of Lenin

which, our guide told us, contained more bronze than any other bronze head of Lenin in the entire USSR.

One afternoon, while Mischa and the local representative of The Agency were elsewhere, we were picked up by a saucy little band of Buryat and Russian girls who, after they had persuaded Otto to take some pictures of them, conducted us to a recreation park on the river bank, which had a little wood in it. It was a squalid place, full of drunks, and the ground was covered, not with hundreds, but with thousands of the silver-coloured caps of vodka bottles, and also of cola bottles, which had been stamped into the earth and whose significance no doubt will be a subject of controversy among archaeologists at some future date. Sitting under the trees on the park benches were numbers of boys, chewing gum and drinking the cola, with their bright red, 350 cc motorcycles propped up around them. At intervals a little band of girl athletes, who were running round and round the park, hove into view and the boys shouted rude things at them. Apart from the caps of the vodka bottles it was exactly like Clapham Common.

All this time the girls, when they were not trying to cadge a ride from some young bloods who were zooming up and down the river in speedboats, displayed an almost embarrassing interest in us. Later, having exchanged addresses and bought them ice creams, we announced that we had to go back to the hotel for dinner. Immediately, without saying another word to us, not even goodbye, they went away.

During our stay in the city we made a couple of long and interesting excursions into the surrounding country. The first of these was to a fishing village called Oymur on the shore of Lake Baikal, east of the Selenga delta. We went there crammed into a Ulanjov jeep, with Semyon Katnikov, the regional fishery inspector, and a mono-syllabic but excellent Buryat driver. At first the road, which had been broken by frost and the hundreds of lorries that used it, fol-lowed the left bank of the Selenga; then it wound up through a thick larch forest to a col in the Khamar Daban Mountains, from which it descended into the delta, where a woman was putting up a '54/418 kilometre' sign in the road, the distances from Ulan-Ude and Irkutsk. Then, having crossed two branches of the Selenga, by a bridge of boats and a ferry that was swung across it on a cable by a powerful tug, the Ulanjov went down with clutch trouble in the main street of a lonely village in the steppe. By the time we reached the settlement it was one o'clock.

It was a grey day, with a bitter wind from the north, and the lake looked grim. At the end of a jetty the fishermen, middle-aged European Russians and Buryats, looked grey and cold, too, in spite of their big black sheepskin coats and fur-lined hats with earflaps. That morning they had made one of the first hauls of *omul* of the season, and it was obvious that they had been told by the regional fishery inspector to await our arrival before unloading it. Luckily, it was a small catch, and while they worked they showed every sign of being friendly.

Later we feasted in the cabin of a motor vessel with its captain, the inspector and the chief of the fish-processing plant, a young-looking man of about fifty, who seemed to be on easy terms with everyone. We ate *ukha*, a soup made with *omul* and flavoured with bay leaves, long strips of the salted fish as a second course, and drank endless toasts in *starka vodka*, which was rudely strong: a meal prepared by the captain's wife, a Ukrainian. Then we put to sea, punching out into the lake in the teeth of the wind towards the snow-covered mountains on the far shore for ten miles or so, until we were clear of the silt brought down by the Selenga; and there a bucket was let down and hauled up, full of sweet-tasting but horribly cold water which we all had to drink.

The fishing port and the processing plant, which contained vast quantities of salted and smoked *omul* and was guarded by chained and savage dogs, were separated from the main village of Oymur, which was about half a mile away. Those of the 1500 inhabitants who were not actively engaged in fishing or processing grew potatoes, carrots and wheat, cultivated fruit trees and engaged in furniture-making. The main street of the processing plant place was a wide dirt road and, at either end, where the one-storey wooden houses finished, there was nothing to be seen but sky. Inside, these houses were spotlessly clean. Their stoves were of whitened brick and each big iron bed had its bedding neatly piled up on top; and spotless, too, were the planked yards outside with the galvanized wash-tubs sitting in them, and the whitewashed outside privies, although I wondered what effort of will would be needed to use them with the temperature hovering around −40°F. Possibly they had other arrangements inside the houses, which were heated by steam from the fish processing plant. Certainly, Oymur was to some extent a show-place, or we would never have been taken there, but the houses were exactly the same, inside and out, in the village where the jeep had broken down and into which we had been invited. There was no reason to think that they would have been very different in any other village in the delta of the Selenga. With the tree-clad mountains of the Ulan-Burgasy Range rising out of the steppe behind it, and the long foreshore, above which the remains of the big, clinker-built sailing and rowing boats that the fishermen had used until recently were gradually disintegrating on the short grass, it was a memorable place.

Then, after another meal at the chief processor's house (tea with swamp berries in it, which looked a bit like bilberries; boiled potatoes, which had a sweetish taste; home-baked brown bread, strong butter, boiled eggs and biscuits which tasted like shortcake), we went home through the cold twilight, catching the last ferry across the river, on the far bank of which the lights of the cellulose factory at Selenga, where the night shift was now at work, illuminated the sky.

16

In the Land of the Buryats
We Laid Down and Died

Folke fit to be of Bacchus' train, so quaffing is their kinde
  Drink is their whole desire, the pot is all their pride,
The sob'rest head doth once a day stand needful of a guide;
  If he to banket bid his friends, he will not shrinke
On them at dinner to bestow a dozen kinds of drinke;

> Master George Turberville, secretary to an English embassy to Moscow, 1568

ON the evening of our third day in Ulan-Ude we dined in the restaurant of the Selenga Hotel. Clean, efficient, cheerful waitresses, dressed in green uniforms and with greens bows in their back-combed hair, served us an excellent dinner: pork steaks with fried eggs, sautéed potatoes, delicious raw cabbage, good bread and a large carafe of apple juice, a popular drink in the restaurant. There was also a good supply of vodka, champagne and other Russian and Bulgarian wines, in fact everything anyone could possibly wish for, with the exception of the demon beer, which seemed to be reserved for alcoholics and which even here, at Ulan-Ude, was served from kiosks in back streets to never-ending queues of unshaven men.

The bill for this dinner came to only 8 rubles for the four of us. Then we talked to the statuesque manageress who told us that her daughter, who was a doctor, was shortly leaving for a holiday in Hungary and Czechoslovakia.

All this time the band was producing music for all tastes, one moment playing a slow fox-trot, the next launching into blasts of rock which scared the living daylights out of the more sedate couples who were ambling round the floor, driving them back to their tables.

Most of the girls were pretty sedate anyway, although one or two were wildly beautiful, and genteel with it: holding their knives and forks as if they were signing two peace treaties at once; munching the same minute bit of pork for minutes at a time in order to be able to smile across at their escorts, some of whom were army officers, without showing what they had secreted inside their pretty little mouths; patting their hairdoes; and from time to time taking bird-like sips at the *sladkoye shampanskoye*, the sweet champagne of Georgia – all of which Otto, with what can only be described as the cruel humour of the fitting rooms, parodied, demonstrating talents that made one feel that he might be in the wrong business.

At this moment, while we were all thoroughly enjoying ourselves, and even doing a spot of dancing, the local representative arrived, a youngish, incredibly gloomy and sour-faced individual, who made Mischa seem like W. C. Fields playing Micawber. He even gave Mischa the pip.

We had heard of this man back up the line, as far back as Novosibirsk. 'Un drôle de type, complètement lugubre', was how an Agency man we had met there (who spoke French like a Frenchman, looked like a Frenchman, dressed like a Frenchman and would have been French, except that he was Russian), described him.

He was also a professional photographer, with a battery of equipment, and the nearest he came to a state approaching animation was when he described a whole new outfit of Nikons and lenses that was now on the way to him from Japan.

Meanwhile, his latest acquisition was a specialist Russian camera, fitted with a lens that moves through an extremely wide angle while the film is being exposed, the sort of camera that is useful for making panoramic pictures of the inside of the Shelekhov Aluminium Plant, or the whole of the Yablonovyy Range. He was so pleased with this camera that he now used it for everything, including pictures of human beings taken at 15 feet, with the result that they looked as if they had been run over by a steamroller. It was unfortunate that Otto's professional integrity led him to tell him so, as it made things even worse.

'And now,' Mischa said, having ordered vodka in an endeavour to break the silence that had fallen upon our table, 'we must discuss what we are going to do tomorrow. Tomorrow we shall ...'

At this moment the manageress arrived to say that Moscow was on the line for Mischa, and we were left to speculate on what it was that he and The Agency had dreamed up for us between them. It was obviously a visit of some sort. He was scarcely likely to tell us that we could stay in bed all day, or go water skiing on the Selenga. What could it be, I wondered: the local mortuary, the meat processing plant, a furniture factory – the possibilities were endless. It was unlikely to be to a lunatic asylum. It was most likely to be meat, or furniture. It might even be that most terrible of all torments devised for visitors behind the Iron Curtain, an extended tour of a wire-making factory, with an hour or so at the conference table with the directors thrown in.

In the course of ten years in Fleet Street I had visited a number of communist wire-making factories: in Albania, where the numbers on the faces of the clocks were all in Chinese characters; in Rumania, in Hungary and in Bulgaria, in which country I had been taken to two. After my first wire factory, in Bulgaria, I knew as much as I ever wanted to know about a process which, even when it is being conducted flat out, is more utterly boring than anyone who has not seen it happening with his own eyes can possibly imagine.

'Oh, God,' I prayed, silently, sinking a vodka at the same time, 'don't let it be a wire factory.'

Soon, Mischa was back, looking rather jolly. 'Tomorrow,' he said, 'we are going to visit the Banner of Lenin Collective Farm in the Mukhorsibir District, where you will have the opportunity of seeing how the Buryat people live. It is not far from the borders of Mongolia.'

I have rarely experienced such a feeling of relief, like a man reprieved from the gallows while already standing on the trap. With any luck, now, I would emerge from a communist country without seeing the inside of a wire factory, and I would be able to send up my name to the editor and compiler of *The Guinness Book of Records* for inclusion in the 1979 edition.

The next morning, as usual, so many telephone calls had to be made to ensure that everything was going to be smooth running en route, and at the Banner of Lenin Collective Farm, that it was 10.30 before we finally got away.

We travelled in two motorcars: Mischa, Wanda, the driver and me in one vehicle; Otto and the man with the panoramic camera in a brand new Russian Fiat, which he had only recently acquired and, equally recently, learned to drive. The car, he told us, had cost him 7000 rubles, which seemed to prove that there was money about.

I must say I didn't envy Otto, travelling with this man. While trying to edge his car forward in order to park it in front of the hotel he inadvertently put it into reverse and shot backwards, running into a man who was just leaving the building, fortunately doing no harm to him, except to his nervous system. Furious, he got out of his car and began to harangue this unfortunate pedestrian.

'What's all that in aid of?' I asked Mischa.

'Because, he says, the man should not have been behind his motorcar.'

'But it was his fault. He should have looked where he was going. Besides, he doesn't know the difference between first gear and reverse.'

'In the Soviet Union,' Mischa said, 'it is the responsibility of the pedestrian to keep out of the way of the motorcar.'

I knew this was nonsense, and so did Mischa, and later the driver of our car, the taciturn Buryat who spoke a few words of English, confirmed that it was – 'Driver was wrong', he said. What this incident did show was when the boys from The Agency were playing on the team together, they presented a very united front.

We crossed the Uda and left the city by a road lined with trees and modern, four- and five-storey blocks of flats. Beyond it was the basin of the Selenga, extending away to the south-west: a wide, concave plain, in which drifts of sand were threatening to overwhelm the fields of chocolate-coloured earth; and from it rose bare, rounded hills, like enormous tumuli, some of them encumbered with the machinery of the Soviet Union's early warning system which here covered only a small stretch of its 9000-mile southern flank – a modest estimate of its length, even allowing for just some of its windings from the Black Sea, through central Asia and along the frontiers of Mongolia and China to the Pacific.

To the right of the road was the railway line to Ulan Bator in Mongolia and to Peking on which a team of women were spreading ballast. Beyond it was the Selenga with its grassy islands, full of aspens and wolf berry (*volichiya*) bushes, on any one of which it would have been nice to sit down and do nothing for a bit. And beyond the river, and the plain beyond that, there were mountains with a sprinkling of snow on them.

The only other human being to be seen was a small Buryat boy in blue denims, riding a horse past a small cemetery which had been built here in the middle of nowhere, on a hill.

Now the road climbed up on to a tree-fringed escarpment above the Selenga, from which we had our last glimpse of it with the white navigation marks shining in the sunlight, winding away to the south-west below crumbling, sandy bluffs. Here, having left the river behind us, we entered a region of grassland steppe, in which wheat was sprouting from earth that was all sorts of shades from red to tan but was only a thin covering for the sand, which was nowhere more than a foot or so below the ground and which, everywhere, was trying to break through to the surface, aided by the wind that blew across these seemingly endless expanses: where it had succeeded there were sand dunes.

In the steppe there were big flocks of sheep guarded by Buryats astride tough little ponies. A shepherd, with the help of two or three dogs, was driving a flock up from a little river to some pens outside a village where there was a hoarding with a poster on it giving the target figures for the area for the Tenth Five-Year Plan, which was due to end in 1980.

The Banner of Lenin Collective Farm, which we finally reached just after midday, was about 60 miles from Ulan-Ude, and about another 60 from the Mongolian border. It was some farm. It was 25 miles long from end to end and covered 74,131 acres, all of it almost treeless steppe. It supported 48,000 sheep and lambs, 2500 cows, 350 horses and 80,000 geese and it employed 2500 people, who lived in five villages. About half of these were Buryats whose job it was to raise and tend the flocks and horses; and the remainder were Ukrainians, Byelorussians, Poles and Tartars who divided between them the work of cultivating the soil, looking after the cattle and feeding the geese.

Their production target for 1977 was 700 tons of meat, 1060 tons of milk, 130 tons of wool and 2000 tons of grain (mostly wheat with some maize for feed); and to help them attain it they had 90 tractors, 40 harvesters, 40 lorries and other vehicles. I was not told whether all this machinery was in commission at any one time, and I forgot to ask.

All these facts and figures, which I religiously wrote down because I didn't want to offend our hosts, were spelled out at a somewhat lengthy conference which was held immediately on our arrival in the office of the Chairman of the Collective, an impressive but rather frightening forty-two-year-old Buryat named Nikolay Tserendashyev who, in spite of his dark suit and white collar, looked as if he would have been equally, if not more, at home riding with the horde of Batu Khan and sacking Kiev. Among others present were the Secretary of Party Organization, Ignat Ivanov (bald, blue suit), Vasily Perevalov, a representative of the District Party Committee (tall, young, dark hair, light overcoat), and Dashabyl Dambaev, Chairman of the Village Council of the Collective. 'Old bloke, wearing specs and medals', I wrote, heavily engaged on all fronts while Otto, who had by this time photographed the whole lot of them from so many angles, so many times that he had enough pictures in 35 mm format to paper the entire room, was showing every sign of suffering from lack of photographic opportunity.

Eventually the meeting groaned to a halt and we went out into the village and had a fleeting glimpse of its modern wooden houses, its fine schoolhouse (to which all the children of the collective came as boarders from Monday to Friday), the silver-painted statue of Lenin, on a plinth outside the schoolhouse, currently addressing a non-existent audience, and the tractor and combine harvester parks. The sun had gone in now, and the sky was covered with grey clouds.

Then we were driven away in a convoy of cars out into the steppe, along a wide dirt road – an ideal place for learning to drive for the man from Ulan-Ude, who was repeatedly explaining to Otto, with

relish, that it would soon be time to go back to the hotel. The steppe
stretched away through all points of the compass, further than the
eye could see, far beyond the confines of the collective: an enormous, pale sea of grass, still waiting for the now long-overdue rain
to fall on it and make it green and tall and full of flowers. Now,
in what was a time of unseasonable drought, in its uniform drabness
it was difficult to know where it ended and the sky began, this
nothingness with so few things in it, and even these only on the
edge of it: a white homestead towards which a man was driving
a horse-drawn *telega*, a Buryat on horseback watching over a flock
– beyond that it was empty. It almost qualified for the description
that Lilya, the conductress of the *Rossiya*, had given of the Steppe
of Ishim on what now seemed that far-off Sunday morning when,
for the first time, I looked out across it – 'Good place, no pipple.'

Nevertheless, this tour of inspection, as all such tours, was not
an unqualified success. This was because so much effort had gone
into organizing the occupants of the steppe so that they would break
into various forms of activity as soon as we appeared, which,
although well-meant, and intended to facilitate photography, destroyed any semblance of spontaneity. After a bit I began to experience the same sensations as an ageing monarch must, surrounded
by equally grizzled courtiers, when he enters a room and the occupants either stand up or, if he has expressed a wish for an informal
visit, continue with their poker work, leaving him nothing to say
but 'Everything all right, eh?'

In this fashion we visited a sheep station. Its 560 sheep were pre-
sided over by Mrs Dashyev, a splendid, impassive Buryat lady,
whose husband we had seen out on the range. Here, we were supposed to have been shown bread making; but because we were late,
the bread had already been taken out of the oven. The house was,
of course, breathtakingly clean and it was difficult to believe that
the Buryats, who are now among the most cultivated and well educated of all the Siberian peoples, were before the Revolution among
the dirtiest – so dirty that the railway-builders hesitated to employ
them in case they spread typhus among the other workers; although
not as dirty as the Evenks, whose habitations were so full of bugs
and lice that they used to bring in ants' nests and allow the ants

to eat their fill, knowing that in winter the extreme cold would polish the latter off.

The Dashyevs had eight children, ranging in age from five to twenty-five, five sons and three daughters. Three of the children were students in Leningrad, one was studying at the Medical Institute at Tomsk and one was in the Army. Apart from the one in the Army, the rest, she said, would all return to the collective, to give it the benefit of their training. Whether they wanted to return it was impossible to say, and seemed impolitic to ask. Until 1975 the Government imposed a complete ban on the issue of domestic passports, which most other Soviet citizens already had, to collective farm workers, putting them in the same position as the serfs before their emancipation in 1861. Although passports are at long last being given to them, many will not receive them until 1981.

Now, having passed through a modern Buryat settlement without stopping, the 'motorcade', for that is what it was, turned into a lush green valley in the hills, full of cattle and with a stream winding through it; roared past a goose farm which we would like to have seen (even a sight of a fraction of 80,000 geese would have been something to remember); and came to rest in the village of Kalinova.

This village was the oldest and largest in the collective. It was established before the present collective was founded in 1955, and long before the foundation of the earliest collective, which was in 1930. Its inhabitants were all European Russians, and its single street with its substantial wooden houses decorated with carvings, its pretty light-haired girls looking out at us from the gaily panelled windows, its fruit trees and its fenced gardens into which stray cows were trying to poke their noses all had a distinctly European air.

These people were descendants of the Raskol'niki, the Old Believers, who in 1658, the year of the Raskol (the Great Schism), broke away from the Russian Church after the introduction of a revised liturgy by the Patriarch Nikon of Moscow. It was at this time that their persecution as heretics began. After the exile to the Pechora River of their leader, the Archpriest Avvakum, who was burned at the stake there in 1681 (by which time thousands of them had voluntarily submitted to be burned rather than recant), they either fled or were exiled to become colonists to the Arctic forests of European Russia and to Siberia, to Yakutsk, to the Ob region, and to the Altai – in fact, anywhere they could continue to practice their faith.

In Siberia, soon after their arrival there, thousands of these Old Believers engaged in an extraordinary aberration of their revealed religion, burning themselves to death in order to escape the fires of hell. Some fled to Poland, and from there, in 1764, they too were expelled to Siberia where they settled in Transbaikalia. Up to this time another name for these Old Believers who had gone to Poland had been 'Poles', but in Transbaikalia they became known as Semeys.

The Raskol'niki, of whom in the 1880s there were estimated to be 15 million – there were 1 million in Perm alone – abstained from tobacco and alcohol, and those who lived in the Altai and in Transbaikalia regarded even the drinking of tea as a sin. They also regarded the railway as an invention of the Devil and refused to work on it.

Among other dissenting groups were the Skoptsi, extremely skilled farming people who castrated themselves in order to be certain of salvation – they were declared illegal by Catherine the Great and exiled to Siberia – and the Dukhobori, a sect founded in the eighteenth century, which denied all authority except God's. They were also sent to Siberia, after first having been exiled to the Caucasus. There, and wherever else they went, they created their own unique blend of havoc which they eventually extended to Canada, when they were allowed to go there in this century.

The Raskol'niki, who like the Skoptsi were excellent colonists, were noted for the beauty of their houses, both inside and out, and their artefacts; and we saw examples of these houses which had been transported with their entire contents from the Ulan-Udinskiy district to the Ethnographical Museum, near Ulan-Ude.

By now it was mid-afternoon and we sat down to breakfast, for that was what our hosts called it, in the house of Ivan Kovalov, which was nothing like a real Raskol'nik house as there was no sign of the domestic altar or the forbidden religious books which were a characteristic of the houses of the Old Believers in past times.

This enormous meal, which was served by Kovalov's wife and
sister, both of whom looked like an advertisement for some health
food, and were encased in identical print dresses, took a considerable time to eat, punctuated as it was by numerous toasts drunk in
vodka. It consisted of masses of boiled pork, cabbage and spring
onion salads, boiled eggs, and home-made bread, butter and honey,
washed down with green tea with milk in it. When we had finished
it, without seeing anything else, full of pork and vodka, we were
whirled back to headquarters.

There, in the canteen, twenty minutes after finishing breakfast
at the house of Ivan Kovalov, we found a banquet awaiting us, set
out on a long table by three Buryat waitresses wearing white head
cloths and aprons. The principal decorations were half a dozen
bottles of champagne, innumerable bottles of vodka and a bottle
of five-star Azerbaijan brandy.

It was obvious that this was going to be something quite out of
the ordinary, a full-scale Buryatan orgy, a more refined version of
those referred to by earlier travellers in Transbaikalia: something
that we were not in a state to cope with, brimful of breakfast, green
tea with milk in it and vodka. Like rabbits hypnotized by a pack
of weasels we took our seats, with Mr Tserendashyev, the Chairman
of the Collective, at the head of the table at my end, and the Secretary of the District Committee, who had Wanda on his left, far
too far away from me to be of help if the necessity arose, at the
other end. The intervening places were occupied by the rest of our
party and the welcomers, now swelled in number by the addition
of three, obviously important, Buryat ladies, and of a silent elderly
male one who was put next to me, on my left, separating me from
the Chairman. 'The Chairman wishes me to tell you that only two
other foreign friends have visited the Banner of Lenin Collective
Farm. One was from East Germany, the other from France, and
this was many years ago,' said one man from Ulan-Ude.

Then the food came, not in ordinary quantities but mounds of
it which, when they were set on the table, made it impossible to
see the persons who were sitting on the other side of it. There were
mutton dumplings called *buza*, the size and weight of cannon balls,
glazed mutton ribs a foot long, sausages made from sheep gut, and

a host of subsidiary dishes. And there was no question of refusing. The Buryats made it abundantly clear by way of the man from Ulan-Ude, who because he was a non-drinker had been chosen as interpreter, that not to eat, and not to continue to be seen eating, would be considered an offence against their ancient laws of hospitality.

And all the time the toasts kept coming. First in champagne and then, when that was finished, in vodka; and, as with the food, the same, deadly protocol obtained. There was no sipping, there were no heel-taps. These people simply threw back their heads and whatever they were drinking – champagne, vodka, five-star brandy from Azerbaijan – was gone. And every time I obeyed their laws the gnarled hand of the old man on my left who was fulfilling the function of loader, extended across my line of vision and refilled my glass. At the end of the second hour, which was the last time I remember looking at my watch, all of us, apart from Wanda, who early on had refused to knock off her drink at a single gulp, however important the toast, and had been excused from doing so on the grounds that she was a woman, were in dead trouble. The copiousness of the supply of alcohol and the plenitude of toasts were more than ordinary flesh and blood could withstand. Otto was already gone – not literally, because he was still seated at the table, but his nose was almost level with it, like the Dormouse at the Mad Hatter's Tea Party. Mischa was as white as a sheet. Among the Buryats, the chairman showed no signs of having drunk anything at all, although he had proposed by far the largest number of toasts; neither did my Buryat wine-pourer, whose job in life was to keep me supplied, nor the three Buryat ladies who, being women, were also excused the excesses of the Buryat table. I wondered what had happened to the lone French visitor and the man from East Germany. Had they too been subjected to this treatment? If so, where were they now – buried somewhere in the vastness of the steppe?

'And now,' said the man from Ulan-Ude, fixing me with a cold eye in which, even in my distressed state, I thought I could detect a tiny flicker of triumph, 'the Chairman of the Banner of Lenin Collective Farm is asking our English friend to make a speech.'

I got to my feet. Later the following day I remembered what I had said.

Ladies and Gentlemen, workers of the Banner of Lenin Collective Farm, we are most grateful for the extraordinary hospitality which you have shown to us and which we shall, certainly, never be able to forget. Nor shall we forget you Buryat and other Soviet people, as long as we live. We come here from distant lands, and therefore might not be expected to appreciate the great and splendid efforts you have made, and are continuing to make, in order to wring a living from this difficult soil.

[Apparently, this bit did not go down terribly well with the Chairman who did not regard the soil of his Collective, which was giving a return of 2,000,000 rubles a year, as being difficult.]

Nevertheless, please do not think that I, for one, do not understand the meaning of manual toil. Although I am a writer in England I, too, work on the land [little did they know that all I had was two acres; half of it cyder orchard], and I, too, know what manual labour means. In proof, I show you my hands [which, fortunately, were calloused as a result of my efforts that previous winter to turn a meadow into an ornamental garden by taking off the top turf]. And now let us drink to the fruitfulness of the Earth and Peace between our respective nations.

Apparently, although I never managed to drink the toast, I was given a standing ovation. It didn't matter what I was given. I was finished, and I never heard it. The next thing I remember was being driven away from the farm and stopping in a wood, in which darkness was already falling. There we got down and went into a clearing where the Chairman and all the male members of his party were waiting for us, surrounded by a number of stout, wooden boxes.

These were immediately opened and their contents set out on a cloth on the ground. They comprised what was left after the banquet of the dumplings, the mutton ribs, the sausages and various sweet dishes which I could not even remember seeing previously, together with fresh supplies of champagne and vodka. According to Wanda, when I realized what they intended I clung to a tree crying 'Wanda, Wanda, save me from the Buryats!', while Otto remained in the Fiat being sick out of the window.

The next morning, on our last day at Ulan-Ude, I woke feeling fine, as if the debauch at the Banner of Lenin Collective Farm had never happened – which was fortunate, as we were going to visit the Ivolginsky Datsan, the last remaining Buddhist monastery of the Buryats in the USSR.

The *datsan*, a collection of wooden buildings surrounded by a wooden palisade, stood alone in a green, marshy plain, with cattle grazing in it, between the left bank of the Selenga and the mountains we had seen the day before while on the way to the farm.

It was a brilliant, spring-like morning. When we arrived a number of shirtless teenage Buryat boys, wearing jeans, and a pretty little girl of about eight who spoke a bit of English were biffing a handball about on the grass outside the enclosure. It was a happy scene; but although it was a churlish thought it was difficult to believe that they were there by accident, especially as the man from Ulan-Ude made a point of telling us that young Buryats now had better things to do than bother about the shrines of an outmoded religion. Later, the little girl said that they all came from the town of Ivolginsk which was two or three miles away. Whatever the truth was, as soon as they had been photographed, they gave up playing.

The temple, which stood immediately inside the front gate, was a typical, richly decorated building of Chinese inspiration, with curved roofs. When I got back to England and was able to look at some drawings and photographs made before the Revolution, I found that it was almost identical with the Datsan of the Khamba Lama at Selenginsk, a place near the shore of Lake Gusinoy, the Goose Lake, which is known to Buddhists as the Gelung Nor. This lake lies a good 70 miles to the south of the Ivolginsky Datsan which is only about 15 miles or so from Ulan-Ude.

At Selenginsk the seminarists spent ten years studying theology, medicine, astrology and philosophy. Whether the *datsan* still stands there, abandoned or preserved, or was dismantled and moved to this new site is not clear.

We were met at a side gate by the Third Lama, a small, shrivelled man. The First Lama, who was, presumably, the Khamba Lama, and the Second Lama were both away at a conference in Leningrad, he said. It was difficult to get very much information from him, partly because both Mischa and the man from Ulan-Ude demonstrated a reluctance to interpret, which Communist officials always show when in the presence of priests, and partly because the Third Lama was reluctant to speak. Inside the temple, which was a lofty hall, there was all the apparatus of lamaism, or most of it, although

no butter lamps were burning, perhaps because now only six cere-
monies take place in it each year; but according to the Third Lama
it was still a place of pilgrimage, to which pilgrims came from Mongolia, Tibet and as far away as Ceylon.

There were large statues of Buddha, hundreds smaller of *burkhans*
(images of Buddha and the saints executed in *papier mâché*, or it
could have been plastic), paintings, banners, trumpets, drums and
prayer wheels. There was no sign of the extensive library of religious
books that had existed at Selenginsk, some of which were in the
Buryat language, and all of which were written after the conversion
of the Buryats to Buddhism, because previously they had no alpha-
bet. We were told that the previous temple had been burned to the
ground in 1976 and had been rebuilt in six months, which was
possible but seemed improbable. Outside in the enclosure there
were other shrines, housing other *burkhans*, and in one part of it
a body of Buryat workmen was building another large, finely gilded,
red-painted wooden building to house ex-votos. There was no sign
of the white elephant, carved in wood and mounted on wheels,
which at the time Kennan and Frost visited the Selenginsk Datsan
used to be harnessed to a four-wheeled cart with a shrine on it in
the form of a two-storey temple and dragged in procession on cere-
monial occasions.

After Kennan's conducted tour of the *datsan*, and having been
spectators at the 'Dance of the Burkhans', performed by dancers
representing Mongolian demons and wearing enormous black helmet masks, they had been asked to dine with the Khamba Lama,
who asked them what their opinion was about the shape of the earth.

Kennan replied that he thought it was shaped like a great ball.

'I have heard so before,' said the Grand Lama, looking thoughtfully
away into vacancy. 'The Russian officers whom I have met have told me
that the world is round. Such a belief is contrary to the teachings of our
old Tibetan books, but I have observed that the Russian wise men predict
eclipses accurately; and if they can tell beforehand when the sun and
moon are to be darkened, they probably know something about the shape
of the earth. Why do you think the earth is round?'

'I have many reasons for thinking so,' Kennan said, 'but perhaps the
best and strongest reason is that I have been around it.'

After a long talk, in the course of which Kennan discussed the sphericity of the earth from every possible point of view, the Grand Lama appeared to be at least partly persuaded, for he said with a sigh, 'It is not in accordance with the teachings of our books; but the Russians must be right.'

It was not until many months later that I came upon an interesting passage in *The Empire of the Tsar* by the Marquis de Custine, which an English friend living in Moscow had advised me to read. It was written in the early 1840s, soon after his return from an extended visit to Russia, in the course of which he took the opportunity to talk with persons of all classes.

Russian hospitality [he wrote] is so hedged around with formalities as to render life unpleasant to the most favoured strangers. It is a civil pretext for restraining the movements of the traveller, and for limiting the freedom of his observations ... the observer can inspect nothing without a guide; never being alone, he has the greater difficulty in forming his judgement upon his own spontaneous impressions ... Would you see the curiosities of a palace, they give you a chamberlain, with whom you are obliged to view everything, and, indiscriminately, to admire all that he admires; a camp – an officer, sometimes a general officer, accompanies you; ... a school, or any other public institution, the director or the inspector must be previously apprised of your visit, and you find him, under arms, prepared to brave your examination; if an edifice, the architect himself leads you over the whole building, and explains to you all that you do not care to know, in order to avoid informing you on points which you would take interest in knowing.... In this manner they tyrannise over us in pretending to do us honour. Such is the fate of privileged travellers. As to those who are not privileged, they see nothing at all.

17

The Far-Flung Fringes
of the Empire

EARLY the following morning, 11 June, the day we were due to
board the *Rossiya*, I stood in the hall of the Selenga Hotel watching
the lady house painters who had just finished putting the finishing
touches to the main entrance door, and were about to knock off for
a well-earned rest.

Before doing so, one of them went to the reception desk and asked
for a piece of paper on which she wrote what I presumed to be the
words WET PAINT in Russian. Then, not having thought to ask the
girl in reception for a pin she stuck it on the wet paint, from which
a draught of air instantly removed it. After she had done this three
times with the same result, she tried once more but it was again
blown away.

Shrugging her shoulders, with an air of despair, she followed her
companion into the back parts of the building.

By now the hotel was waking up, and when I saw a lady in a
smart, black coat making for the exit I hurried towards her, pointing
at the door and saying 'Wet Paint'. Ignoring me as if I had been
a beggar asking for alms, she barged through it and emerged in the
open air looking like a zebra. The same thing happened to a man
wearing a dark suit, who actually glared at me when I tried to save
him.

I then told the girl at the reception desk, who spoke English,
what was happening and she, too, shrugged her shoulders. She also
disappeared, presumably to avoid getting involved in what looked
like becoming a whole lot of unpleasantness.

In the next ten minutes something like a dozen people went out
through the door, all of whom emerged on the other side muttering

angrily when they realized what had happened and displaying their damaged garments to passers-by, none of whom showed the slightest interest. Some made things worse by spitting on the paint marks and rubbing them with their handkerchiefs.

What was extraordinary was that none of them complained to the management; and I became so engrossed in thinking about this that when I, too, went out through the door a few minutes later I, too, forgot that it had just been painted.

The *Rossiya* was due to leave Ulan-Ude for Chita and points east at 4.32 pm local time (11.32 am Moscow time). It was unfortunate that we arrived late at the station – which was crowded with real gypsies, not theatrical ones – because when we got there we found that there was another passenger train parked between us and the *Rossiya*, and in order to reach it with our luggage, which had now been vastly increased in bulk by a parcel of *omul*, three packages each containing a quilted cotton jacket, and two magnificent black sheepskin coats which Mischa and Wanda had bought at a knock-down price from the store at the fish-processing plant at Lake Baikal, we had to make innumerable journeys up the steps of a car on the other train, through it and down the other side and then along the line for some way before reaching our car on the *Rossiya*. When we finally succeeded in getting everything on board we found that, not only had we not been given two-berth compartments, but once again we had been split up and given places in two four-berth compartments, each of which was already occupied by two people. Fortunately, the two Russian gentlemen in the compartment that Wanda and I were due to occupy kindly offered to move into the one into which Otto and Mischa had been put, and, once again, we were able to travel together.

The car opposite our own on the other train was occupied by soldiers, and from our compartment we had an unprecedented view of its lavatory accommodation through its window which, unlike the lavatory windows on any other Russian train I had ever seen, or on any other train anywhere else in the world I had ever seen, was made of clear glass.

Both trains left a little late and in the course of the next few minutes we were treated to the extraordinary spectacle of a succession of Russian soldiers each one of whom, on entering the lavatory, stood astride the pan and, as if he was performing a drill movement, lowered his trousers, in doing so revealing one of the most closely guarded military secrets of the Soviet Union – that its soldiers, like those of kilted, Highland regiments in the British Army, are not issued with underpants. If this is a calumny and they are issued with underpants, then they had forgotten to put them on.

The *Rossiya* clonked out through the environs of Ulan-Ude along the right bank of the Uda River, past wooden houses sandwiched between it and long rows of apartment blocks, all sizzling like sausages in the hot sunshine; past the spur that carried the railway to Naushki, Ulan-Bator and Peking; and past a sinister enclosure surrounded by a 20-foot-high palisade, above which nothing could be seen but the rooftops of some buildings, with guard towers at each corner, equipped with searchlights and manned by armed sentries.

For a time, too, it followed the Great Siberian Trakt until, at a place called Onokhoi, where it crossed the Uda, the road diverged from the railway in order to follow its own, more ancient way to Chita, over the Yablonovyy Range.

At Petrovskiy Zavod, 90 miles from Ulan-Ude, the *Rossiya* halted for fifteen minutes while its electric engine was exchanged for another model, or it may have been two. By this time I had lost interest in the types and numbers of types.

Here a couple of inspired drunks acted out an unrehearsed comedy on the platform which involved them in performing a sort of tribal dance round the station-master, who seemed not to be aware of their existence – station-masters seemed to be more tolerant out here than they were further to the west.

At Petrovskiy Zavod in 1790, in the reign of Catherine II, an iron works was built, and there were still a couple of more modern iron works close to the station, from which railway trucks were carting away slag from the crucibles.

It was to this place that a number of the Decembrists, including Prince Trubetskoy and Prince Volkonsky, were sent from Chita, and it was there that their wives, who had renounced their titles in order to be with them, had joined them and given them some comfort in the wilderness, when they were not engaged in digging and other menial pursuits. The first to make the 4000-mile journey from Moscow was Princess Trubetskaya. She was followed by Princess Maria Volkonskaya who brought her clavichord with her in a sledge.

Now the *Rossiya* ran up the wide valley of the Khilok River, between it and the Yablonovyy (the 'Apple Tree') Range, which was covered with pastures of pale green grass with cream and brown cattle grazing in them and fields of dark earth with wheat coming up in it, all brilliant in the last rays of sunlight. It was a quarter to nine local time, and in a few minutes the sun disappeared behind the mountains, but even so an hour and a half went by before it was completely dark. Then the only sign of illumination in this immense but now invisible landscape was provided by the headlights of the *Rossiya* as it bored into the darkness ahead, and by the fires of the herdsmen and shepherds in the fields.

After eating our habitual ration of bread, sausage and cheese, but this time accompanied by several bottles of beer (this version of the *Rossiya* appeared to have inexhaustible quantities of beer on board, which suggested that some more than usually important person might be travelling on it), we went to bed.

We were now in the sixth time zone beyond Moscow, and before switching out the light and without seriously thinking about it, I set our alarm clock for what I thought was 11.50 pm. This was the time at which I estimated, with the *Rossiya* rumbling along at about 40 mph, we would reach a tunnel mentioned by Baedeker, through the Yablonovyy Range. This tunnel is 93 yards long and has the words 'To the Great Ocean' inscribed at the western end of it, and 'To the Atlantic' at the other. I subsequently learned that it was not a tunnel at all but a cutting on the watershed which had been roofed in to protect the trains from rock falls, but one which, whatever it was, caused the first passengers on the line to groan with apprehension when they went through it in 1900. The work on this section of the line, from Mysovaya on Lake Baikal to Sretensk on the Shilka River, had taken five years to complete and it had been accomplished only with the help of 4000 convicts and other exiles from the gold and silver mines who had been employed under the

usual terms of remission of sentence, which they accepted with
eagerness. At what I still thought to be 11.50, but was really 12.50
local time, I staggered out into the corridor in order to see the *Ros-siya* enter the tunnel, followed by the curses of the other occupants
of the compartment who had also been woken by the alarm.

I opened a window (this train, besides having bottled beer, also
had windows that opened) and stuck my head out. It was running
through torrents of rain, along what looked like a ledge on a mountain side, with great chunks of granite, streaming with water the
colour of tinned salmon in the lights from the windows of the train,
looming up on the edge of it. At last, I thought, we were on the
watershed of the Yablonovyy Range and just coming to the tunnel!

In fact, the *Rossiya* had long since passed through the tunnel and
was already descending the southern slopes following a stream, the
waters of which would eventually end up in the Pacific, but I did
not know this, and I stayed at the window for ages, craning out
of it, with the rain pouring in, seeing one lonely hamlet with white
shuttered houses and an occasional glare of light when we passed
a small station or a siding, until the *Rossiya*, which all this time had
been roaring southwards, turned north-east up the Ingoda River,
and I finally discovered the truth.

At 3.30 am on the morning of 12 June (9.30 pm Moscow time
on the 11 June) the *Rossiya* reached Chita, 3902 miles from Moscow
and 1933 miles from Vladivostok, the capital of the Chita *oblast*;
a grudging, grey light began to seep into the world, revealing a horde
of potential passengers who proceeded to swarm aboard to the
accompaniment of the strains of piped Buryatan music.

In 1903, when it was finally completed, Chita became the western
junction of the Chinese Eastern Railway, on which work was begun
in 1897 by Russian engineers and artisans and thousands of Chinese
coolies. The difficulties and obstacles they encountered were if anything worse than those that had been met with in building the
Trans-Siberian, and included plague, brigands and marauding
Chinese and Boxer armies who tore up whole sections of the track
when the spirit moved them, permafrost, swamps, wide rivers,
deserts and ranges of almost impenetrable rock. When it was finished
it carried Trans-Siberian passengers to Vladivostok by way of Har-

bin and Ussuriysk on the Ussuri River. It was now possible, after September 1904, when the Transbaikal Loop was completed, to buy a ticket to Vladivostok in London and travel all the way there by train. In 1914 *Bradshaw's Continental Guide* gives the time as twelve days. It was not until 1916, however, when the 1200-mile Amur section of the Trans-Siberian was completed from Kuenga on the Shilka River to Khabarovsk, that it became possible to make the entire journey from Moscow to Vladivostok on Russian soil.

In the course of the following forty-eight hours, stopping at thirty stations along the way, the *Rossiya* covered 1454 miles, penetrating some of the wildest and least inhabited country on the entire Trans-Siberian Railway.

It ran through country loaded with coal, iron ore, tin, molybdenum, wolfram and gold. Both gold and silver had been mined under the tsars in Transbaikalia by slave labour; but it was not until Stalin came to power that its other riches were also exploited by this inefficient means.

It burrowed its way through endless, mountainous *taiga*, dense forests of pine, fir and larch; further east, near the left bank of the Amur, through woods of mixed leaf-bearing trees, it ran across plateaux on which wheat and potatoes were the principal crops, and to the east, by the Amur, through country in which sunflowers grew; it crossed grasslands which supported cattle and sheep that, like the crops, could survive only along the southern edges of these regions of eastern Siberia and the Far East, close to the border of China. For even in these comparatively low latitudes, the temperature falls in winter to between $-22°$ and $-56°$ F, and in some places there is snow on the ground for up to 180 days a year. These are areas where the ground is locked in permafrost to a depth of 320 feet below the surface. It is not surprising that, of the peoples who live in this part of the world – Russians and Byelorussians make up the bulk of the population, together with some Ukrainians, Jews, and a few Evenks on the northern fringes of it – 60 per cent live an urban existence, and that outside the narrow strip along which the railway runs the population drops to 1 or 2 to the square mile.

Beyond Chita on this first morning the line followed the left bank of the Ingoda River which rises away to the south-east in the mountains near the Mongolian border. Soon the *Rossiya* ran into fog and the driver switched the headlights on. Here the Ingoda was only about 100 yards wide. Its surface was without a ripple, like glass, and as the train ran downstream alongside it, it produced a variety of elongated reflections of various objects on the far bank – trees, navigation marks, an occasional village and what were here whitewashed houses, a fisherman – like distorting mirrors.

Around 5 am local time we were brought tea by a cheerful, dotty-looking, blonde conductress, and at about the same time the sun rose and shone through the fog ahead, itself rather like a giant headlamp. Soon the fog began to thin and eventually it dispersed completely except for some long horizontal bands which hung above the larch and birch forests in the Cherskovo Mountains through which the Ingoda was now burrowing its way. The only human being in sight in the whole of this expansive landscape was a man, still very drunk from the night before, who, when he saw the *Rossiya*, fell flat on his back. It was Sunday morning.

Now the Ingoda was gaining momentum. It was full of eddies, and fish were rising in it; in a few minutes it was joined by the Onon, which rises in a range of mountains in Mongolia eastwards of Ulan-Bator: together they became the Shilka.

In 1162 Genghiz Khan, later to become Ruler of the World, was born on the banks of the Onon, the son of Bulantsar, a Mongol chieftain, whose tribal lands were the steppe between the Onon and the Kerlulen River. When Yulun, the child's mother, opened his clenched fist she found a piece of coagulated blood in it resembling a red stone; and when Bulantsar, the father, who was also the chief of the tribe, returned from a successful campaign, in the course of which he had slain a rival chieftain named Temuchin, this red stone was regarded as an auspicious omen, so the child was named Temuchin.

In 1206 Temuchin, now himself chief of his tribe, and having by this time conquered all the neighbouring tribes in Mongolia, summoned their chiefs to the banks of the Onon where he proclaimed himself Genghiz Khan (the 'Perfect Warrior'), and he then proceeded to reorganize their combined armies, which were by now enormous, into bodies that numbered hundreds, thousands and tens of thousands, each 10,000 forming a *tumen*.

Genghiz died in 1227, in his portable palace on the banks of a river in Mongolia, or on the borders of China – its whereabouts are uncertain – leaving an empire that extended from the China Sea to the river Dnieper, and hordes of cavalry, the finest that the world had ever seen. His body, preceded by outriders who are said to have killed every human being they encountered on the way, in order that lesser men should not witness the passing by of his corpse, was taken to his horde on the Kerlulen and from there to a burial place, possibly on the banks of the river, the actual whereabouts of which are as controversial as the place where he actually met his death.

William of Rubruck, a Flemish Franciscan sent by Louis IX of France as an envoy to the Great Khan of the Mongols at Karakorum in Mongolia, has left an interesting account of a Mongol camp a few years after the death of Genghiz. Their way of life was very similar to that of the Buryats before the Revolution.

Three days after leaving Sudak in the Crimea, in May 1253, he and his party, travelling in slow and hideously uncomfortable carts, saw their first Mongol *yurts*. They were circular, made of felt which was either blackened or whitened with chalk, clay or powdered bones, which was stretched over intricate wooden frameworks. Openings in the top allowed the smoke from the fires to disperse.

The interiors were embroidered with motifs of vines, trees, birds and beasts, and the *yurts* were carried, when the Mongols were on the move, on immense waggons drawn by as many as twenty-two oxen. Bedding and valuables were packed in chests made from plaited osiers and transported on high carts drawn by camels.

Women lived on the eastern side of the *yurt* (which was always pitched with its entrance facing south) and men on the western side. Felt images were suspended above the living places of the husband and his principal wife. The entrance was closed by a rug and the teat of a mare and the udder of a cow hung down on either side, mares being milked exclusively by men, cows by women. From the mares' milk the men fermented *kumiss*, which tasted of almonds and was extremely intoxicating. Men had wives, 'as many as they would', and any of their female slaves could act as concubines. In winter they wore furs next to the skin. The men shaved a square patch on top of their heads, leaving a tuft to fall over their eyebrows. Marriageable girls were taken by force with the connivance of their fathers, the marriage being consummated by what was virtually rape.

The *Rossiya* ran on down the left bank of the Shilka, which was broadening out and full of wooded islands; and at 3.35 am Moscow time (9.35 am local time) reached Priiskovaya, the junction for the town of Nerchinsk, where it stopped for a five-minute rest.

In tsarist times Nerchinsk, which was founded in 1654, was the headquarters of the Nerchinsk Silver Mining District, which comprehended an enormous area of utter wilderness in the ranges north of the Shilka and south of it towards the Chinese border. Sixty miles downstream was Sretensk, terminus of the railway until the Khabarovsk line was completed in 1916, and 150 miles beyond Sretensk were the great gold deposits on the Kara River. All the silver and gold mined in these areas became the personal property of the tsars. Here, on the southern fringes of the Empire, thousands of convicts and other exiles who had been sentenced to hard labour, having walked there from Irkutsk along the Trakt, a journey of two months or more, worked until they died, either from overwork or lack of food, or by their own hands (soaking matches in water and drinking the liquid was a common way), or from the floggings that they were given with the *plet*, a three-tailed rawhide whip. A hundred strokes was a normal sentence, and it left the victim's back a raw mass of flesh. Whatever the cause, when they finally did die, their deaths were not recorded.

Kennan and Frost visited the Kara Goldfields and some of the silver mines in the Nerchinsk area. By the time they reached the Kara River in October 1885, winter had set in, and the temperatures were around ten or fifteen degrees below freezing. There were no roads and the only way it could be reached was by boat in summer or by sledge over the ice in winter. There they found that the various prisons, mines and convict settlements extended along the river bank for about twenty miles and contained about 1800 hard labour convicts and 800 women and children who had accompanied them there. Hard labour convicts were issued with one coarse linen shirt and one pair of linen trousers every six months; one cap, one pair of thick trousers, and one grey overcoat every year; a *polushuba*, a sheepskin coat, every two years; one pair of *brodni*, loose leather boots, every three and a half months in winter; and one pair of *kati*, or low shoes, every three weeks in summer. Their hours of work were from 7 am to 5 pm in winter, 5 am to 7 pm in summer. Breakfast was brick tea and black rye bread and their midday meal was the same, eaten on the site in the open, in winter beside a camp fire. Their last meal of the day was eaten while sitting on their wooden sleeping platforms, locked up in their barracks: hot soup, meat, bread and sometimes more tea.

The day was cold and dark, a light powdery snow was falling, and a more dreary picture than that presented by the mine can hardly be imagined. Thirty or forty convicts, surrounded by a cordon of Cossacks, were at work in a sort of deep gravel pit, the bottom of which was evidently at one time the bed of the stream. Some of them were loosening with pointed crowbars the hardpacked clay and gravel, some were shovelling it upon small hand-barrows, while others were carrying it away and dumping it at a distance of 150 or 200 yards. The machine was not in operation.... [The machine separated the gold particles from the sand.] The convicts, most of whom were in leg-fetters, worked slowly and listlessly, as if they were tired out and longed for night; the silence was broken only by the steady clinking of crowbars, a quick, sharp order now and then from one of the overseers, or the jingling of chains as the convicts walked to and fro in couples wheeling hand-barrows. There was little or no conversation except that around a small camp-fire a few yards away, where half a dozen soldiers were crouching on the snowy ground watching a refractory tea-kettle, and trying to warm their benumbed hands over a sullen, fitful blaze. We watched the progress of the work for ten or fifteen minutes, and then, chilled and depressed by the weather and the scene, returned to our vehicle and drove back to the Lower diggings ...

A description of a similar scene, this one written by one of the forced labourers, occurs in Solzhenitsyn's *One Day in the Life of Ivan Denisovich*. The result of these labours in what were called the 'cabinet mines' was that the Tsar received about 3600 pounds weight of pure gold a year.

In the Nerchinsk region Kennan and Frost visited some silver

mines in which the prisoners worked several hundred feet underground. It was to these that a number of the Decembrists and thousands of revolutionary Poles had been sent. In one of these mines
the air was so foul and thick with the fumes of dynamite that their
candles constantly went out, and in another all the galleries for
hundreds of yards at a time were lined with ice. Some of the oldest
galleries and caverns had been excavated in the reign of Catherine II.

What was worse than working the mines, for the 950 or so hard
labour convicts, at least a third of whom were unemployed at any
one time owing to the inefficiency with which they were run, were
the appalling living conditions. At Alagachi, where 'the country,
which we could see for thirty miles, looked like a boundless ocean
suddenly frozen solid in the midst of a tremendous Cape Horn gale
where the seas were running mountain-high', Kennan and Frost
were taken to an old prison house, probably built when the mine
was first opened in 1817. In one room in it, which was being used
as a hospital, there 'were eight or ten low beds, upon which, under
dirty, and in some cases bloody, sheets, were lying eight or ten sick
or wounded convicts, whose faces were whiter, more emaciated, and
more ghastly than any I had yet seen. Two or three of them, the
warden said, had just been torn and shattered by a premature
explosion of dynamite in the mine.' In another part of this dreadful
prison, the sleeping quarters of the so-called fit men, there was a
continuous red band around the walls, as if it had been painted:
the blood of thousands of bedbugs, squashed by the prisoners while
lying on the *nari* (the sleeping platforms).

Beyond Priiskovaya the *Rossiya* ran for another twenty miles
down the Shilka, along the foot of cliffs and across ravines, passing
a few scattered houses and at one place, on the far bank, an old
white church built of stone or brick with another equally ancient
building close to it which may have housed the priests who served
the church, standing utterly isolated in a meadow between the river
and the great forests of larch and birch that soared above it.

Then it turned away from the river and began a long ascent to a
watershed in the Olekminskiy Range, at first through open, steppe-
like country covered with forget-me-nots and here and there a field
of wheat and an occasional white barn, through which the Kuenga,

a small and pretty stream, flowed down to meet the Shilka. Then it began to climb more steeply, with the river growing smaller, sometimes running down through miniature rapids, at other times almost disappearing in equally miniature swamps, full of white flowers growing out of what looked like hassocks and sometimes purling down through villages of wooden houses under wooden bridges, with no one about in them on this late Sunday morning.

We were in hilly, wooded country now. It was cold, and there was snow among the larches on the mountainsides as we ate a late breakfast of salted *omul*, part of the great parcel of the stuff we had been given at Lake Baikal, some of which we had already given away – to maids at the hotel and to the conductresses on the train – without in any way seeming to have reduced the quantity we still had with us.

Around half past three, while the radio operator was giving us a Russian version of 'Auld Lang Syne' on his piped music apparatus, the train entered a concrete tunnel in a cliff and roared out the other side above a stretch of river in which an excavator the size and shape of a Mississippi steamer, except that it was equipped with tracks, was lumbering up the bed, scooping up huge mouthfuls of rock and gravel. Finally, around 5.15 in the afternoon, having panted up through two perfect hairpins and gone through another tunnel with the sentries (who guard every tunnel and important bridge on the railway) shivering at either end, the *Rossiya* reached the watershed of the Olekminskiy Range, 4430 miles from Moscow, and began running away downhill, high above valleys which were now bathed in the golden light of what had become a beautiful evening. Meanwhile we took ourselves off to the restaurant car, which was also bathed in a golden light but which gastronomically had become a disaster area. Of eighteen items on the menu, only caviar and fried eggs were 'on' – there was not even a single dose of the 'smashed potatoes and boiled tongue' which someone in a fit of insane optimism had added to the menu in pencil and then crossed out again. There was no more beer and the only vinous drinks were *portvein*, a syrupy looking dessert wine from Azerbaijan, and medium dry champagne.

There was also no service. At another table a party of four Swiss men and girls were trying without success to have themselves served

with milk by making mooing noises at the staff and pulling imaginary udders.

'What can you do with these bastards?' said one of the girls, a
Miss Oerlikon, who it later transpired had had an English nanny
and had been to school in Berkshire.

'And you are coming all this way without a cow? Fine Swiss
people you are,' said Otto, taking out his always-ready-for-action
Canon Dial camera – which immediately got our table the service
of the manageress, who informed him that photography in her
sumptuous restaurant car was forbidden. So we ordered fried eggs
and a bottle of *palusookhoye*, medium-dry champagne at 5.40 rubles,
which turned out to be *sladkoye* (sweet), and while we were wining
and dining a big black ant from the *taiga* which happened to be
passing managed to get inside Otto's pants and bite him. This would
teach him to try and be funny with a girl named Oerlikon who knew
more about what went on around Sunningdale than Otto knew
about St Gallen.

At 2.05 pm Moscow time (8.05 in the evening), the *Rossiya* rolled
into Amazar. On the platform the usual welcoming committee of
local ladies was dispensing good cheer in the form of red cabbage,
spring onions, boiled potatoes and bits of chewing gum shaped like
sausages which looked as if they had been rolled between their
thighs. Apart from being a graveyard for old steam locomotives,
of which there were hundreds if not thousands in this part of Siberia
(all awaiting the moment when the electricity is cut off for the last
time and there's no more oil, to make a comeback), it was a hell
of a place. Roll on Khabarovsk, now only 949 miles away!

At nine o'clock the sun went down, by which time each one of
us – German, Slovene, Russian and English – was afflicted by a
terrible melancholy. We were also feeling sick, as a result of drinking
the *sladkoye*.

After we passed through Erofei Pavlovich, named after Erofei
Pavlovich Khabarov, the dreadful Cossack explorer, we slept or
tried to sleep while the *Rossiya* ran for 120 miles or so through some
of the wildest country on the entire trip, more or less all the way
along the 54th parallel, through a region of swampy *taiga* and
permafrost, through Bam station from which a line has been built

200 miles northwards, to the Chulman coking coal fields in Yakutia north of the BAM, from which the Japanese have contracted to buy a large slice of the production.

I woke around 5.30 am on 13 June. On the *Rossiya* it was still 12 June. You have to be careful about post-dating cheques on this train if short of the necessary. We had just passed a place called Bolshoi Never. You could tell we were still in the permafrost because the telegraph poles had either sunk deep into the melted muck above it, sometimes almost up to the insulators, or else were keeling over at crazy angles, threatening to break the connections. Here there were numbers of amphibious vehicles lying around in the mire, waiting for their drivers to come back after a weekend in town.

Down the line to the east the sky was a flaming red with the forest an impenetrably black wall silhouetted against it and the branches of the tallest trees like spikes along the top of it. Then the sun came roaring up, flooding the forest to the left of the line with a lurid light as if it was on fire, and turning the telegraph wires into glistening silver threads.

We were out of Eastern Siberia now, in the Far Eastern Economic Region, about two and a half million square miles, the largest region in the USSR but with a population of scarcely one person to every one of them. We were in upland country, and from time to time, to the right of the line, long vistas opened up, down wooded valleys towards the Amur, here about 40 miles to the south of the railway, and one could see cumulus and vapour trails high over China. The road beside the line was sometimes asphalt, sometimes earth turned to thick mud through which lorries and jeeps ploughed their way. It was rare to see a car. This was four-wheel-drive country.

Occasionally the *Rossiya* stopped at old-fashioned wooden stations, painted green or blue, which had waiting rooms with huge iron stoves in them extending from the floor to the ceiling and looking like cannon. At Shimanovskaya, 4831 miles from Moscow, a number of male passengers sloped off behind a woodpile, to emerge after a while carrying bottles of vodka. It was here that a militiaman seized both my hands and said that photography was forbidden, of everything.

We were emerging from the permafrost now and the *Rossiya* was running through birch forests full of little lakes, on some of which men were fishing from rowing boats, and when the train stopped you could hear hundreds of birds chattering away. Then, while we breakfasted off more of the *omul*, of which we were beginning to tire, the country began to open out. In the fields the wheat was already 18 inches high, which showed that we were really out of the permafrost zone, and there were lush meadows full of buttercups and bog cotton, and grassy banks covered with yellow lilies and lupins. Even the forest was changing. The everlasting larches and birches were thinning out and being replaced by oaks. Around one o'clock we crossed a big river, the Zeya, a tributary of the Amur (as were all the rivers we were crossing now). There were gold mines on its upper waters and in the ranges away to the north of the line. By now we were ravenous and we all trooped off to the restaurant car to find that it had been miraculously replenished with food, although the drink situation was the same; and there, with the temperature up to 86°F, we ate fish soup and minced steak, washed down with lemonade. All the time now the big, brilliantly painted containers from Japan and the United States were rushing past on their flat cars on their way to Europe. All that day the *Rossiya* travelled eastwards under a cloudless sky. Then, towards evening, away to the north, an enormous swirling cloud as black as night appeared over what was a practically limitless horizon and came racing towards the railway. In order to get a better view of this phenomenon I rushed to the back of the train and looked out of the window of the last car. By now it was nearing the line and not more than 100 feet above it. An apocalyptical wind began to blow, bending the trees and tearing the leaves from them, and forked lightning began to shoot earthwards from it while at the same time the sun continued to shine, bathing the whole landscape in a ghastly, yellowish light. Then, when the cloud was over the *Rossiya*, it released a deluge of rain, which was accompanied by prolonged and deafening peals of thunder. It was at this moment, just as we reached the 8020th kilometre mark from Moscow, that *Rossiya* No. 1 roared past in the opposite direction, inward bound from Vladivostok, streaming water and illuminated by the lightning which was now continuous, a magnificent sight. I shared this grandstand view of a Siberian storm with a very drunk Russian who was armed with a half-full bottle of vodka, and he was so overcome by the spectacle that in the course of those few minutes he finished it off. Soon this great cloud was gone beyond the Amur where it would presumably give the Chinese the same treatment as it had given us, once more leaving the sky overhead clear and blue as if nothing had happened.

At Zavitaya, which we reached just before 6 pm (11 am Moscow time) the *Rossiya* entered the seventh time zone from Moscow, and now it began to rain again. We were insatiably hungry, so hungry that we began to wonder if we had worms. By seven o'clock we were back once more in the restaurant car, which now had a distinctly cosmopolitan air as it contained, as well as the usual Russians and the Swiss, an English couple, two West Germans and an Australian, all of whom must have been lurking in the two-berth compartments since leaving Ulan-Ude, as this was the first time we had set eyes on them.

Outside, on the platform at Arkhara, laid out at the foot of a silver-painted statue of Lenin in the rain that was now belting down, with its lid on and with important looking seals on it, was a brand new, unpainted wooden coffin. Some of the staff of the restaurant car, including the cook, were so excited by this presumably unusual sight that in spite of the rain they got out to have a look at it, and the whole episode put them in the best of spirits, which was also pleasant for the customers.

'What a lucky joker', the Australian said, as the *Rossiya* pulled out, leaving the coffin and whatever was inside it either to be picked up by whomever it had been consigned to at Arkhara, or else to be sent further down the line by a local, stopping train.

'Six feet by two of Russian earth, a landowner at last.'

Now the sky cleared again and in the twilight the *Rossiya* followed a beautiful, green valley between wooded hills. At a place called Obluchye, where we stopped for ten minutes, we came as near as to China as we would anywhere while on the *Rossiya* (we would be changing to another train at Khabarovsk for the run to Nakhodka). Here, we were only about 15 miles from the Amur

River, but there was nothing to be seen as by now it was quite dark.

Nor did I see OBLUCHYE written up on the station in Russian and Yiddish; it is reputed to be, and it was something that I had promised myself I would see, but in the course of this long journey from Ulan-Ude I had completely forgotten about it until it was too late.

Obluchye is the first town, coming from the west on the railway, in the Jewish (Yevresk) Autonomous *oblast* which is popularly known as Birobidzhan. Birobidzhan is also the name of its capital, which was fabricated by amalgamating the names of two rivers, the Bira and the Bidzhan, which flow through its territory into the Amur. It became an autonomous republic in 1934 when Stalin, having failed to turn the Jews into collective farmers in western Russia, had the bright idea of moving the younger ones out of the bosoms of their still Orthodox elders and sending them to this bleak, lonely, swampy 13,895-square-mile area which lies in a big bend of the Amur and which, on that side, forms the border with China for a couple of hundred miles or so. There they would be able to till the soil and develop into good, conventional, Soviet Communist citizens.

Unfortunately, many young Jews who set off for Birobidzhan in a first flush of enthusiasm soon became disenchanted with it and returned whence they came. Another possible reason for their reluctance to remain, and one that does not seem to have been given sufficient consideration, was that, soon after the end of the war, Ivan Fyodor Nikishov was elected as their representative to the Soviet of Nationalities, one of the two Chambers (the other is the Soviet of the Union) that together form the Supreme Soviet of the USSR.

From 1938 onwards, for a period of nearly ten years, Nikishov, one of the cruellest and most merciless of men, was head of Dalstroy. This was a vast organization set up in 1931-2 to develop north-eastern Siberia and in particular the huge gold deposits in the Kolyma River area, using slave labour in an area where winter temperatures are among the lowest in Siberia.

In the first ten years of its existence Dalstroy, otherwise the Far Eastern Construction Trust, imported slaves into its territory by way of Magadan through Nagayev Harbour on the Sea of Okhotsk, which the slaves had to build, at the rate of about half a million a year. The mortality would have had to be enormous to require such influxes, and it was. Of the 12 million slaves who died in the USSR between 1936 and 1950, 3 million died in the Kolyma gold fields.

In 1944 Henry Wallace, at that time Vice-President of the United States, was invited to visit Magadan, the administrative centre of Dalstroy operations, and while there he and Professor Owen Lattimore, who accompanied him, were taken on a tour of inspection of a camp which had been given a face-lift and in which the prisoners were kept out of sight for the duration of the visit, their places being taken by bogus prisoners who were members of the NKVD. There they were entertained by Nikishov and his wife, herself an ex-NKVD camp guard as ruthless as he was; and there Wallace admired her embroidery, which had been done by one of the female prisoners. Lattimore's assessment of Nikishov, who had been decorated with the Order of Hero of the Soviet Union 'for his extraordinary achievement', was that he was a man 'having a deep sense of civic responsibility'. Little wonder that with such a representative the Jews departed in shoals.

By 1968 only 15,000 out of Birobidzhan's total population of 174,000 were Jews. By 1974, by which time the population had risen to 181,000, only 11,400 were Jews, less than 7 per cent of the population. Of these, a large number work in the garment industry, as did their forefathers in European Russia, and Birobidzhan is now the biggest producer of made-up textiles in the Far Eastern Region. It also produces combine rice harvesters, which have been exported with great fanfares of publicity to Iran, Iraq and Cuba, and building materials. Apparently it sits on a huge deposit of raw cement.

Although I had missed seeing the Russian–Yiddish nameplates on the station at Obluchye, I was not yet beaten. Surely, I reasoned to myself, similiar signs must exist at the station at Birobidzhan. After all it *was* the capital. According to my timetable, the *Rossiya* was due to arrive there at 6.47 pm Moscow time (which at Birobidzhan was the gruesome hour of 1.47 am, where it would remain for only five minutes. What could be easier than to get down there and photograph these signs for posterity? At the rate they were going, in another ten years there wouldn't be any Jews left in Birobidzhan.

I confided this idea to Otto, and eventually sold it to him, on the grounds that for him to pass through the only place on the Trans-Siberian Railway with any noteworthy agglomeration of Jews in it would be an affront to them, even though they didn't know that he was in the vicinity. Once I had succeeded in persuading him he became enthusiastic and began loading up a Leicaflex or a Nikon, I forget which, with some extremely fast film called GAF, and connecting it up with his infra-red flash synchronizer.

He was not so enthusiastic when I woke him at 1.15 am – I had already been up for half an hour, afraid of arriving too late on the scene, which was what had happened to me at the tunnel through the Yablonovyy Range. Outside, beyond the confines of light that shone out from the corridors of the *Rossiya*, there was nothing to be seen of what was supposed to be steppe, only the blackest of black night which was further blanketed by rain.

Photographers, whether amateur or professional, are not renowned for their sense of humour while pursuing their craft, but I must say that Otto when not sited behind one of his innumerable instruments was very funny, and particularly when being Jewish. For the next half hour we entertained one another while passing through this stygian land of the Jews by identifying imaginary Jewish enterprises in the god-forsaken landscape, talking in Yinglish, something I might have questioned the propriety of if Otto had not been Jewish, but something that I myself was fairly adept at, having spent twelve years in the wholesale garment industry.

Eventually, after what seemed hours, a faint blur of light away to the east announced the existence of this New Jerusalem beside the Amur.

'I'm using GAF, at 500 ASA. I'll give it a 30th at f8, but it'll have to be from about twenty feet,' Otto announced as the *Rossiya* came into the station.

Fortunately the dotty-looking conductress, who liked us, was in charge. By the time she had got the steps down and we had got on to the platform, a few muffled figures were shuffling through the rain towards the station building which had a facade so dimly lit that it would have been difficult to make out if it had a twice life-size poster of Lenin on it, let alone a couple of signs in Russian and Yiddish.

'I think I'll have a trial shot,' said Otto to no one in particular, pointing his apparatus at the rear of the train as we moved towards the station buildings, 'just to make sure it's working OK.'

It was. There was an incandescence brighter than a thousand suns. Then he did it again, this time pointed at the station, then once more, by which time angry shouts could be heard and figures began emerging from the building. Quickly, we hopped back into the *Rossiya*. The conductress, who was screaming with laughter, pulled up the steps, shut and locked the door and the *Rossiya*, which had created a record by staying at Birobidzhan for less than its scheduled time, something that it had never done before in the course of the entire journey, began to pull out and roll away to Khabarovsk.

If the pictures that Otto took of the facade of the station at Birobidzhan are anything to go by, there is no sign in Yiddish on it. If there is one then it is probably on the elevation facing the street.

After this ludicrous adventure I slept only fitfully, and at about a quarter past four we all got up in order to prepare to disembark from the *Rossiya* at Khabarovsk. Dawn was just breaking over a grey, sodden landscape with nothing in it. The train was stationary in the steppe, opposite a marsh from which rose the croakings of innumerable frogs and strange, whistling noises made by water birds. Then the *Rossiya* let out a mighty bellow and began to move forward, and about ten minutes later she rumbled out on to the biggest bridge on the entire railway, the twenty-two span girder bridge across the Amur, here nearly a mile and a half wide and more like a large inlet of the sea than a river. Then the *Rossiya* was running among hills, past an oil refinery that was belching flames, and slid into the station at Khabarovsk, 5331 miles from Moscow. It was 9.35 pm on 13 June Moscow time, 4.35 am at Khabarovsk on 14 June. Now the *Rossiya* only had 478 miles – 14 hours and 10 minutes

– to go before it reached the Pacific at Vladivostok. Even before we had left the station its twenty-minute halt at Khabarovsk was already used up, and it pulled out. I felt sad to see it go, and cheated not to have completed the journey to Vladivostok, like a visitor to Tibet who fails to see the Potala.

18

Amurkabel

It is hard to imagine our life nowadays without electricity, or electricity without conducting means manufactured by our Plant, such as aluminium–steel wires for overhead lines, mine cables, ship cables, general-purpose wires, extra-flexible trailing cables for movable current collectors, high-voltage aluminium sheathed cables and armoured cables....

Amurkabel

'YOU will now go to your rooms and rest. Breakfast will be at 8.30,' said the friendly, neighbourhood Intourist guide after a bus journey through completely empty streets, with the other members of the *Rossiya's* cosmopolitan dining club who had alighted here. 'Then you will begin your tours of Khabarovsk at 10.30.'

Wanda and I decided not to rest, and we set off on a personally conducted tour of the city in which, apart from the lady street-cleaners who were now out and about, we were the only people abroad: past the statue of Khabarov, outside the railway station, which was being used as a guano depository by some gulls; downhill along wide streets, past big blocks of flats, less sorrowful than those at Bratsk; uphill through one of the older parts of the town where the streets were lined with trees, old stone buildings and wooden houses; then down through the Park of Culture to an embankment on the right bank of the Amur, here 2700 miles from the source of its ultimate tributary, the Onon, where fishermen were out in force and in which barges were being shoved upstream against the current by motor vessels that pushed instead of tugged. From there we went up past what had formerly been the Museum of the Russian Imperial Geographical Society, founded by the same Baron Korf who had put the wind up the Tsar in his report about the Yellow Peril; through a children's playground where we, too, played with the toys; and came out on a rocky eminence with an immense view across the Amur to the treeless steppe beyond and an even better one upstream where two isolated, detached mountains rose into the air close to the Chinese border. No sign of the statue of Count Muravyev-Amursky, who founded Khabarovsk in 1858 which, at least until the Revolution, stood on this eminence. Its plinth was still there but the statue had been taken away and replaced by one of Lenin. It was a mouldy thing to have done, especially as there was already a metal one of him in Lenin Square, outside the hotel.

From here, having paid silent tribute to Count Muravyev-Amursky, whose statue has probably been melted down to make yet another statue of the founder of the Soviet Union, we went down to the landing stages for the river steamers, which, with their office buildings and waiting rooms on top of them, looked like arks; and there got into what might have been trouble with a policeman for photographing them.

Then, having admired the offices of the Amur Steamship Company on Komsomolskaya Square, a fine building of the *belle époque*, we returned to the hotel by way of Karl Marx Street, where the principal shops were. Apart from seeing the inside of Baron Korf's Museum, the Fine Arts Museum, the Tower beside the Amur in which a number of Austro-Hungarian military bandsmen who had been made prisoners-of-war had been shot in 1918 for refusing to play the Russian National Anthem and the Arboretum, and taking a conducted tour of the bridge over the Amur, we seemed to have done Khabarovsk.

'Listen, Mischa,' I said at breakfast, which we consumed together with the local rep. from The Agency, 'I know we've only got one day in Khabarovsk now, but on the way back from Nakhodka we've got another day or two here if we want them. Before we came to Russia I sent your people a list of things I would really like to see. For instance, I would like to go to some village in the *taiga*, and see how the people live.'

'Unfortunately it is impossible to visit a village in the *taiga*, because of the insect that causes encephalitis.'

'The *clesh*?'

'Yes. None of you have been inoculated against it.'

'Well, why can't we visit that man who captures Siberian tigers alive? Ivan Bogachev, I think his name is?'

'Ivan Bogachev is dead and, besides, the reserve is near the Ussuri River and you are not allowed to go without special permission.'

'But I asked for special permission.'

'It has not come through.'

'Well, what about visiting the men who look for *ginseng* roots, or the ones who go after the deer for their horns, the *panti*. I asked for permission to see them, too.'

'The permissions for these have also not come through,' Mischa said, rather wearily, as if he was answering a lot of unanswerable questions posed by a child, which in effect was what he was doing.

'Well, at least, can we see the Arboretum?'

'Yes, you can see the Arboretum this afternoon,' said Mischa, 'but this morning we are going to Amurkabel.'

'What's Amurkabel?' Otto asked, emerging from what appeared to be a trance.

'Amurkabel is the largest wire-making plant in the Far East. It employs 2500 workers.'

'Listen, Mischa,' I said. 'You and Wanda and Otto can all go to the wire-making factory if you want to. Personally, I've seen so much wire in so many wire factories in my life that if it was all put into a heap it would cover more ground than the Matto Grosso.'

'If you do not go to Amurkabel,' Mischa said – by now he was becoming very angry – 'you will cause grave offence and I will be forced to report to Moscow that you are a trouble-maker. You are a writer, and you are supposed to be writing a book about Siberia and the Trans-Siberian Railway. I do not care whether you write it or not, but you must go to Amurkabel.'

We all went to Amurkabel.

Amurkabel was housed in a largish factory on the outskirts of the city. Next to it there were some blocks of flats that housed the workers. When we arrived the technical information bureau chief, a Mr Beresnev, and a number of faceless satellites were waiting for us.

'The cars of the workers,' said Mr Beresnev proudly, pointing to fourteen vehicles parked outside, as we swept through doors held open by professional door-openers into the administration building.

'But there are 2500 workers. Do only fourteen have cars?'

'Only half the workers are on shift,' said Mr Beresnev, completely unperturbed. 'This is the day shift.'

'But the day shift's 1250 people!'

'They don't need their cars because they live next door,' said Mr Beresnev, and I began to wonder if I was going round the bend.

After enduring the *mineralniye vody* treatment for an hour or so we were taken on a tour of the plant, shown the various machines that reeled up cable core coming from a continuous-process vulcanizer, coated the wire with enamel, and braided it with fibre glass, as well as machines for drawing the wire out from whatever stuff it was made from, and so on. Amazingly, none of them was working, and apart from one or two men and women who were either repairing machines or walking around stroking them with oily cloths, there were no workers.

'Where is everyone?' Otto said, loaded down with equipment and fed up with all this. 'How am I supposed to take photographs of a factory with no workers in it?'

'This is the dinner break,' said Mr Beresnev. 'All the workers are in the canteen.'

'Well, then, let's go to the canteen.'

When we reached the canteen, it was populated by about forty or fifty men and women, many of them elderly, some of them wearing white coats – none of them wearing the sort of dungarees that the machine-minders had on. It was obvious from their garb that, whoever they were, they all hailed from the clean-hands departments, and that this was *their* canteen. There was not a single grease mark of the sort that the grimy beings we had seen could not have failed to leave on the surface of the spotless tables; and, anyway, the canteen was much too small to accommodate even a third part of the day shift. Wherever the workers ate it was not here.

'Well, where are the workers?' Otto said.

'Unfortunately,' said Mr Beresnev, 'they have just gone back on shift. But now,' he went on, indicating a table at which other managerial persons were hovering, waiting for us to join them, covered with a spotless cloth and with a whole battery of wine and other glasses at each place setting, 'it is time for us to eat.'

'Tell me,' Mr Beresnev asked, leaning across the table towards me, in the course of what was proving to be a copious and excellent luncheon. 'Do you believe in God?'

It was an unusual question to be asked by the technical information bureau chief of a wire factory, even though it was 5300 miles east of Moscow.

'Mr Beresnev,' I said, 'I don't know what your feelings are about this matter, but one thing I am certain about is that, if there is no such thing as God, you wouldn't be showing me round your wire factory.'

Later that afternoon a small, highly intelligent woman, who had an excellent command of English, took us round the Arboretum of the Far East Forestry Research Institute. It was a charming, old-fashioned place, founded in 1935 on the site of a tree nursery, set up about 100 years ago to supply Khabárovsk with saplings. Now hemmed in by buildings, it was almost miraculously preserved, together with its 1300 sorts of trees and shrubs indigenous to the Soviet Far East.

While we were ambling about it, Mischa showed signs of impatience, as he always did whenever we visited anything faintly old or of pre-revolutionary date; but at last he succeeded in getting us back into the waiting cars. There was a further delay while our guide went off to get for me the last copy the Arboretum possessed, other than its file copy, of a descriptive pamphlet to it written in English.

'Vod is dis life,' she said, ignoring Mischa and his colleagues, as she presented it to me, 'if full of care, ve haf no time to stand and stare.'

19

Night Train to
the Great Ocean

THAT evening at 6.25 pm local time (11.25 am Moscow time) we boarded the *Vostok*, the night train to Nakhodka. By this time the *Rossiya* had already been six hours in Vladivostok, and in another four hours and fifty minutes would be starting on the return journey to Moscow.

The *Vostok* was made up of a half-dozen green passenger cars, drawn by an electric engine, and from the outside looked no different to any normal Russian passenger train. On the inside it was fantastic, a train-that-never-was, something that might have been designed by Beaton for Garbo, using for money the three-year box office take from *My Fair Lady*: the perfect train, kept forever behind the wall in Plato's Cave, of which only distorted shadows are seen in the outer world, all shining mahogany, brass and scintillating glass.

Each of the two-berth compartments was loaded with mahogany, some of it gilded. The mahogany armchair was covered in red plush (and so was the brass door chain) and the coved roof was also banded with mahogany. The finely chased door furniture was solid brass, and the screws in the brass door hinges had been aligned by some artisan so that each of the cuts in the heads of the screws was parallel with the ones below it and next to it. The mahogany table had a brass rim round it; there were brass rails around the luggage compartment overhead to stop the cabin trunks crashing between one's ears, the ashtrays were solid brass, and the cut-glass ceiling light had a brass finial on it.

On the floor there was a thick red and green Turkey carpet. On the beds snow-white pillows had been arranged in a manner that suggested that this work had been performed by a parlourmaid who had majored in household management around 1903. The sheets were freshly ironed and so were the white voile curtains which were also supported on a brass rail.

In the bathroom, with which the compartment was connected by way of a mahogany door, there was a full-length looking glass, a stainless steel washbasin as big as a font, furnished with nickel-plated taps (the sort that stay on once you have turned them on), and the stainless steel lavatory basin had a polished mahogany seat. The shower head was attached to a flexible tube. The towels were thick and sumptuous and the heavy water carafe held two litres. Illumination in the bathroom was provided by a frosted glass window which gave on to the corridor. On the outside this window was embellished with an art-nouveau motif, also in solid brass, and in the corridor this motif was echoed in the decoration of the ceiling lights. The corridor, in which golden curtains oscillated with the movement of the train (which, admittedly was far more bumpy than that of the *Rossiya*), was provided with a number of tip-up seats, also upholstered in red plush, for those who had grown weary while on the way to and from the restaurant car, and the carpet was the same as those in the compartments.

And everything worked. If this was not enough, our particular car was equipped with the most beautiful conductress I had seen on the Russian or any other railway system. She was reputed to be of Czech origin. Perhaps the whole thing came from Czechoslovakia, for it was newly built, and she with it. If it was built in Russia, where had the Russians found the artisans to build it? From the same source that produced the men and women who refurbished the Summer Palace at Tsarskoye Selo?

The train trundled out of Khabarovsk past allotment plots, soldiers laying track in a siding; over level crossings with long queues of lorries, their drivers fuming; through marshalling yards in which disembodied, gravelly voices were giving instructions through loudspeakers mounted on poles; past long trains of red, yellow and black tank waggons being shoved up inclines by bright green diesels, the *Vostok* mooing, the factory chimneys belching black and yellow smoke; running past stagnant ponds and fatigued-

looking trees, out into the country where the ponds were clearer,
red in the now-setting sun: out between the two hills, now with
mist rising around them, that we had seen from the one-time site
of Muravyev-Amursky's statue that morning. On to Vyazemskiy,
a very-close-to-the-Chinese-frontier town which was immediately
to the west across the always invisible Ussuri. There the train halted
for five minutes, long enough for Wanda to borrow a bike from the
station-mistress and go for a ride on it.

It was a brilliant evening. To the east the country was open and
rolling. The fields along the line of the railway were full of straw-
berries in flower, currants and raspberries and sweetcorn.

All through the twilight the *Vostok* rolled along the frontier with
long views, across expanses of open plain, of hills and mountains
that were in China. To the right of the line in one section there
was a continuous wire fence with a splayed top. It was about seven
feet high and showed signs of being electrified. Beyond it there was
a wide strip of freshly raked earth. At kilometre mark 8672 the fence
turned away westwards towards the heights above the Ussuri on
the Russian side, where the watch towers were silhouetted against
an apple green sky that had small, black bands of cloud floating
in it.

Then we had dinner. If the restaurant car was anything to go
by, there was not a single Russian passenger on this train. In fact,
the *Vostok* was not a train run for the benefit of Russians. It was
the boat train for the Russian ferry service from Nakhodka to Yokohama and Hong Kong, and the passengers, all of whom were from
capitalist countries, were bearers of valuable foreign currency. The
Japanese on board were nothing like the little men in black suits
who work for Mitsubishi and get married by numbers, but up-to-
date people who regarded a suit as something you got buried in.
The Americans were mostly one-time love children from Haight-
Ashbury, now grown up and thinking about their mortgages: the
men had moustaches and suits from the Cable Car Clothiers, and
their girls were in easy-to-pack cotton jersey; and from what one
could hear, all of them had made the great leap forward into the
Psychobabble era while living in Marin.

But it was fun in the restaurant car with the lovely big drinks

coming. No shortages on this train, of anything, and the pretty waitresses smiled and stopped to chat, after bringing to you items that
were always 'off' on the *Rossiya*. But in spite of it all I still thought
nostalgically of the *Rossiya*, simply because we had spent so much
time together.

While we slept soundly as a result of this bout of unusual good
living, the *Vostok* continued to run southwards through the flat,
marshy country, bitterly cold in winter, hot and humid in summer,
between the Ussuri and the Sikhote Alin Range, which extends for
750 miles along the Pacific seaboard from Nikolayevsk, near the
mouth of the Amur, to Vladivostok. It is in the mountains of the
Sikhote Alin that the finest procurable ginseng roots, *Panax schin-
seng*, are to be found at the foot of cedar and larch trees. And this
was the not-so-happy hunting ground of a Chinese sect known as
Va-pa-tsui, who used to search for these roots – not so happy
because the area was infested with Siberian tigers, which used to eat
them, and with robbers who used to knock them on the head and
take their *ginseng* away.

At Ussuriysk, 5710 miles from Moscow and now only 141
miles from Vladivostok, the *Vostok* left the Trans-Siberian Railway and turned away to the south-east on the branch line to
Nakhadka.

The last 478-mile stretch of the Trans-Siberian, between Vladivostok and Khabarovsk, which we were now not on anymore, was
built by a motley collection of hard-to-come-by labourers –
15,000 Chinese coolies were brought in, and from Sakhalin Island
across the Tatar Strait, soldiers, exiles and convicts were brought
over, many of whom were murderers, and who continued to rob
and murder the inhabitants of Vladivostok when they escaped from
their guards, which they frequently did. In the course of its construction every conceivable kind of natural and unnatural disaster
occurred. There were outbreaks of anthrax and fever, the Ussuri
rose frequently and inundated the works, and the famous Siberian
tigers struck terror into everyone's hearts. It took more than
six years to build it and was not fully operative until November
1897.

I woke around five-thirty and the delicious Czech conductress took me down the train to a car where an elderly conductor, who looked as if he might be of Manchurian origin, had just unlocked his samovar and was making tea. Outside there was fog and drizzle, and occasionally we passed a *dacha*-like house standing in a clearing in the oak woods. At a quarter to six, Muravinaya Bay, an arm of the Pacific, or more accurately of the Sea of Japan, hove in view momentarily across a dreary expanse of marsh, with a solitary white hut with a light burning standing in it and a line of telegraph poles stretching across it, a grey stretch of water on a rocky, fog-bound coast.

By now I had discovered that there were a couple of coaches at the rear of the train with real Russians in them, and I set off to explore, but was brought back by the Czech conductress. And now we passed through several towns in which there were ribbon developments of wooden houses, plants producing steam heat and delivering it through huge silver pipes, coal mines with old-fashioned winding gear, slag heaps and, at one place near the sea, what looked liked salt pans.

Then, just after seven o'clock, the train began to descend a wide, mist-filled valley, the steep sides of which were densely wooded with tall, deciduous trees, and in which the villages of white-painted houses had more geese than human beings visible in them, down to the Suchan River which rises in the same massif as the Ussuri.

At nine o'clock the *Vostok* was running down the right bank of the Suchan River on a ledge cut out of the sheer cliffs that rose above it. Beyond the river there was a low range of mountains covered with smoking cloud, and in the meadows down by the water big herds of cattle were huddled together, steaming. It was damnably cold for June.

Near Kuznetsovo the *Vostok* passed a new spur of the railway, a double-track line which crossed the river and led away in the direction of Vostochnyy, the Eastern Port, which is being built on the shores of Vrangel Bay, east of Nakhodka. It will be completed in 1990, and when the BAM railway begins to operate it will become its coal terminal on the Pacific.

Now the *Vostok*, uttering wild, bellowing noises as it went, ran past a big isolated bluff which rose out of the valley floor. Then, quite suddenly, there was the Pacific, lots of it, greyer than the grey sky above, and with a Chinese-style sugar loaf hill rising above the coastline away to the north. As the *Vostok* curved away to the right from the river a mass of merchant ships, anchored in the outer roads, came into view. Then it ran in behind the port warehouses with dozens of cranes rising beyond them and there were fleeting glimpses of ships moored alongside, piles of what looked like silver ingots, and behind a disused bus in an open lot a momentary view of some small boys puffing away at cigarettes. Finally, at 9.25 am local time (2.25 am Moscow time) on 15 June, the *Vostok* rolled into Tikhookeanskaya Station at Nakhodka, 569 miles from Khabarovsk, 5900 miles from Moscow. We had made it. The journey was over.

'And now,' Mischa said, 'We are going to a conference with the Mayor of Nakhodka.'

We were sitting in the lounge of a hotel on the outskirts of the town. From its windows there was a view that included Partizanskaya Creek, the sugar loaf hill which was called the 'Sister', and some spoil barges. It was as cold and grey as ever. With us was a 'journalist' who never left us and never opened his mouth in our presence, except to put food in it: if he was a journalist, which seemed highly unlikely, he must have worked for a paper catering for the deaf and dumb. There was also a rather nice girl from Intourist.

'Listen Mischa,' I said. 'As we were coming into Nakhodka on the *Vostok* you asked me if I wanted to meet the Mayor and I said I didn't. Remember?'

'I don't want to meet the Mayor, either,' said Otto.

'There isn't any point in my meeting the Mayor,' Wanda said. 'I don't want to photograph him and I don't want to interview him.'

'What we really do want to see is the fishing port, and we also want to go on board one of the big fishing ships,' I said. 'And before that we want to see the ferry leave for Yokohama.'

'It is all arranged, the meeting with the Mayor. He is already waiting for us. It was arranged from Khabarovsk. Besides, there is no fishing port at Nakhodka,' Mischa said. By this time he was becoming angry.

'Well if there's no fishing port, how do you account for Nakhodka being the base for your ocean-going fishing fleet in the Far East?'

'That is so,' said the girl from Intourist, proud of her native place. 'There is a fishing port. It is the biggest.'

'You're playing us a dirty trick, Mischa,' I said, really very angry myself by this time. 'Just because you want to get some copy out of the Mayor of Nakhodka there's no earthly reason why we have to go too. You go. We want to see the ferry leave for Yokohama.'

'Watch what you're saying, Newby, or it will be the worse for you,' he shouted, and went off in a fury, taking the journalist and the Intourist girl with him, no doubt to give her a rocket for letting him down over the fishing fleet.

After a few minutes he came back, with the journalist but without her, having cooled down a bit by this time.

'The fishing port is being reconstructed, and you cannot visit it,' he said. 'I have cancelled your visit to the Mayor, and will go and see him myself. He was extremely displeased. This gentleman and the Intourist guide will accompany you to the ferry terminus.'

We stood on the quay outside the ferry terminal building, which resembled a huge, old wooden hunting lodge in Red Indian country, watching the other passengers from the *Vostok* going up the gangplank of the good ship *Baikal* past a frontier guard who stood at the foot of it. The Japanese were so heavily laden with loot from Europe that some of them failed to get up the gangplank with it and had to make two journeys. Soon the ship's side was manned by dozens of our newly found, and equally soon to be lost, friends, all waving.

They continued to wave for the next thirty minutes until twelve noon, when the *Baikal* cast off and the tugs began to take her out, until she was far from the quay, and we had no alternative but to wave back at them all this time, without stopping, as the three of us were the only people seeing them off.

'Lucky bastards,' Otto said. 'Providing they don't run into a typhoon in a couple of days they'll be sniffing cherry blossom.'

'In June, in Yokohama?' I said. 'You must be joking.'

Late the following afternoon I stood with Wanda on some high ground above the port area beside an enormous hoarding with a poster stuck on it which showed a female worker making WHAM! POW! with her clenched fist and shouting 'Peace to the People!' There was a bitter wind from the north-east, the sea was choppy and the temperature was around 41°F. Looking down on the fishing port, which in spite of what Mischa said seemed to be flourishing, its fish-canning and can-making factories, its miles of quay, its ship-building yards, its 300-ton floating crane, one of two in the USSR (the other is in the Black Sea) which had been towed round the Cape of Good Hope, and its big dry dock which had been brought 15,000 miles from Klaipedia in Lithuania by the same route, it was difficult to believe that at the end of the war there had been nothing here but a few shacks. Now Nakhodka was a city of 120,000 people and the biggest commercial port in the Soviet Far East; and when Vostochnyy, the Eastern Port, really gets going, around 1990, it will have five times the annual turnover of Nakhodka, which is now 9 million tons a year, 75 per cent of which is foreign trade cargo. We had been to Vostochnyy, by boat across the bay, and had damn nearly frozen to death there. It was almost completely automated and utterly eerie, out there in the wilderness, with huge yards for exporting lumber which was moved about by Hitachi travelling gantries each of which could lift 16 tons; and it was also a stop-off for containers from the United States and Japan which from here were sent by the Trans-Continental Route to Europe. It was being built with Japanese capital, and somewhere there on the shores of Vrangel Bay the 10,000 men and women who were building it were living in huts, although we saw no more than half a dozen all the time we were there.

Over both these ports and the Tchadaudja Oil Harbour (over the hill from Nakhodka) and also over the city itself, an air of super-secrecy and security brooded. The whole place was crawling with frontier guards. When foreign sailors wanted to go ashore for the evening they were met at the gangplank by buses which took them straight to the International Seamen's Club and, when the evening was over, straight back to the ship. In winter the only thing that doesn't freeze at Nakhodka is the sea, which is why it was built there.

'I've had enough of Nakhodka,' Wanda said. Her teeth were chattering. 'It's a hell of a place. What's more I've had enough of Siberia, and we've all had enough of Mischa, and I'm fed up with your damn maps. I want to go home.'

So we did.

Bibliography

ATLASES

Atlas SSR (Atlas of the USSR), 2nd ed. (Moscow 1969).
The Times Atlas of the World, comprehensive edition; 4th ed. (London 1973).
The Times Survey Atlas of the World (London 1922).
The Times Atlas of China (London 1974).
The Oxford Regional Economic Atlas. The USSR and Eastern Europe (London 1956).
Fullard, Harold (ed.), *China in Maps* (London 1968).
Fullard, Harold (ed.), *Soviet Union in Maps* (London 1972).

MAPS

Northwestern Asia, 1:5,000,000 Sheet 5, Series 1106 Edition 1-AMS. Ordnance Survey for Ministry of Defence.
Northeastern Asia, 1:5,000,000 Sheet 6, Series 1106, Edition 1-AMS. Ordnance Survey for Ministry of Defence.

TIMETABLES

Various Soviet Railway timetables and Station Route Book. Price, J. H., *Thomas Cook International Timetable* (Peterborough, monthly).

GUIDES ETC.

Admiralty Sailing Directions: *Arctic Vol I; Bering Sea and Strait; East Coast of Siberia and Korea* (London).

Baedeker, Karl, *Russia with Teheran, Port Arthur and Peking* (Leipzig 1914).

Bradshaw's Continental Guide for Travellers through Europe, introduction by J. H. Price (London 1914, reprinted 1972).

Dmitriev-Mamonov, A. I. and Zdziarski, A. F. (eds), *Guide to the Great Siberian Railway*, trans. L. Kulol-Yasnopolsky; rev. John Marshall (St Petersburg 1900. Reprinted Newton Abbot 1971).

Louis, V. and L., *The Complete Guide to the Soviet Union* (London 1976).

Mitchell, T., *Handbook for Travellers in Russia, Poland and Finland*, 2nd rev. ed. (London 1868).

Moore, W. G., *The Penguin Encyclopaedia of Places* (London 1971).

Wagret, M. P. (ed.), *Nagels Encyclopaedia Guide*, USSR (Geneva 1973).

Whitaker's Almanack (London, various dates).

Armstrong, Terence, *Russian Settlement in the North* (Cambridge 1965).

Atkinson, Mrs, *Recollections of Tartar Steppes and their Inhabitants* (London 1863).

Atkinson, Thomas Witlam, *Oriental and Western Siberia and Chinese Tartary* (London 1858).

Atkinson, Thomas Witlam, *Travels in the Regions of the Upper and Lower Amoor and the Russian Acquisitions on the Confines of India and China* (London 1860)

Baker, J. N. L., *A History of Geographical Discovery and Exploration* (London 1931).

Barzini, Luigi, *Peking to Paris. An Account of Prince Borghese's Journey Across Two Continents in a Motor Car* (London 1907).

Byron, Robert, *First Russia Then Tibet* (London 1933).

Chekhov, Anton, *Letters*, selected and edited by Avraham Yarmolinsky (London 1974).

Cochrane, J. D., *A Pedestrian Journey through Russia and Siberia. Tartary from the Frontiers of the Frozen Sea and Kamchatka* (London 1825).

Collins, Perry McDonough, *United States Commercial Agent at the*

Amoor River. A Voyage Down the Amoor: With a Land Journey Through Siberia, and Incidental Notices of Manchooria, Kamschatka, and Japan (New York 1864).

Collins, Perry McDonough, *Overland Explorations in Siberia, Northern Asia and the Great Amoor River Country; Incidental Notices of Manchooria, Mongolia, Kamschatka, and Japan, with Map and Plan of an Overland Telegraph Around the World* (New York 1864).

Conolly, Violet, *Beyond the Urals* (London 1967).

Conolly, Violet, *Siberia Today and Tomorrow, A Study of Economic Problems* (London 1975).

Conquest, Robert, *The Great Terror* (London 1968).

Conquest, Robert, *Kolyma. The Arctic Death Camps* (London 1978).

Couling, Samuel, *The Encyclopaedia Sinica* (Shanghai 1917).

Custine, The Marquis de, *The Empire of the Czar, or Observations on the Social, Political and Religious State and Prospects of Russia,* translated from the French (London 1843).

Czaplicka, M. A., *Aboriginal Siberia* (Oxford 1914).

Dallin, David J. and Nicolaevsky, Boris I., *Forced Labour in Soviet Russia* (London 1948).

Dawson, C. (ed). *The Mongol Mission, Narratives and Letters of the Franciscan Missionaries in Mongolia and China in the Thirteenth and Fourteenth Centuries,* translated by a nun of Sherbrooke Abbey (London and New York 1955).

Encyclopaedia Brittanica, 9th ed. (Edinburgh 1898).

Fleming, Peter, *The Fate of Admiral Kolchak* (London 1963).

Fraser, John F., *The Real Siberia* (London 1902).

Gunther, John, *Inside Russia* (London 1958).

Hookham, Hilda, 'Builders of the Trans-Siberian Railway', *History Today* (August 1966).

Kaiser, Robert G., *Russia the People and the Power* (London 1976).

Kalesnik, S. V. and Pavlenko, V. F., *Soviet Union, A Geographical Survey*, various editors and authors (Moscow 1976).

Kennan, George, *Tent Life in Siberia and Adventures among the Koraks and other Tribes in Kamchatks and Northern Asia* (New York 1870).

Kennan, George, *Siberia and the Exile System* (London 1891).

Kropotkin, Peter, *Memoirs of a Revolutionist* (New York 1899).

Lansdell, Henry, *Through Siberia* (London 1883).

Le Fleming, H. M. and Price, J. H., *Russian Steam Locomotives* (Newton Abbot 1972).

Levin, M. G. and Potapov, L. P. (ed.), *The Peoples of Siberia*, English translation ed. Stephen Dunn (Chicago 1964).

Lydolph, Paul, *Geography of the USSR*, 3rd ed. (London, New York 1977).

Michie, Alexander, *The Siberian Overland Route from Peking to Petersburg. Through the Deserts and Steppes of Mongolia, Tartary, &c.* (London 1864).

Mitchell, M., *Maritime History of Russia* (London 1949).

Nordenskiold, A. E., *The Voyage of the Vega Round Asia and Europe, With a Historical Review of Previous Journeys along the North Coast of the Old World*, trans. A. Leslie (London 1885).

McWhirter, Norris and Ross (ed.), (New York, London 1973 and 1977). *Guinness Book of Records.*

Pares, Bernard, *A History of Russia*, (5th ed). (London 1947).

Pokshishevsky, V., *Geography of the Soviet Union* (Moscow 1974).

Polo, Marco, *The Book of Ser Marco Polo the Venetian, concerning the Kingdoms and Marvels of the East*, trans. and ed. Colonel Sir Henry Yule; 3rd ed. rev. Henri Cordier (London 1903).

St George, George, *Siberia, The New Frontier* (London 1969).

Scott, John, *Behind the Urals* (London 1942).

Semyonov, Yuri, *Siberia, Its Conquest and Development*, trans. J. R. Foster (London 1963).

Silverlight, John, *The Victors' Dilemma* (London 1970).

Smith, Hedrick, *The Russians* (New York 1976).

Summers, Anthony and Mangold, Tom, *The File on the Tsar* (London 1976).

Theroux, Paul, *The Great Railway Bazaar* (London 1975).

Treadgold, Donald, *The Great Migration* (Princeton 1957).

Tupper, Harmon, *To the Great Ocean. Siberia and the Trans-Siberian Railway* (London 1965).

Westwood, J. N., *A History of Russian Railways* (London 1964).

Zonn, J. G., *Through Siberia by Train* (San Francisco 1976).

Index

Eric Newby
Love and War in the Apennines £3.99

After the Italian Armistice of 1943, Eric Newby left the prison camp in which he'd been held and evaded the advancing Germans by going to ground high in the mountains and forests south of the river Po. He was sheltered and protected for over three months by Italian peasants, and his account of these idiosyncratic and selfless people and of their bleak lifestyle is interwoven with a tale of dangerous, funny and bizarre incidents and of his hopes of the local girl who was to become his wife.

'The men, women and children, weather and woodsmoke are as fresh as yesterday' OBSERVER

'An exciting story, superbly told' PUNCH

'Italian village life, full of notable characters . . . and the reactions of one sensitive man to being out of the war in the middle of one'
DAILY TELEGRAPH

Slowly Down the Ganges £4.50

The story of the 1200-mile journey made by Eric Newby and his wife from Hardwar, where India's holy river enters the great plain, down to where the waters of the Hooghly flow into the Bay of Bengal. Travelling in a variety of boats and by rail, bus and bullock cart, they met an engaging assortment of characters and the dusty enchantment of India, all evocatively described with Newby's brilliant talent.

'Vintage Newby' GUARDIAN

'No journey into an unmapped interior to carry the word or find a lost explorer was more obstinately seen through to its end than this do-it-yourself pleasure trip' THE TIMES LITERARY SUPPLEMENT

'Any book by Eric Newby is an event' LEN DEIGHTON

Eric Newby
Something Wholesale £3.99

My Life and Times in the Rag Trade

Eric Newby's adventures during the years he spent as a commercial traveller
in the improbable trade of *haute couture*, from his repatriation as a
prisoner-of-war in 1945 until he embarked upon *A Short Walk in the
Hindu Kush* in 1956, were as full of chaos and bizarre incident as any that
befell him before or after. *Something Wholesale* is his hilarious and
splendidly macabre account of the confusion and disorder that was his life
apprenticed to the family firm of Lane and Newby. It is also an affectionate
portrait of his father, a delightful eccentric who spent most of his time
averting disasters or actively participating in them, his heart more in his
abiding passion, sculling, than in the preservation of the tottering edifice
that was his business.

'I read it at once and liked it awfully' EVELYN WAUGH

A Short Walk in the Hindu Kush £3.99

Eric Newby made a classic journey, from Mayfair to the wild mountains of
the Hindu Kush, north-east of Kabul. As a more recent generation of
travellers has discovered, Afghanistan can be an inhospitable place; as this
truly diverting and evocative book shows, it is also one of the most
spectacularly beautiful wildernesses on earth. With a preface by Evelyn
Waugh.

'The funniest travel book I have ever read' OBSERVER

'Tough, extrovert, humorous and immensely literate'
THE TIMES LITERARY SUPPLEMENT

Eric Newby
Round Ireland in Low Gear £4.99

'In the autumn of 1985, more or less on the spur of the moment, we decided to go back to Ireland. We were not going to travel in the guise of sociologists, journalists or contemporary historians. We were not going there, we hoped, to be shot at. We were going there to enjoy ourselves, an unfashionable aspiration in the 1980s . . .'

When Eric and Wanda Newby set out to find Ireland they set out on two wheels apiece. Their chosen mode of transport was described by *The Bicycle Buyer's Bible* as – in one case – a *Crossfell* and in the other – a *Wild Cat*. To the Irish, they were simply 'boikes'. A whole catalogue of expensive essential extras later, one of the all-time greats of travel writing was equipped to journey *Round Ireland in Low Gear* – with Wanda 'to keep him out of trouble'.

Lashed by storms of winter, fuelled by Guinness and warmed by thermal underwear, they set out on their travels along the highways and by-ways of the isle of Erin, with every pannier packed with maps, spare parts and a veritable library of books on Ireland's stones and stories.

They traced the footsteps of saints and hermits, visited the ruins of castles and the remains of follies, sought out Armada wrecks and cities lost in time. More immediately, they were expelled from Lismore by fearsome ladies and chased by even more fearsome dogs. They talked poetry on the banks of the Grand Canal and peat-cutting with a master of the craft in the great Bog of Allen. They drank in pubs of sepulchral bleakness and stayed overnight in B&Bs of daunting rectitude. From the horse fair at Spancil Hill to Croagh Patrick's holy mountain, they left very few of old Ireland's stones unturned to produce a volume of the finest and funniest travel writing in many a long season.

All Pan books are available at your local bookshop or newsagent, or can be ordered direct from the publisher. Indicate the number of copies required and fill in the form below.

Send to: **CS Department, Pan Books Ltd., P.O. Box 40, Basingstoke, Hants.   RG21 2YT.**

or phone: 0256 469551 (Ansaphone), quoting title, author and Credit Card number.

Please enclose a remittance* to the value of the cover price plus: 60p for the first book plus 30p per copy for each additional book ordered to a maximum charge of £2.40 to cover postage and packing.

*Payment may be made in sterling by UK personal cheque, postal order, sterling draft or international money order, made payable to Pan Books Ltd.

Alternatively by Barclaycard/Access:

Card No. | | | | | | | | | | | | | | | | |

Signature:

Applicable only in the UK and Republic of Ireland.

While every effort is made to keep prices low, it is sometimes necessary to increase prices at short notice. Pan Books reserve the right to show on covers and charge new retail prices which may differ from those advertised in the text or elsewhere.

NAME AND ADDRESS IN BLOCK LETTERS PLEASE:

....

Name———————————————————————————

Address—————————————————————————

————————————————————————————————

————————————————————————————————

————————————————————————————————

3/87